Changing Church and State Relations
in Hong Kong, 1950-2000

We thank Xu Bing for writing Hong Kong University Press in his Square Word
Calligraphy for the cover of this book. For further explanation, see p. iv.

A new series on socio-economic and cultural changes in Hong Kong

HONG KONG CULTURE AND SOCIETY

Series Editors
Tai-lok LUI

Department of Sociology,
The Chinese University of Hong Kong

Gerard A. POSTIGLIONE

Faculty of Education,
The University of Hong Kong

Panel of Advisors
Ambrose KING

The Chinese University of Hong Kong

Alvin SO

The Hong Kong University of Science
and Technology

Siu-lun WONG

The University of Hong Kong

Other titles in the series

The Dynamics of Social Movements in Hong Kong
edited by Stephen Wing-kai Chiu and Tai-lok Lui

Consuming Hong Kong
edited by Gordon Matthews and Tai-lok Lui

Toward Critical Patriotism: Student Resistance to Political Education in Hong Kong and China
Gregory P. Fairbrother

At Home With Density
Nuala Rooney

HONG KONG
Culture and Society

Changing Church and State Relations in Hong Kong, 1950-2000

Beatrice Leung and Shun-hing Chan

香港大學出版社
HONG KONG UNIVERSITY PRESS

Hong Kong University Press
14/F Hing Wai Centre
7 Tin Wan Praya Road
Aberdeen
Hong Kong

www.hkupress.org
(secure on-line ordering)

© Hong Kong University Press 2003

ISBN 962 209 612 3

British Library Cataloguing-in-Publication Data
A catalogue record for this book is available from the British Library.

Printed and bound by Condor Production Ltd., Hong Kong, China

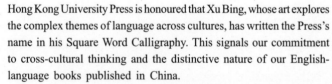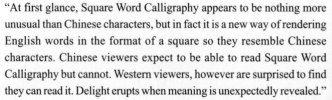

Hong Kong University Press is honoured that Xu Bing, whose art explores
the complex themes of language across cultures, has written the Press's
name in his Square Word Calligraphy. This signals our commitment
to cross-cultural thinking and the distinctive nature of our English-
language books published in China.

"At first glance, Square Word Calligraphy appears to be nothing more
unusual than Chinese characters, but in fact it is a new way of rendering
English words in the format of a square so they resemble Chinese
characters. Chinese viewers expect to be able to read Square Word
Calligraphy but cannot. Western viewers, however are surprised to find
they can read it. Delight erupts when meaning is unexpectedly revealed."
— Britta Erickson, *The Art of Xu Bing*

Contents

Series Foreword

Most past research on Hong Kong has been generally aimed to inform a diverse audience about the place and its people. Beginning in the 1950s, the aim of scholars and journalists who came to Hong Kong was to study China, which had not yet opened its doors to fieldwork by outsiders. Accordingly, the relevance of Hong Kong was limited to its status as a society adjacent to mainland China. After the opening of China, research on Hong Kong shifted focus towards colonial legitimacy and the return of sovereignty. Thus, the disciplined study of Hong Kong was hindered for almost half a century, and the richness of a society undergoing dramatic economic, social and political change within the contemporary world was not sufficiently emphasized.

The unfolding of culture and society in Hong Kong is no longer confined by the 1997 question. New changes are shaped by local history as much as by the China factor. Rather than being an isolated entity, Hong Kong is an outcome of interaction among local history, national context, and global linkages. An understanding of the future development of Hong Kong requires sensitivity to this contextual complexity.

The volumes in this series are committed to making Hong Kong studies address key issues and debates in the social sciences. Each volume situates Hong Kong culture and society within contemporary theoretical discourse.

Behind the descriptions of social and cultural life is a conceptual dialogue between local agenda, regional issues, and global concerns.

This series focuses on changing socio-economic structures, shifting political parameters, institutional restructuring, emerging public cultures, and expanding global linkages. It covers a range of issues, including social movements, socialization into a national identity, the effect of new immigrants from the Mainland, social networks of family members in other countries, the impact of the colonial legacy on the identity of forthcoming generations, trade union organization within the shifting political landscape, linkages with Southeast Asian societies, Hong Kong's new role between Taiwan and the Chinese mainland, the transformation of popular culture, the globalization of social life, and the global engagement of Hong Kong's universities in the face of national integration.

Gerard A. Postiglione
Tai-lok Lui

Series General Editors

Foreword

Faith, Citizenship and Colonialism in Hong Kong

Christians are supposed to be distinguished from the rest of society by their moral commitment and, above all, to be inspired by concern for the well being of others. Both the Old and New Testament impose on the believer an unlimited duty of care for the dispossessed, the deprived and the underprivileged.[1] In assessing the record of Christianity in any community, it seems entirely fair, therefore, to set higher standards than would be applied to other organizations and to weigh church performance against these Christian precepts. Christians are, of course, members of society and are moulded by the same political and economic experiences as the rest of the community and swayed by the same aspirations and anxieties. The crucial question is whether their Christian convictions make any significant difference to the way in which they behave as members of society.

The Historical Context

In retrospect, it is tempting to accuse the Protestant and Catholic Churches of entering into an alliance with British colonialism after World War II which diminished their ability to act as Hong Kong's social conscience. Could they not have done more to foster social justice, to promote democracy, to encourage the workforce to struggle for its rights and to defend the well being of the vulnerable in society? Should they have assumed a more 'prophetic' role, as the Church did in South Korea for example?

The Churches' performance has to be measured in the historical context which their members faced. Throughout the second half of the twentieth century, the entire Hong Kong community deliberately refrained from challenging the existing political and economic systems. Unlike elsewhere in Asia, there was a remarkable absence of radical political groups, and the trade union movement displayed little militancy after the early 1950s. This self-denying covenant extended to the Chinese Communist Party and its organisations although the Chinese government publicly denied the legitimacy of British rule.[2] Even during the violent 1967 anti-colonial campaign, Beijing stopped short of calling for an end to either colonialism or capitalism in its denunciations of the British.[3] During the 1970s, the Party increasingly stood aloof from the student activists who were bent on challenging prominent features of colonial rule.[4] The political landscape was dominated by an almost universal passivity rationalized by a belief that Hong Kong would not be allowed to survive any attempts to introduce radical reforms.

The colonial administration, nevertheless, found it difficult to tolerate criticism. It was afflicted by a long-standing fear that the Chinese community, including its business leaders, felt no commitment to Hong Kong.[5] In the early post-war period, the colonial administration was prepared to take direct action to stifle opposition from the Christian community. In 1953, a Jesuit priest published an article in a cultural magazine criticizing Hong Kong for appointing judges from the Civil Service whereas the United Kingdom selected them from the legal profession, a practice which reinforced the independence of the judiciary.[6] The Attorney General decided to prosecute the Jesuit editor for contempt of court on the grounds that this article was likely to bring Hong Kong's administration of justice into disrepute. The priest was found guilty and fined.[7]

At the same time, religious leaders of some standing were frequently the objects of considerable suspicion within the upper ranks of the Civil Service. The Protestant Bishop, R. O. Hall, was perhaps the best example of this blend of social acceptance and political mistrust, for he was viewed by many colonial officials as either excessively naïve or far too 'leftist' for comfort. In the eyes of many contemporaries, the Churches were on the side of social programmes that often seemed dangerously radical, although, institutionally, they did not seek such a role.

Practical Charity

In the 1940s and 1950s, survival rather than reform was the overwhelming priority. The influx of population was on such a scale that Hong Kong's people lacked even the most basic medical, housing and educational services. The community's material needs rather than the Christian message had to be the Churches' first concern if they were to be true to the New Testament.[8] They cooperated with the state and its policies and built the schools, the clinics and the hospitals which the colonial administration failed to provide because of its commitment to laisser faire, low taxation and small government.[9]

At the institutional level, the Churches acted as the state's agents in these fields. At the individual level, however, it is plain that Christians acted as a powerful though informal pressure group and played an important role in gaining greater commitment from the colonial administration to improved social services. The professions included a substantial number of Christians. These were prominent, both as clerics and as lay persons, in the various statutory and advisory bodies that the government established to develop housing and social service programmes.[10] It is notable that the Churches' involvement was essentially a humanitarian response rather than part of a strategy to proselytize. For example, Catholic schools did not give priority to admission of Catholic children even though these children were thereby denied the opportunity of a Catholic education as prescribed by Church law.[11]

Confronting Colonialism

The 1960s saw the emergence of a more confrontational attitude within the community, which the Churches were to reflect. As their social service programmes expanded, the need for additional financing became urgent. The Churches were no longer able to mobilize all the funds they needed from overseas, and they became dependent on the Community Chest and government subventions to maintain their welfare programmes. There was a clear danger that they would be demoted from partner to client. This development was counterbalanced by the appearance of activist 'protest' organizations, particularly in the housing field, though by the standards in other modern cities, they were far from radical.[12]

The Churches played a significant part at the institutional level in changing community attitudes. The Protestants became outspoken about the lack of social conscience in Hong Kong and the failure to tackle urgent social problems whose solutions were self-evident. The Catholic Church was inspired by the Second Vatican Council which ended in 1965 to call on the laity to participate in an ambitious review of every aspect of religious life. This exercise included detailed discussions of a document 'which indicted everything from lack of labour protection to the capitalist-orientated Legislative Council. One observer described its tone as more savage than even the effusions by local communists.' In parallel, a priest set up a new labour organisation to fix 'the machinery of society [that] injures people.' It never matched the achievements of the Christian Industrial Committee established later under Protestant auspices but it was a start.[13]

The colonial administration resented the Churches' new role. The Governor, Sir David Trench, warned a gathering of 20 Christian groups that he believed their religious principles disqualified them from commenting on the government's activities. Among his comments was the claim: 'We are all familiar with — and often admire — people of strong religious conviction whose hearts are so full of love that it unfortunately impairs their judgment in practical situations.'[14] The warning was ignored. Throughout the 1970s, the political landscape became dominated by community protests and pressure groups. Staff from Protestant and Catholic institutions were conspicuous in organizing these activities.[15] There is ample evidence that, once again, Christians had sought conscientiously to act as the leaven in society, inspired by their religious convictions to work in the more demanding social services and to promote social reform at considerable personal cost.[16]

A New Citizenship

In the 1980s, the role of the Churches shifted dramatically. By this stage in Hong Kong's development, the colonial administration had accepted its responsibilities for such basic social services as universal compulsory education, comprehensive care for the disabled, welfare benefits for the elderly, the infirm, and the single-parent family. There were disputes about the quality of service and the level of provision, but the state's obligations to the community's social well being had been established. The conflict now was over democratic reform and the arrangements for Hong Kong's post-colonial future.

In the previous period, the professional and middle classes had taken the leading role because effective solutions to social problems required professional expertise as much as public lobbying. After the start of Sino-British negotiations on the Joint Declaration in 1982, matters became both clearer and simpler. Livelihood issues remained a matter of widespread concern, but the public's keenest anxieties related to the preservation of the Hong Kong way of life after 1997. Although many of the individuals and groups that had led the 'protest' politics of the 1970s remained prominent in the new '1997' politics, they played a very different role. The political landscape had been transformed by the introduction of elections to the Legislative Council in 1985. There was now a forum in which the government could be held accountable to the community even though the public's representation was by way of limited and indirect elections.[17] As 1997 drew nearer and disputes over democracy intensified, grassroots concerns and livelihood issues slipped down the political agenda.[18]

The new political environment shaped the programmes of the Churches. Their members accepted an obligation to help overcome the threats to the survival of the Hong Kong community. But this reaction was not simply the humanitarian response of the first two decades after World War II. In that period, the Churches had answered the appeal of the homeless and the destitute by mobilising the generosity of their more fortunate members in Hong Kong and overseas. The activism of the 1960s and 1970s had also been marked by a sense of guardianship towards the vulnerable and deprived. But the Churches were potential casualties after 1997, both institutionally and as individual members of society, if Hong Kong did not make the transition from colonial rule intact. Indeed, the Churches were more at risk from the Chinese Communist Party than most other parts of Hong Kong society.

But there was an additional factor. The Churches themselves had expanded the role which they believed their members ought to undertake if they were to live up to their religious commitments. From the very beginnings of the Christian faith, its followers were supposed to be exemplary citizens, ready to respect the state and its laws except where these violated the Christian conscience.[19] But that duty was now expressed in terms of personal responsibility in order to match modern concepts of citizenship and civil society. In the Catholic Church, the process had begun in 1891 when Pope Leo XIII had defined the Church's role as the guardian of social justice in his encyclical *Rerum Novarum*. In 1965, the Church had proclaimed that as an institution in modern plural societies, it stood aside from political activities not directly related to its religious mission. Its members, nevertheless, had the duty to participate fully in the government of their societies together with the rest of their fellow citizens.[20] In 1991, Pope John Paul II, having previously distanced the Church from both Marxist and capitalist ideologies, applauded the downfall of oppressive regimes that had violated the rights of workers and hailed 'new forms of democracy ... which provide hope for change in fragile political and social structures.'[21]

Post-colonial Churches

This heightened awareness of the meaning of Christian citizenship in the modern world had a profound impact on the Churches' response to the challenge of 1997. In many ways, they lived up to the expectation that they should behave as model members of the community. They managed to set aside their preconceptions about future prospects based on the experience of witnesses to the Christian faith in the People's Republic of China, and they avoided hostile intransigence and defensive isolationism. For its part, the Chinese government was determined to cite Hong Kong as an example of religious toleration. The official news agency recorded with considerable satisfaction, for example, an Anglican and a Catholic bishop's reports of increased freedom for their churches during the first five years of the Special Administrative Region.[22]

The Churches, in different ways and in varying degrees, established a relationship with the post-colonial Hong Kong, its evolving society and its new administration that reflected a commitment to its people's wellbeing and a confidence in the relevance of the Christian message. Both Protestants and Catholics expected the post-colonial era to bring changes to their role. In private, senior clerics asserted that radical changes in the government's organization of educational and other social services were not inspired solely by a desire to reform their performance or achieve financial economies. They also felt conscious of a desire within the new government to lessen the dependence on religious organizations for the provision of these services. But it was not on this issue that confrontations with officials developed after 1997 but on human rights.

The government's treatment of Mainland residents with claims to the right of abode in Hong Kong provoked vigorous criticism from the Christian community even though the official policy had wide public support.[23] The Catholic Bishop, Joseph Zen Ze-kiun, was relentless in urging officials to recognize the right of families to be reunited. He was no less trenchant in his opposition to the government's ban on the children in these cases from attending school. Although the Catholic Church received most of the media attention on this issue, other Christian groups were no less committed. Their joint efforts were not welcomed by officials, and the Hong Kong Christian Women's Council complained, for example, that because of its involvement in the campaign, its status as a tax-free, charitable body had been questioned by the authorities.[24]

The Christian community was even more united in its response to the government's attacks on the Falun Gong, which had been banned on the

Mainland by the Ministry of Public Security in July 1999.[25] When the Chief Executive, Tung Chee-hwa, added his voice to the denunciations of the Falun Gong, the Christian community as a whole, together with Buddhist and Muslim representatives, joined forces to oppose any attempt to ban the group in Hong Kong.[26] Significantly, their public stand on this issue came the day after Ye Xiaowen, Director of the State Council's Religious Affairs Bureau, had issued a harsh warning against the Falun Gong at a forum in Hong Kong.[27]

China's most senior official in the field of religion also took this opportunity to criticize the Catholic Church. He repeated the Chinese government's attack on the canonization in 2000 of 120 Catholics who had died for their faith between 1648 and 1930 but whom a Chinese official described as 'missionaries and their henchmen who committed monstrous crimes against the Chinese people.'[28] The Chinese government's Liaison Office in Hong Kong told the Hong Kong diocese to be 'low key' in celebrating the canonization, advice which was not heeded. The Special Administrative Region government, however, kept a careful distance from this exchange.[29]

The post-colonial administration understood that respect for religious freedom was an important benchmark for the way that the principle of 'one country, two systems' was implemented. This political reality was symbolized by the respects paid publicly on the death of Cardinal John Baptist Wu in 2002 by the Chief Executive and Chinese government officials in Hong Kong.[30] The strains between Church and State could not be concealed but there was considerable political sense in observing the courtesies.

Charting the Transition

The transition of the Churches from the traditional colonial setting of Hong Kong in the aftermath of World War II to the mature Christian community of post-industrial, post-colonial Hong Kong is analysed with considerable skill by Dr Beatrice Leung Kit-fun and Dr Shun-hing Chan. They trace the pattern of development from the social and economic crisis that followed the post-war refugee influx to the emergence of a social conscience within the community. They present a detailed critique of the relationship between the colonial administration and the Churches as they weigh up their contribution to the provision of social services.

The two authors make a considerable contribution to our understanding of the dilemmas which confronted not only the Churches in adjusting to the transition from British rule but also the strains on the wider community. They present an analysis both of how Christian institutions reflected the concerns of society as a whole and of how the Churches' policies were shaped by their individual members. Because of the contribution which the Churches made to Hong Kong's social infrastructure during the colonial era and because of the impact of their responses to the post-colonial challenge, the Christian community has a greater importance in Hong Kong's recent history than is often recognised. Dr Leung and Dr Chan have shown why the Churches were institutions of such influence and impact during the last fifty years.

Leo F. Goodstadt

Adjunct Professor, Trinity College, University of Dublin,
Honorary Fellow of the University of Hong Kong,
and former Head of the Central Policy Unit (1989–1997)
of the Hong Kong government

Acknowledgements

There are many we wish to thank for helping us write this book. Our research began in late 1996, when Beatrice Leung received a direct allocation grant from Lingnan University to study Church-State relations of Hong Kong in the transition to 1997. The project has later expanded to include Church-State relations in the Hong Kong SAR. As for the roles that the two authors played in the book, Beatrice Leung was primarily responsible for drafting the sections on the Catholic Church (chapters 3, 4, 5 and 6), and Chan Shun-hing for the sections on Protestant churches (chapters 3, 4, 5 and 7) and chapter 2 on the theoretical models. We jointly wrote chapters 1 and 8, the introduction and concluding chapters.

We are grateful to Lingnan University for providing a grant for this research project. In addition to the sponsoring institution, we wish to thank Father Louis Ha, the director of the Archive Office of the Hong Kong Catholic Diocese, and Miss Cheung Yuen-mui, the archive officer who allowed us to use statistical figures and photographs of the Catholic Church. Thanks are due to the Hong Kong Christian Council and Hong Kong Christian Institute for providing photographs of Protestant churches. Many thanks are also due to Miss Margaret Lo and Mr Patrick Ng Koon-kwan for their help in collecting research data for this project.

Friends have read different chapters of this book while it was an ongoing project. We want to extend our special thanks to Mr Leo F. Goodstadt, adjunct professor, Trinity College, University of Dublin, and Honorary Fellow of the University of Hong Kong, and the former chief policy adviser to the Hong Kong government as Head of the Central Policy Unit (1989–1997), for his support in writing a preface for this book and his valuable comments on the drafts at various stages. Professor William Liu of the University of Illinois gave his valuable comments on the final draft. Miss Moira Deidre Shaw, deputy editor of the *Sunday Examiner,* helped to proofread the English of various chapters. Dr Elspeth Thomson of the Institute of East Asia, National University of Singapore, and the assistant editor of the new journal *China: An International Journal,* provided very useful comments and helped edit the whole manuscript. Her patience in going over the entire manuscript draft with a fine-tooth comb is very much appreciated. Bishop Zen Ze-kiun and Father Lido Mencarini, P.I.M.E. allowed us to interview them and spoke about Catholic issues by revealing some incidents that were not known to the public.

Finally, we wish to thank Professor Tai-lok Lui and Professor Gerard A. Postiglione, general editors of the Hong Kong Culture and Society Series of Hong Kong University Press, for their encouragement and attention.

Beatrice Leung
Shun-hing Chan

CHAPTER ONE

Introduction

The impact of Church-State relations on the history of Europe and the United States has been enormous and remains an important issue of debate today. For centuries, Christianity has influenced the cultural and political development of Europe. As a result, it is closely associated with the West. In general terms, Christianity, and the churches in particular, has played a double role in the Western political system. At times, the churches have thrown their support behind a government, and thereby strengthened its political legitimacy. On other occasions, the churches have condemned and criticized a government in order to challenge its rule or promote political reform. Church-State relations are complex, with many factors influencing how the two interrelate.

The relationship between Church and State has never been static. Relations have been affected by constant changes in the wider social environment of people and politics. Secondly, the Christian church is not a unified organization, but is instead made up of different denominations and groups — a divided clan. The three major Christian groups that make up the clan — Catholicism, Protestantism and Orthodoxy — have their own political ideologies. Furthermore, within the Protestant group there are many different sub-groups, each with its own political viewpoint and set of beliefs. Thirdly, as a whole, the Christian churches have a common set of faith-prescribed values and morals, which should, in theory, guide the churches in their relationship with the State. However, many factors, especially self-interest and desire for power in the political environment, have always affected how the churches have related to the State and at times Christian values and morals have come second. Hence, the study of Church-State relations should go beyond the official documents of a government and beautiful religious discourse. It should investigate whether power and interest have played a part in that relationship.

Hong Kong has its own unique socio-political culture and system which is not identical to that found in the West. Catholic and Protestant missionaries were invited by the Hong Kong government to serve the army and local people soon after the British occupied the colony in 1841. Before World War II, the churches assisted the Hong Kong British colonial administration by offering educational, social and medical services to the poor and destitute. In return, the government granted land and financial subsidies to the Christian churches for their social service work, thus laying the foundations of a 'contractual relationship' between the government and Christian churches. This unique form of Church-State relations flourished after World War II when the British government feared the infiltration of Communism into Hong Kong. From the 1950s to the 1970s, the Christian churches were encouraged by the government to provide educational, social and medical services to the wider community. During the 1980s, however, Church-State relations began to change as both the Catholic and Protestant churches began to play a more prominent role in the socio-political arena. In the lead-up to the handover of Hong Kong to China (July 1997), the churches became increasingly involved in politics and social action. They demanded assurances from Britain and the Chinese government that religious freedom and political reform would be protected after the handover. These changes led to the development of an 'untraditional' form of Church-State relations. As the handover neared and the Chinese government entered Hong Kong's political arena, the bilateral relationship between the colonial government and Christian churches expanded into a triangular relationship now including China. Close scrutiny of the changing Church-State relations in the Special Administrative Region (SAR) of China will be essential in the years to come.

Researchers from various disciplines have analysed aspects of Church-State relations in Hong Kong from their own specialist perspectives. Based on the British-US model formulated by Francois Houtart, Li Ng Suk-kay (1978) in her political science thesis examined the relationship between the Catholic Church and the Hong Kong government. She reached the conclusion that the colonial government in Hong Kong made use of the Catholic Church to further its own aims. Looking at Church-State relations from a historical perspective,

Lee Chee-kong (1987) sought to explore the relationship between the Protestant churches and Hong Kong society during the pre-Second World War period. He argued that the Protestant churches played the role of a 'servant' in the colony. Lee showed that by staging campaigns, such as the 'anti-keeping handmaid campaign' in 1938, the churches successfully pressured the government into initiating social reform. In an academic article, sociologist Shun-hing Chan (1995) analysed Church-State relations using the theory of 'institutional channelling' as promoted by researchers of social movements. He argued that as a result of the Protestant churches becoming faithful partners of the government they were forced to sacrifice their voice as a 'prophet'. When acting as 'prophet' the churches comment on social, moral and political issues in the context of Christian faith and criticize or monitor the behaviour of a government. Wong Chi-wai (1995) in his political science thesis examined the relationship between the Protestant churches and the Hong Kong government in the 1980s. He focused on the changing relationship between the churches and the State, and the future development of such relations. Ko Tinming (2000) in his sociology thesis examined the political involvement of Hong Kong Protestant church leaders from the 1980s to the 1990s, concluding that a number of Protestant ministers had participated in Hong Kong's political affairs to varying degrees.

Concepts and Theoretical Framework

This book investigates Church-State relations in Hong Kong from the perspective of the relationship between the state and society at large. In particular, the research focuses on the content, formation and development of Church-State relations between 1950 and 2000. At times, however, historical events prior to 1950 have been referred to in order to elaborate certain points or provide background. Patterns of interaction between the State and Church have been examined along with how that relationship has impacted Hong Kong's political development. The 'government' referred to in this book is the Hong Kong colonial government before 1997 and the Hong Kong SAR government after 1997. The mainland Chinese government is occasionally referred to in some of the chapters in this book because its religious policies have, at times, affected Hong Kong. However, Beijing's religious policies are not a focal point of discussion. The 'church' refers to the Catholic and Protestant churches. While the Catholic and Protestant churches in Hong Kong are independent organizations, they share a common cultural heritage and face the same Hong Kong political environment and government. However, they respond differently to political change due to their differences in organizational structure and culture.

The approach of this research starts from the social theory of state-society relations, and this is taken as a theoretical framework from which Church-State relations in Hong Kong are examined. The study of Church-State relations has a long history in the West, with much conducted within the field of theological studies. Christian scholars who have assessed Church-State relations from the perspective of Christian philosophy and political theory have done considerable work (Barth 1960; Stone 1983; Feige 1990; Jungel 1992). Within the field of sociology, Church-State relations have been discussed largely in the area of sociology of religion, particularly using social theories on religion and society formulated by Karl Marx, Emile Durkheim and Max Weber.[1]

While acknowledging the contributions of this work, it must be said that it has some limitations. As Christian scholars do not generally engage in empirical study, their writings are not particularly useful in understanding the pattern of Church-State relations in a particular historical context. The classical theories of Marx, Durkheim and Weber provide profound insights and their theories point to particular dimensions of Church-State relations. However, the local political environment is often extremely complex and the theories of the classical sociologists of religion can often provide only guidance, not a theoretical framework.

In this research, Church-State relations are studied from the perspective of State-society relations, and the Church is viewed as one of many social organizations. The researchers looked at the interaction between the Church and government from an organizational perspective. Simply put, the unit of analysis in this research is the organization, that is, patterns of interaction between the government and churches at an organizational level.

The study of Church-State relations in Hong Kong has both theoretical and practical significance. On the theoretical level, traditional theories of Church-State relations come mostly from the West, notably Europe and the United States. As such it is assumed that the Christian faith and churches are part of the mainstream culture. The government and the churches share certain values and ideological views (Smith 1972; Curry 1986; Bradley 1987; McBrien 1987; Robbins and Robertson 1987). Outside Europe and the United States, another paradigm of Church-State relations is derived from countries with socialist/communist governments. This paradigm makes the assumption that communist/socialist governments automatically seek to oppress and control the Christian churches (P. Ramet 1987, 1990; S. P. Ramet 1998).

Over the past thirty years, researchers have also studied the impact of Christianity and the churches on the dynamics and political development of many Latin America and African countries.[2] In the process of their work, however, some have found that models of Church-State theory developed in European, North American and a number of socialist/communist countries are highly problematic when applied to Latin America and Africa. They are now making efforts to develop a new model of Church-State theory more suitable for these countries (Levine 1992; Pattnayak 1995; Swatos, Jr. 1995). The authors of this book share that same vision, and seek to develop a theoretical model that can better explain Church-State relations in Hong Kong, in the hope that such a model might prove useful in other Asian countries (Leung 1996b).

In addition, the study of Church-State relations is closely related to the study of the development of democratization and civil society. One of the reasons why researchers find Church-State relations in Latin America and Africa so interesting is that they have witnessed how Christianity and the churches have been a positive force in the process of democratization and a major source of strength in promoting civil society. In Asia, Christianity in the Philippines, South Korea, and Taiwan has been a powerful force behind political development (Parker 1938; Hanson 1980; Carino 1981; Wong 1992; Yang 1997). The study of Church-State relations in Hong Kong can help untangle the complex relationship between Christian faith and political development, and provide new insights into the development of democratization and civil society in the territory.

On a practical level, Church-State relations have been an inseparable part of Hong Kong's history, though researchers have largely neglected this aspect. This study of Church-State relations should help fill some blanks in Hong Kong's history. For example, it suggests that the churches played the role of 'contractor' or 'deputy' to the government. This resulted in an uneven relationship of power between the churches and government and limited the churches' capacity to adopt the role of 'prophet', mentioned above. The study of Hong Kong's Church-State relations reveals how the government was able to absorb certain forces in society that had the potential to turn against it, and how it was able to manipulate those same forces into becoming faithful partners.

This research also shows how, as the years passed, Church-State relations changed as some Christian groups began to adopt the role of prophet by monitoring and criticizing the government. This helped to facilitate social and political reform and reveals how the churches advanced the process of democratization and the building of a civil society in Hong Kong.

Data and Methodology

According to data covering the years 1951 to 2000 in *Hong Kong,* a Government Information Service Department publication, the percentage of Christians in the Hong Kong population has been approximately between 8 to 10 per cent since 1950. For example, the Hong Kong population in 1970 and 1975 was 4,127,800 and 4,379,900 respectively and the Christian population (Catholics and Protestants) was 400,000 in 1970 and 440,000 in 1975, which was 10 per cent of the Hong Kong population. From the 1980s the Christian population decreased slightly. The Hong Kong population in 1980 and 1985 was 5,147,900 and 5,466,900 respectively. The Christian population fell to 9 per cent of the Hong Kong population with 456,800 in 1980 and 500,000 in 1985. The Hong Kong population in 1995 and 2000 was 6,307,900 and 6,865,600 respectively, while the Christian population was 514,140 in 1995 and 529,700 in 2000, a drop to 8 per cent of the Hong Kong population (Table 1).

The Christian population makes up approximately 12 to 13 per cent of all religious believers in Hong Kong (Table 2). According to two surveys conducted in 1988 and 1995, the followers of folk religion form the largest population of believers, at 23 per cent and 15.3 per cent respectively. The Protestants and the Buddhists rank second, with Protestants forming 7.2 per cent in 1988 and Buddhists 11.6 per cent in 1995. However, if Catholics and Protestants are taken together as Christian, then the number of Christians totaled 12.1 per cent in 1988 and 12.9 per cent in 1995, a percentage slightly higher than the number of Buddhists.

'Church' is defined here as an organization that professes a belief in some transcendental being and codifies behavioural norms that presumably are in accordance with this belief. 'State' is defined as a set of organizations vested with the authority to make binding decisions for people and organizations juridically located in a particular territory and to implement these decisions using, if necessary, force.[3] As the scope of this study covers fifty years from 1950 to 2000, it was necessary to conduct both historical and field research in order to understand how Church-State relations varied in different periods of time.

The two authors of this book have themselves dual roles, being both academics and active church members. Beatrice Leung Kit-fun is a Catholic nun and member of the Sisters of the Precious Blood congregation. She is also an associate professor in political science. Shun-hing Chan is an assistant professor in religion and philosophy and a Protestant who has received theological training. Hence, the two authors were able to consider the topic from the viewpoint of insiders and outsiders.

Table 1   Hong Kong Population, Numbers of Catholics and Protestants, 1950–2000

Year	Hong Kong Population	Number of Catholics	Number of Protestants	Total (Catholics and Protestants)	Ratio of Total Number of Catholics and Protestants to Hong Kong Population (%)
1950		(33,848)			
1951	2,000,000	40,000	20,000	60,000	3%
1955	2,400,000	73,499 (60,000)			
1960	3,190,000	158,419 (146,464)			
1965		(220,280)			
1966	3,716,400	234,500			
1970	4,127,800	247,953 (241,813)	152,047	400,000	10%
1975	4,379,900	265,000 (265,806)	175,000	440,000	10%
1980	5,147,900	266,800 (266,843)	190,000	456,800	9%
1985	5,466,900	269,000 (267,429)	231,000	500,000	9%
1990	5,859,100	258,200 (253,362)	285,000	543,200	9%
1995	6,307,900	254,140 (257,457)	260,000	414,140	8%
2000	65,600	229,700 (229,723)	300,000	529,700	8%

Source: Data from each year of *Hong Kong* published by the Government Information Services Department, Hong Kong. The numbers in parentheses are provided by the Archive Office of the Hong Kong Catholic Diocese.

Table 2   Distribution of Religious Groups in Hong Kong in 1988 and 1995 (%)

Religious groups	1988	1995
No religion	58.3	60.2
Folk religion	23.0	15.3
Buddhist	6.6	11.6
Protestant	7.2	8.4
Catholic	4.9	4.5
(N)	(1,644)	(2,275)

Source: Data from May M. Cheng and Wong Siu-lun, 'Religious Convictions and Sentiments.' In Lau Siu-kai et al., eds, *Indicators of Social Development: Hong Kong 1995*. Hong Kong: Hong Kong Institute of Asia-Pacific Studies, The Chinese University of Hong Kong, 1997, 301.

The material and data were drawn from three sources. For the 1950 to 1980 period, the main sources were the Hong Kong Public Records Office, government publications, such as White Papers and reports, and files and documents collected by the churches. Various studies on Hong Kong's history, such as on British and American foreign policy on China, and missionary correspondence also proved useful. For the post-1980 period, the material pertained mainly to the activities of the churches or Christian social groups in response to social and political change, as well as church-related controversies. It included statements, proposals and comments issued by the churches or Christian social groups. Other useful material was found in church leaflets, booklets, newsletters, extras, collected essays, position papers, books, newspaper reports and commentary articles. As active members of their churches Leung and Chan took part in, or were able to observe many of the major incidents outlined in their book. Personal and insider contacts also provided the two authors with valuable information about certain Church-State controversies. Although not conducted as formal interviews with structured questions and recordings, the authors' discussions with church insiders were also useful.

The Structure of the Book

The 'contractual relationship' model is employed here as the conceptual framework for analysing Church-State relations in Hong Kong. The first chapter provides some historical background and describes the socio-political context of this study. It also contains a general review of Church-State relations in Hong Kong, introducing the themes of 'contractual relationship', traditional relationship and untraditional relationship. This paves the way to a full discussion of these themes in the following chapters.

Chapter 2 considers some theories on Church-State relations and how they apply to Western nations, socialist/communist States and Asian countries. Some of the inadequacies and difficulties experienced in applying such theories to Hong Kong are pointed out. Here the concept of a 'contractual relationship', which is derived from John McCarthy and his colleagues' theory about governmental 'institutional channelling', is presented as offering a better framework from which to study Church-State relations in Hong Kong (McCarthy, Britt and Wolfson 1991).

Chapter 3 explores the partnership between Church and State during the colonial period and how, through the Churches' provision of social, educational and medical services, they cooperated closely with the government. It also includes an in-depth discussion of the causes and affects of this partnership and the various stages of development of Catholic and Protestant educational, social and medical services. Chapter 4 examines the changing political environment from the 1980s to 1997, and the response of the Catholic and the Protestant churches. The events surrounding the Xin Weisi controversy and the Selection Committee are analysed in detail.

Chapter 5 investigates the emergence of a new socio-political role of the churches as advocated by progressive church leaders and lay Christians in the 1980s. The next two chapters examine changes in the political culture of the Catholic and Protestant churches in the 1990s as the handover of Hong Kong to China approached. A change of attitude within the Catholic Church towards the new Hong Kong SAR government, and the new form of Church-State relations between Protestant church leaders is reviewed. Chapter 8 summarizes the major findings of the study and discusses their theoretical and practical implications.

CHAPTER TWO

Church-State
Relations Models

The study of Church-State relations emerged in the West, in countries where Christianity was the traditional religion. In the United States for example, the Church-State separation model was not only enshrined in the constitution, but was also regarded as resulting from the advanced development of political philosophy and religious liberty. Outside the US, other forms of Church-State relations have attracted the attention of scholars, especially those found in Communist/socialist countries where State domination over the Church has often resulted in an undermining of religious liberty. In this chapter, these theoretical models and their relevance to Asian societies are discussed and the theoretical framework of 'institutional channelling', a heuristic model considered very useful in the study of Church-State relations in Hong Kong is introduced.

The Separation of Church and State: The US Model

The political philosophy demarcating the separation of Church and State in the US can be found in the First Amendment of the Bill of Rights. In the opening sentence, it is stated: 'Congress shall make no law respecting an establishment of religion or prohibiting the free exercise thereof.' The bill of rights is incorporated into the due process clause of the Fourteenth Amendment, and is thereby binding on the actions of each state in the union. In 1802, Thomas Jefferson brought the 'wall of separation' into the permanent lexicon of American relations between Church and State when he wrote a letter to the Danbury Baptist Association in which he explained his understanding of the meaning of the First Amendment's religion clauses (Howard 1985, 85):

> Believing with you that religion lies solely between man and his God, that he owes account to none other for his faith or his worship, that the legislative powers of government reach action only, and not opinions, I contemplate with solemn reverence that act of the whole American people which declared that their legislature should 'make no law respecting an establishment of religion, or prohibiting the free exercise thereof', thus building a wall of separation between Church and State.

These oft-quoted clauses and Jefferson's theory of a 'wall of separation' reflect two significant foundations of Church-State relations in the US. Firstly, the separation of Church and State stands as a constitutional principle that promotes democracy and protects the religious freedom of all Americans equally. Secondly, this principle emerges as a unique American contribution to political theory (Feldman 1997, 4).

Although this model of Church-State separation in the US is highly regarded, scholars have also questioned whether it can be applied to other countries. The first difficulty is the original meaning of the religion clauses. It is argued that the congressional framers and State legislators understood non-establishment to mean no sect preference. When the First Amendment was adopted, the general sentiment in America was that Christianity ought to receive encouragement from the State, in so far as it was not inconsistent with the private rights of conscience and the freedom of religious worship. Thus, the amendment conditioned the manner in which the government aided religion, rather than banning all aid (Bradley 1987, 121).

The second challenge was directed at how Church-State separation was actually applied in the history of the US. It has been argued that for almost two hundred years after the First Amendment of the Bill of Rights, America's Christian roots often influenced State court decisions. For example, in the *Church of the Holy Trinity v. United States* (1892), a court upheld the US Congress' constraint on the importation of alien unskilled workers. It noted: 'These, and many other matters which might be noticed, add a volume of unofficial declarations to the mass of organic utterances that this is a Christian nation.' In *United States v. MacIntosh* (1931), an application for US citizenship by a man who refused to promise that he would fight in any and all wars in defense of the country was denied, on the following grounds (Demerath III and Williams 1987, 78):

> We are a Christian people, according to one another the equal right of religious freedom, and acknowledging with reverence the duty of obedience to the will of God. But, also, we are a nation with the duty to survive; a nation whose contribution contemplates war as well as peace, whose government must go forward upon the assumption, and safely can proceed upon no other, that unqualified allegiance to the nation and submission and obedience to the laws of the land, as well as those made for war as those made for peace, are not inconsistent with the will of God.

The above examples show that the value and principle of Church-State separation was an ideal rather than a reality in the history of the US. As N. J. Demerath III and Rhys H. Williams have noted, it was a 'mythical past' (1987).

Furthermore, scholars note that a growing tension between Church and State gradually emerged in the US after World War II. Thomas Robbins identifies two kinds of issues or conflicts involving the relationship between Church and State in contemporary America. The first kind is called 'Church autonomy conflicts'. According to Robbins, a potential Church autonomy conflict is created when a branch of federal, state or local government proposes to impose some regulatory constraint on a religious group, a group member or an institution connected in some manner to a religious group or organization. An actual Church autonomy conflict arises when a claim is made by religionists opposing the regulatory measure on the grounds that it burdens the 'free exercise of religion'. The second kind is called 'State neutrality conflicts'. State neutrality cases involve either a proposed form of assistance that the State will provide to a religious group or the alleged expression of religious faith by a public institution. State neutrality disputes highlight the Establishment clause of the First Amendment, which is generally viewed as prohibiting the State to sponsor religion or public favouritism among competing religions (Robbins 1987, 67–70).

Robbins has further constructed a typology of American views on Church-State issues that fully reflects the complexity of the situation in the US today. By differentiating between support versus antipathy to the separation of Church and State, a dichotomy or continuum can be drawn to highlight four kinds of agenda. The first kind can be called a 'separationist' agenda, which consists of the vigorous defense of the rulings made by the Supreme Court in the Establishment and Free Exercise clauses. Separatists tend to be hesitant about allowing the State to support a religion and they also generally oppose enhanced State regulation of religious practices. Opposite to the separatists is the 'Statist' agenda, which favours both enhanced regulatory constraints being imposed by the State on religious practices and enhanced State support for religion. Statist orientation can be endorsed either by a caesaro-papist or by a theocrat. The third kind can be called 'secularist' orientation, which approves of enhanced State regulation of religion but would oppose greater State support for any religion or governmental religious expression. Opposite to the secularists is a consistently pro-religion or supportive orientation, which demands the State to give greater support for religion but rejects any collateral increase in governmental regulatory prerogatives (Robbins 1987, 70–3). Robbins's observation reveals that even the ideal of Church-State separation is being undermined by growing tensions in contemporary America.

Even though the model of Church and State separation is a political philosophy produced in the US, it is possible to ask whether such a theory would make sense in other countries. As pointed out by some critics, the separation of Church and State is a notion possible only in societies that have the following conditions: Firstly, the society is clearly able to differentiate between sacred and secular, between what belongs to God and what belongs to Caesar. Secondly, there is a state or government (in the Western model) that is clearly distinguished from society and culture. The concept of such a state emerged only in the sixteenth century. Thirdly, a religion can be organized into some form of concrete religious organization properly denoted as a 'church'. Many religions do not have the same degree of institutionalization as Christianity and many countries have neither the historical experience nor the know-how to approach 'Church' and 'State' as rival or complementary institutions. It is rather difficult to promote or apply such a political philosophy in countries that do not have such conditions, in particular in Asia (Bradley 1987, 121–2; Wickeri 1996, 26).

State Domination of the Church: The Communist Country Model

Church-State relations in Communist/socialist countries have also attracted the attention of social scientists. In recent years, Sabrina Petra Ramet's research on Communist countries in Eastern Europe and the former USSR have produced interesting results. She attempted to construct a theoretical framework on Church-State relations in Communist countries (P. Ramet 1987, 1990; S. P. Ramet 1992, 1993, 1998). For her, the basic discrepancy between Church-State relations in Communist and non-Communist countries is that Communist regimes see religious organizations as potential political rivals or policy tools. Communist regimes then tend to construct religious policies to control or manipulate religious organizations and to weaken the bases of grassroots loyalty. For example, one of the tasks for the Department of External Church in the former USSR's Council of Religious Affairs, was to act as an ancillary of the foreign policy apparatus. Its responsibility was to work with religious organizations in the realm of international relations in order to strengthen ties with other nations (S. P. Ramet 1987, 3–10).

Sabrina Ramet vividly delineates the characteristics of Church-State relations in Communist countries as: believers have the right to believe in, and to gather in a community to worship their god, but belief in a religion is the 'private affair' of an individual. In other words, religion is not accorded any legitimate public role in the discussion of social and political affairs. Regarding the relationship between Church and State, they are technically separated. However, the State often pays subsidies to priests' salaries, censors or controls church publications, issues State licenses for the practice of priestly functions, monitors sermons in church and approves and rejects prospective church appointees for ecclesiastical leadership positions.

Communist regimes usually tended to depict Church-State relations as positive. However, when a church overstepped any of the State-set boundaries on its activities, the Communist regime would use two tactics to bring it back into line. Firstly, the Communist regime would try to isolate the outspoken member of the clergy and lure the churches into a more acquiescent relationship with the regime. Or, the regime would defame the outspoken clergy in the press, harass him or her through governmental bureaucracy, or fabricate charges in order to make an arrest.[1]

To enhance the study of Church-State relations in countries outside the US, Ramet developed a theoretical framework based on the Eastern Christian churches that centres around three different themes between Church and State, namely, nationalism, co-optation and opposition. By nationalism, she refers to the situation where a church (or religious body) is, on the whole, supportive of a regime's aims, although sometimes is in conflict with it. The term 'nationalism' is used to mean devotion to a cultural-linguistic collectivity, manifested in respect for the history, culture and tradition of a country, and in the aspiration to promote the specific culture and way of life identified as that of the nation. By 'co-optation', she refers to the situation where a church is in a stable co-operative relationship with the State, and from that relationship gains certain benefits, such as subsidies, state salaries, pensions for the clergy or perhaps bare toleration. The church agrees to be 'loyal' and to advance the goals of the regime in specific areas. Hence, a co-opted church is a dependent church. By 'opposition', Sabrina Ramet refers to a situation where a church is conflict with the regime. There are many forms of opposition that a church can take. For example, a church can oppose the presence of a hostile occupier (a conquering neighboring state); or become the outspoken critic of a state that does not favour Orthodox Christianity; or of internal opposition within the church itself, in which alternative views of society become reflected in a struggle for dominance within the church.

From the themes described above, Sabrina Ramet further formulates four patterns of Church-State relations in the Orthodox world. The first pattern is called 'simple co-optive nationalist', whereby the hierarchy of the Church is co-opted and espouses the nationalist line endorsed by the regime. The second pattern is called 'non-nationalist dependent', whereby the Church is too weak to offer any resistance to the polity of the State. The third is called 'nationalist defiant' or 'independent-oppositionist', whereby the Church has a strong sense of nationalism but it at the same time opposing the regime. The fourth is called 'simple co-optive anti-nationalist', whereby the Church is sapped of its nationalist strength due to isolation from the public and is penetrated and co-opted by the regime (S. P. Ramet 1998, 6–19).

Multi-faceted Phenomena: Church-State Relations in Asia

Church-State relations are more complex in Asian societies due to their broad diversity of ethnic groups, languages, cultures and religions. One problem lies in the relationship and differences between religion and Church. The main traditional and influential religions in Asia are Buddhism, Hinduism, Islam, and Confucianism. Apart from the highly Christianized countries such as the Philippines and South Korea, Christianity in Asia is a minority religion. Two fundamental points need to be seriously considered in the study of Church-State relations in such a context. Firstly, Christianity, or the Christian church in Asia as a social institution, is often not considered to be significant or influential compared to the religious institutions of Buddhism, Hinduism and Islam. Therefore, religion and State relations, rather than Church and State relations, should be the focus of attention in Asian societies. This leads to the second point, which is that research into Church-State relations in Asia often results in the study of the socio-political role of Christianity as a minority religion in Asia.

Another difficulty in the study of Church-State relations in Asia is the relationship between Christianity (or the Christian church) and the government. As discussed above, various Asian countries have their own well-established religious traditions, such as Hinduism in India, Buddhism in Thailand, and Shintoism in Japan. The study of religion-State relations in Asia needs to consider the influence of religion on the government or State, and how religions have become embedded in the local culture. Moreover, researchers must look at the interplay between the political structure and religious ideologies. Thus, Church-State relations in Asia include the complex relationship between Christianity (or the Christian churches) and the government, as well as Christianity and Asia's traditional religions. In addition, researchers need to study Asia's Communist regimes, such as those of mainland China, North Korea and Vietnam, and how Marxism, which implies atheism, has been introduced into the religion-State equation (B. Leung 1992a, 1996a; Liu 1996; Chan and Lam 2000). Communist regimes are largely antagonistic towards all forms of religion and generally attempt to use all kinds of measures to control them. Researchers of these Communist countries need to consider the model of State domination of the Church.

In sum, due to the multiplicity of religions and political structures, Church-State or religion-State relations in Asian societies are significantly different from the West. There is not one theory or model alone that can be aptly applied to or used to fully explain the complex range of religion-State relations in Asia. To study religion-State relations in Asia it is necessary to take into consideration the unique circumstances of each country. The study of religion-State relations in Asia is considered to be only in its infancy. Researchers are still exploring which theoretical frameworks and research methods are relevant.

As for the situation in Hong Kong, various scholars have studied issues relating to Church-State relations. For example, the political participation of Protestant ministers (Ko 2000); the contribution of Christianity to democracy (Brown 1996); the social awareness of Catholic intellectuals (Sze 1996); and the like. However, these do not investigate the problem of Church-State relations *per se*. Other studies have tried to explore the nature of Church-State relations in Hong Kong. For example, the role of the Christian churches in the social development of Hong Kong (Li 1978; C. Yu 1996), and the history of Church-State relations in pre-war Hong Kong and in the 1980s (C.-k. Lee 1987; Wong 1995). These are very interesting, but do not provide a suitable theory or systemic explanation for the phenomenon of Church-State relations, which is the research goal of this study.

Institutional Channelling: A Theoretical Framework for the Study of Church-State Relations in Hong Kong

Among the studies of State and society relations in recent years, John McCarthy, David Britt and Mark Wolfson's theory on 'institutional channelling' is heuristic and particularly useful in the study of Church-State relations in Hong Kong (McCarthy, Britt and Wolfson 1991). McCarthy and his colleagues observed that the US government established various kinds of channelling mechanisms. These channelling mechanisms effectively conditioned the activities and development of social movement organizations (SMO) in the country, which finally led to a narrowing and standardizing of the structural forms of many SMOs. The channelling mechanisms included: federal tax laws and policies and their enforcement by the Internal Revenue Service; the action of formal coalitions of fundraising groups; US Postal Service regulations and their impact on access to post; the rules and actions of private organizational monitoring groups; the dynamics of combined charity appeals and, finally, State and local-level fundraising regulations and their enforcement.

It is important to study the channelling mechanisms established by the government in order to understand the relationship between the State and society. State control over society is normally through direct or indirect manipulation. Direct manipulation can take the form of arrest, harassment and State-sponsored violence. However, direct manipulation can lead to collective action of anti-government in society. On the other hand, indirect manipulation can be more successful in influencing SMOs. As observed by McCarthy and his colleagues, State channelling mechanisms have successfully created structural isomorphism in SMOs and led them to follow orthodox tactics and set moderate goals of collective action. Such mechanisms have also created incentives by favouring certain kinds of organization, tactical approaches and collective goals. Thus, in the study of State and society relations, researchers should ask the following questions: How do channelling mechanisms create costs for non-participation in this formal system of organizational labelling? And how do they narrow the range of structures, tactics and substantive goals of those organizations that choose to become legitimate organizations in the eyes of the State?

Channelling mechanisms not only affect the operation of SMOs themselves but can also be used to provide a subtle warning to other SMOs to fall in line. McCarthy and his colleagues discussed in depth how channelling mechanisms influenced SMOs internally and externally. Internally, channelling mechanisms can directly and indirectly affect the activities, goals and structure of SMOs. For example, a government can establish regulations through which a SMO has to change its organizational goal in order to obtain non-profit status. Furthermore, when faced with a multitude of government regulations, SMOs often need to hire a variety of specialists to deal with complex and ever increasing demands in order to ensure the organization's survival and development. For example, SMOs have to consult legal experts and use professional accountants in order to ensure that the organization meets government-set standards. According to McCarthy and his colleagues, 'we should expect conservatising effects as cautious professionals advise organizations of their understandings of appropriate behaviour' (McCarthy, Britt and Wolfson 1991, 66). Externally, SMOs often developed in the same wider communities. Channelling mechanisms can change the formation of boards of directors and the attitudes of board members towards the organization's goals and activities. In particular, the channelling mechanisms of the State can limit the mobilization of resources and tactics used by SMOs.

Although State channelling mechanisms have been shown to comprehensively affect SMOs in the US, McCarthy and his colleagues noticed that some organizations were able to avoid such outside influences. The second question is: what proportion of SMOs is able to avoid being influenced by such State control mechanisms? McCarthy and his colleagues argued that only a small minority of organized groups was able to avoid completely the consequences of these channelling mechanisms in contemporary American society. National or large-scale SMOs were more easily caught up in the tangle of State regulations due to their size and need for a large amount of resources. Local, grassroots SMOs were more easily able to escape the net of channelling mechanisms because their survival did not depend upon having a tax exempt/ tax deductible status. Seemingly, the tax exempt/tax deductible status is the linchpin of the State channelling process.

The channelling mechanisms used by the State to control SMOs affects State-society relations significantly. One of the consequences is a blurring of the boundaries between the State and society and between civil and political affairs. This can seriously impact the political development of a society. Modern Western political thought has been based upon the distinction between State and society, locating the potential for dissent in groups that exist autonomously from the State. If a state's channelling mechanisms can penetrate into the domain of civil affairs and civil leadership, it will result in the narrowing and taming of the potential for broad dissent.

It is possible to argue that McCarthy and his team's theory on institutional channelling is a heuristic concept that can be used in building up a theoretical framework to study Church-State relations in Hong Kong. Neither the Church-State separation model in the US, nor the State domination of the Church model in Communist countries is appropriate for the study of Church-State relations in Hong Kong, particularly during the colonial period before July 1997.

Hong Kong was a British colony before 1997 and Anglicanism was the *de jure* national religion. This formal relationship between the government and the Anglican Church was evident from the Protocol List, in which the Anglican bishop ranked fifth following the Governor, Chief Justice, Chief Secretary and Commander-General. The principle of Church-State separation was largely observed by the Catholic and the Protestant churches. However, any study or analysis of Church-State relations in Hong Kong that stopped here would neglect exploring the complex structure and interplay of power. This research explains that the Hong Kong government invited the Catholic and Protestant churches to become involved in education and social services due to the special historical circumstances of the 1950s. In the years that followed, the government and churches established a contractual or 'deputy' relationship, and as a result, the Christian churches were able to develop huge educational and social service enterprises. The churches' involvement in education and social services came at a cost, however. As the churches received resources, such as land and subsidies from the government, they were placed in an awkward position in so far as it became very difficult to criticize the government's policies for fear of a loss of funding. To use a Christian theological term, the churches lost their ability to act as a 'prophet', or someone whose calling it is to speak out against all forms of injustice, according to the will of God. The above analysis shows that there was a *de facto* relationship of power between the government and the churches and that this relationship greatly affected the churches' role and activities in society.

The colonial government adopted Britain's policies on handling religious and other social organizations. During the colonial period, Hong Kong enjoyed a high level of religious liberty as experienced in many Western nations. Although Anglicanism, and more generally Christianity, appeared to be the national religion, the Hong Kong government treated non-Christian religions in the territory fairly. Historically, the government made no attempt to oppress religious groups. The minority religions, such as Islam, Judaism, Hinduism, Sikhism and Zoroastrianism, were left largely free to operate and establish themselves as communities. Furthermore, after 1949 Hong Kong became refuge to large numbers of religious people fleeing mainland China following the Communist takeover.

Although there is evidence of a power relationship between the government and the Christian churches, and the churches adopted the role of government contractor, it was not a relationship of domination as found in Communist countries. Hence the authors believe that the model of State domination of the Church in Communist countries does not provide an appropriate framework within which to study Church-State relations in Hong Kong.

The concept of institutional channelling as suggested by McCarthy and his colleagues is helpful in understanding the reality of Church-State relations in Hong Kong. From the perspective of organization, the Catholic and Protestant churches in Hong Kong act more like SMOs. They have complex institutional structures, and their own goals and agenda for social participation. Both the Catholic and Protestant churches take part in education, medical and social services in addition to evangelism. Although the Christian faith has a political dimension, and has its own social and political theology, the churches in Hong Kong seldom became involved in political issues before 1980. Their lack of political voice is in stark contrast to the outspokenness of Christian churches in other Asian countries, such as the Philippines, South Korea and Taiwan.

Following the 1980s, the Christian groups that began to comment on or participate in political affairs tended to be frontline, grassroots Christian organizations rather than the official churches. McCarthy and his colleagues' analysis of national and local SMOs can be aptly applied to the division between the official Christian churches and these smaller front-line organizations in Hong Kong. With the official churches receiving large-scale funding and support from the government, many were placed in a position where it was impossible or difficult to criticize the activities and policies of the State. It is possible to say that the Christian churches were trapped in the State's channelling mechanism net. Comparatively speaking, the frontline Christian organizations that became involved in political affairs tended to be independent of the official churches and their survival did not rely on resources provided by the government. The grassroots character of these smaller Christian groups can be identified by their ability and willingness to challenge the official Christian churches' dependence on the government. As these frontline groups were outside the State's channelling mechanism net they were able to criticize publicly the government's political and social policies.

CHAPTER THREE

Traditional Relations Between the Hong Kong Government and Christian Churches

Rendering Education and Social Services While Assisting the Government in Defending Hong Kong from Communism

The Hong Kong government and Christian churches established a working relationship from the start. The churches were given land for buildings and financial subsidies to run a wide variety of social services. It was recognized that the churches were able to offer a higher quality of service than the government, and at a lower price. It cost the government only a quarter of what it would cost if it ran such services itself.[1]

Catholic and Protestant missionaries had come to the colony at the request of the British to serve the spiritual needs of British troops, dying at a rapid rate from the plague and tropical diseases.[2] The missionaries were also asked to educate the children of the British troops and government officials. Before World War II, there were nine government schools, seven Catholic, and four Protestant. All of the Christian schools received financial support from the Hong Kong government.[3]

As a result of the refugee crisis caused by World War II, the government suddenly found itself needing to rely even more heavily on the churches to organize and provide various social services. The Japanese occupation of Hong Kong lasted for more than three years during the War, ending in 1945 when the Imperial Army surrendered to the Allies. Four years later the Chinese Communist Party (CCP) seized power in the Mainland and hundreds of thousands of Chinese flocked into Hong Kong to avoid Communist rule. Hong Kong had approximately 1,639,000 inhabitants in 1941 on the eve of the occupation, but by 1945, only 600,000 people were left. However, an average of 100,000 people, who refused to live under a Communist regime, migrated to Hong Kong each month from 1945 to 1951. By the mid-1950s, Hong Kong had a population of some 2.2 million, and the refugees, irrespective of their former wealth and professional status, required food, housing, medical care, education, employment, etc.[4]

The Christian churches, with access to the abundant resources available through their international connections, were well positioned to help the refugees. Among the refugee population were large numbers of missionaries who had been expelled from the Mainland by the atheist CCP for political and religious reasons.[5] They were able to provide immediate, extra manpower to the established Christian churches.

The first refugees were granted only temporary asylum, as the Hong Kong government believed they would soon return to the Mainland. The government made no long-term plans regarding their education or housing. Given the colony's limited resources, both the government and local newspapers argued that social services should be provided only to those born in Hong Kong — or at least that they should be given priority.[6] After the establishment of the People's Republic of China (PRC), however, and the withdrawal of the Kuomintang (KMT) to Taiwan, the government's attitude towards the refugee population changed.

Apart from the social problems caused by the influx of refugees, the government was also faced with the politically disruptive activities of pro-Nationalists and pro-Communist factions which had brought their ideological struggles with them from the Mainland. The colonial government feared that the Communist cadres in particular, working on secret missions in Hong Kong, could instigate anti-British sentiment among the local Chinese on the pretext of social problems. Riots in the early years of the 1950s and '60s had mostly to do with conflicts between Nationalist and Communist factions.[7]

For its own security, the Hong Kong government was determined to prevent Communist infiltration. It took seriously what it saw as a significant Communist threat from the PRC. Prior to the Japanese occupation, the British had had experience fighting Chinese Communists in guerrilla warfare in the Sai Kung area of the New Territories. Then throughout the occupation Communist guerrillas and couriers continued to operate in the area.[8]

The Hong Kong government also sought to implement the anti-Communist policy of the Foreign Office in London (Miners 1991, xv–xvi). Britain, being a traditional ally of the United States and member of the North Atlantic Treaty Organisation, resolutely agreed to assist in the Cold War effort to eradicate Communism. Indeed, the British supported the embargo in the 1950s against China, despite the hardship it meant for its own colony. The British were well aware of the unrest caused by Communists in other Southeast Asian countries such as Vietnam, Cambodia, Burma, Thailand, the Philippines, Indonesia and Malaysia, and were not going to allow Hong Kong be the recipient of the CCP's revolutionary ideology.

A letter to the Secretary of State for the Colonies from the Hong Kong Governor, Sir Alexander Grantham, clearly illustrates the level of concern over the infiltration of Communists into the education system of the Colony:

> A potentially greater danger than any of those mentioned in your telegrams … is presented by the increasing Communist infiltration into schools … Evidence produced in that case [the recent deportation of five Communists] confirms that the efforts of the Chinese Communists and pseudo-communists in this Territory are being directed at the young and comprise not merely indoctrination but actual recruitment for service with real organisations and forces in South China.[9]

The following month at the opening ceremony of a new school Grantham warned:

> There are those, and to my mind they are the most evil, who wish to use schools as a means of propaganda and poison the minds of their young pupils with their particular political dogma or creed of the most undesirable kind. This we know is what happened in the schools of Fascist States and is now happening in Communist-dominated countries. This deforming and twisting of youthful minds is most wicked and the Hong Kong government will tolerate no political propaganda in schools.[10]

During a discussion in April 1949 with the Secretary of State for the Colonies, Grantham remarked:

> The Chinese Communist Party, when they achieve complete control over China, may wish to have an office in the Colony just as the KMT have now. This would give them a base in our midst which

would be a focus for disaffection and trouble-making. Proposed
legislation will prevent this and will also facilitate control over
subversive elements in education and labour ...[11]

Malcolm MacDonald, British Commissioner-General for South-East Asia, who
had had experience in dealing with the CCP infiltration aimed at subverting
British rule in Malaya and Singapore in the early 1940s, visited Hong Kong
in 1949. He confirmed the above observation about the intended infiltration
of the CCP and suggested that Hong Kong ban all political parties, so as to
prevent the possibility of the formation of a CCP within the colony. He believed
it would be better to prevent its birth rather than have to deal with a much
bigger problem at a latter date.[12]

According to a government internal paper prepared in March 1949, about
34 schools in the urban areas were classified as being actually controlled by
Communists. Another 32 were classified as having leftist elements, including
staff, teachers and 'students'. In the New Territories, 24 schools were controlled
or otherwise manipulated by Communists (Sweeting 1993, 201). In 1952 a new
ordinance on education was passed, empowering the Director of Education to
close down any schools that he believed were engaged in political
indoctrination.

When seeking partners and contractors to share the burden of providing
education and social services to the refugees in the 1950s, the government found
it could trust the Christian churches because most had common socio-cultural
roots and shared the government's anti-Communist ideology. Communism's
atheist ideology was fundamentally at odds with Christianity. Moreover, the
government initially doubted the trustworthiness of many local Chinese charity
organizations and traditional associations, fearing they might become
sympathetic to the Mainland CCP on the grounds of Chinese patriotism.

The government's support for church schools is illustrated by a letter
written in 1950 by Bishop Ronald O. Hall to the Secretary of the Board of
Education in which he took the initiative in suggesting that in order to
counteract the influence of atheistic Communism, the Education Department
should rely on Protestant churches and the Catholic Church to run schools:

> In view of what was said by two members of the Board who do
> not share my Christian faith, I could not say publicly that my main
> concern is with the use of Christian churches by subsidy in primary
> education. The government both in the UK and in its colonial policy
> recognises that by-in-large only religion can resist Communism and
> that non-religious secular primary education on a large scale will

produce an atheistic proletariat as prepared ground for Communist sowing. I very much hope that the Roman Catholic Church will, with encouragement from the department, strengthen and enlarge their primary school work. I think the Director understands my view on this matter, but it's not easy to say it publicly.[13]

The reply from G. P. Ferguson, Secretary of the Board of Education, indicated that he endorsed Bishop Hall's view:

I agree entirely with your view in your penultimate paragraph. I consider myself that religion should play a more and more important part in schools since it is the very essence of cultured civilisation ... I read the report of your address with interest and can well sympathise with your feelings ...[14]

Ideologically, Christianity is fundamentally opposed to atheism but the Christian educational institutions were, however, encouraged to work with the Kaifongs in the provision of schooling when there was acute shortage of educational facilities.

Although some colonial officials did not want to be criticized for using tax-payers' money to support the evangelization work of the Christian churches, for the sake of the colony's stability, it was decided that education could be contracted out to the Christian churches. This indirectly assisted in strengthening religious activities.[15]

For the British, the Catholic Church was not as friendly as it appeared. Italians who were allies of Hitler during World War II dominated the Hong Kong Catholics. It is true that Catholic bishops helped the people of Hong Kong during the war, and the British were indeed grateful. However, the British viewed the Italians with contempt. The Irish Jesuits were less of a problem, but the British had no reason to regard them as 'loyal'. One of the Jesuits in Hong Kong, for example, was well known as the son of a man executed by the British during the Irish Independence. In addition, the one senior expatriate civil servant who voluntarily worked with the Japanese during the war was Irish and was dismissed from the civil service. In reality, most British officials trusted and preferred to work with Chinese rather than Italians or Irish.

There is evidence that the decision-makers in the government and certain church leaders were well aware of the unique position of the Church. The government saw the Church as an existing social force that had the potential to develop into a partner and one that would not become a menace to its authority. It also, of course, could not fail to appreciate the fact that the Christian churches' providing of social services continued to save the government considerable expense, not only in terms of food and clothing, but also in the hiring of planners, social workers and teachers. The churches were also pivotal in preventing Communism from gaining a permanent foothold in the Colony.

After the war, three church leaders (two Catholic and one Protestant) were appointed to the 17-member Education Board that advised the government on the colony's education policy.[16] A government campaign to register children for school was organized in September 1950. A total of 21,906 children between the ages of 5 and 12 registered.[17]

The Church, for its part, believed that participation in work relating to medical care, education and social welfare was consistent with its faith. Social service work was an effective channel for evangelism. Thus theoretically, the Church had every reason to be involved in the building of post-war Hong Kong. Well matched in a unique historical context, they became allies in social development. Indeed, the religious schools went on to become known for offering the best education available in the territory.

It was not until after the 1967 pro-China riot that the government began to encourage the establishment of secular schools run by Chinese associations.[18] In the months following the 1967 pro-China riot, the underground CCP network was almost completely annihilated. With the threat of Communist infiltration removed, the value of the Christian churches as instruments to block Communist infiltration was weakened. Thus government financial aid, once given exclusively to the Christian churches, was also made available to various Chinese social service associations, which had also been offering philanthropic services since the nineteenth century. These included the Tung Wah Hospital Group and Po Leung Kuk and Kaifong Associations.

Other changes were taking place within Hong Kong society. By this time there were far fewer church people in Hong Kong. Many of the foreign missionaries had returned to their native countries and were not being replaced. As Hong Kong's economy recovered and began to grow, those who were left were unable to manage the rapidly growing annual intake of new students.

In 1972 the World Council of Churches (WCC) supported and subsidized the 'Program for Social Development in Tsuen Wan, Tai Wo Hou and Kwai Chung'. Six churches, Protestant and Catholic, jointly initiated the program in those districts. Its aim was to offer leadership training and help local people become better organized and active in their communities. The WCC is an international umbrella organization incorporating most of the mainstream Christian churches that favour ecumenism. Its objectives are to promote global cooperation among the churches and encourage Christians to reform society.

The understanding that the integration of faith and social action is a mission of all Christian churches has generally been recognized as the spirit of ecumenical movement.

This movement had direct influence on the social participation of the churches in Hong Kong. For example, the WCC supported and subsidized a Christian labour organization called the Hong Kong Christian Industrial Committee (HKCIC). Established in 1966, the HKCIC was originally a unit of the Hong Kong Christian Council (HKCC) to spearhead the Christian churches' response to labour issues. The HKCIC later moved towards greater independence from the Council by becoming an auxiliary organization. The HKCIC was and still is active in organizing workers and helping them fight for their rights. It runs educational courses and battles to improve labour laws and social security for workers (Lee and Cheung 1986).

The second change was the discrediting of the organizations controlled by the CCP. Its trade unions were heavily concentrated in public utilities and communications, both in the government and private sectors because 'the Communists adopted in the post war period a deliberate policy of infiltrating these key economic areas.' (England 1971, 238) Although Hong Kong showed little enthusiasm for giving labour representatives a stronger voice in political life, the United Kingdom since the 1930s had been urging its colonies to promote trade unions, and this pressure from London increased after the Labour Party won the 1945 election (Miners 1988, 40–5; Fosh et al. 1999, 240–1). Consequently, the colonial administration felt obliged to encourage the development of trade unions not only among its own 'industrial' workers (marine department crews, for example) but also in major commercial organizations (public utilities in particular).

The 'pro-China' unions were the best organized, as well as law-abiding up to 1967, and their policy was to concentrate on these strategic sectors of the economy (England and Rear 1975, 268). The 1967 riot, which paralysed the economy, brought into question the colonial administration's tolerant attitude towards the 'pro-China' labour movement, while the dismissal of striking workers in both the private and public sectors removed most of the 'pro-China' union officials and most committed members from government employment — and from jobs in strategic sectors.[19] In addition, employers responded by strengthening their own cooperation to present a united front to the colonial administration on labour issues (Ng and Sit 1989, 83–4).

The pro-China schools found themselves in a similar position. As long as there was a gross shortage of school places in the territory, parents were willing to send their children to schools that were openly committed to the communist ideology. The pupils came from a broad social spectrum. One such pupil was Tung Chee-Hwa, the son of a wealthy Shanghai ship owner who was to become Hong Kong's first Chief Executive.[20] By 1967 these students accounted for 12 per cent of the total enrollment in Chinese language secondary schools. The Education Department found their efforts laudable and described them as 'until recently ... more meticulous in cooperating with the Department than other schools' (Goodstadt 1967). However, as the export-led Industrial Revolution made English the preferred language of secondary education, their attraction started to wane along with Chinese language schools generally (F.-y. Yu 1987, 224–9). In 1958, 45 per cent of all secondary students were in Chinese-language schools, but by 1967, the proportion had fallen to 26 per cent (So 1987, 250).

Education and Services Offered by the Catholic Church

As early as 1843, Catholic missionaries began to provide education to both British and Chinese boys.[21] French Catholic missionaries, the Sisters of St. Paul de Chartres, established an orphanage and an old age home in 1848 (Ticozzi 1997, 67–9). However, as most members of the British Hong Kong government belonged to the Anglican Church, the Catholic, mostly Italian, missionaries received less attention than the Protestant.

The American Foreign Missionary Society (Maryknoll Fathers), affiliated with the New York-based American Catholic Relief Service, had been providing social services through their missions in undeveloped areas on the Mainland (Luo 1967, 45–74).[22] After the arrival of the Maryknoll Fathers in Hong Kong in the 1950s, Catholic relief service funds that had been used for China projects were now diverted to Hong Kong to help the refugees.

In 1953, new Catholic schools numbered 22 (14 in the New Territories and 8 in Hong Kong and Kowloon). Ten years later 33 new Catholic schools were added (16 in the New Territories and 17 in Hong Kong and Kowloon), making for a total of 55 in 1963. The number of students attending Catholic schools over the 10-year period, 1953–63 increased from 3,909 to 28,029.[23]

The Catholic Church did not purposely start the role of 'contractor' after World War II. On the contrary, in the 1940s, '50s and much of the '60s, the government relied on the Catholic Church and other voluntary and welfare bodies to provide services which it could not provide or finance. The Church and these other organizations raised large sums of money overseas to finance their activities, which ranged from noodle factories and clinics to rooftop schools and welfare associations.

In 1952, Cardinal Spellman of the United States visited Hong Kong (left, standing) and inspected the relief work offered by American government through the American Catholic Relief Service Centre. Hong Kong Bishop Lawrence Bichani (right, standing) accompanied the visit. Courtesy of the Archive Office of the Catholic Hong Kong Diocese.

Catholic schools expanded rapidly in the 1950s and '60s, partly because of the contractual relationship between the government and the Church, and partly because of great demand by the Catholic population for Catholic education. The Catholic population of Hong Kong increased rapidly from 20,000 in 1941 to 200,000 in 1960.[24] As part of their contractual relationship, the government first built the school building, then invited the Church to run the school with funds supplied by the government. The government at first allowed school halls and playgrounds to be used for Christian religious services. Later, it permitted the churches to buy land adjacent to the school, upon which to build churches, social centres and living quarters for the clergy, at only two-thirds of the lease price.[25]

The government launched a six-year free education campaign in 1971 and a nine-year free education campaign in 1978. The Catholic Church, through its diocesan education commission and Caritas, gave its full co-operation to the campaign by sponsoring more schools. The diocese's support came at a time when the missionary religious institutes, running some of Hong Kong's most elite schools, found they could not take on any more new schools on behalf of the government because of insufficient numbers of religious personnel. In 1996, there were 327 Catholic schools, serving not only the Catholic community but also the wider Hong Kong society. Religious institutes ran half of these, and the diocese and Caritas-Hong Kong ran the rest.[26] Approximately a quarter of Hong Kong's school children were attending Catholic schools. Throughout the 1990s, an average of 91.6 percent of the students attending Catholic schools were non-Catholic. In 1973, Bishop Francis Hsu, a graduate of Oxford University, at the invitation of the government mediated between the government and teachers in a salary dispute. He was able to prevent a threatened teachers' strike during the public examination season and help resolve the labour dispute (Ha 1992).

At the request of the government the Catholic Church also operated various types of specialty schools, such as evening and pre-vocational schools, adult education institutes, as well as schools for the disabled and handicapped. However, paradoxically, while the Catholic education services met the aims of the government, they hindered the Church in reaching its own goals. The Jesuits Fathers and the reputable Wah Yan College are a case in point. In 1920, plans were made to build a Catholic post-secondary college or university. Bishop Pozzoni (1909–24) invited Irish Jesuits to come to Hong Kong to establish the tertiary institute. On arrival in 1926, however, they were instead given responsibility for a residential hall at the University of Hong Kong, then the only officially recognized tertiary education institute in the territory. The learned Irish Jesuits found themselves assigned to run Wah Yan College, a secondary school with two campuses, one on Hong Kong Island and one in Kowloon. This explains why the two Wah Yans soon became elite schools. Many of the Catholic primary and secondary schools became cradles for the elite of Hong Kong society, educating the future leaders of the Democratic Party such as Martin Lee and many members of the civil service, including the first Chief Secretary of the HKSAR, Anson Chan, and the Finance Secretary, Donald Tsang. In 1999, some 75 percent of the HKSAR's leading officials were graduates of Christian schools including Catholic schools.[27]

Most of Hong Kong's prestigious schools were run by international Catholic congregations specializing in education such as the Wah Yan Colleges (the Jesuits), Aberdeen Technical Institute (Salesians Fathers), St. Paul's Convent School in Happy Valley and Causeway Bay (Sisters of St. Paul de Chartres), Canossian St. Mary's College and Sacred Heart School (Canossian Sisters), Maryknoll Sisters Schools in Hong Kong and Kowloon (Maryknoll Sisters), and La Salle College and St. Joseph's College (La Salle Brothers).

The rapid rise in population and expansion of the economy after WWII made the Catholic Church's desire to run a Catholic tertiary institute even stronger. In 1961, its bishop again proposed a plan to erect a tertiary education institute that would offer a liberal arts programme including social sciences and languages, designed to enhance 'whole person development' as advocated by Cardinal John Henry Newman, a distinguished Oxford scholar in the nineteenth century (Newman 1947). The government turned down the proposal and again in the late 1960s and '70s.[28] The Church's plan was not honoured because it did not fit into the government's education policy, which saw tertiary education as a means to develop the future leadership of Hong Kong society in a manner the British desired, and not for whole person development.

Most of the social services provided by the Catholic missionaries were concerned with the sheltering of orphans and abandoned children, and the assisting of the deaf, blind, elderly and those needing direct support and care. This was a traditional pre-evangelization technique brought to Asia from Europe.[29]

Two religious women's congregations — The French Sisters of St. Paul de Chartres and the Italian Canossian Daughters of Charity — came to Hong Kong in 1848 and 1860 respectively, with the chief purpose of rendering much needed social services to the underprivileged. In a letter to the Superior General of the Sisters of St. Paul de Chartres in France, the third Hong Kong Catholic bishop explained why the Sisters were needed:

> I need Sisters to be in a hospital for Irish soldiers, who are mostly Catholics ... I need Sisters in the school for these soldiers' children ... I need Sisters to run a hospital already started for little abandoned children ... I need Sisters to train Chinese girls for future Chinese hospitals and schools.[30]

Thus the French Sisters established an orphanage, asylum for the blind, almshouse, hospital and boarding school adjacent to their convent.[31] The Sisters' wide range of services provided a model that was followed over the decades by other Hong Kong Catholic social service groups. Before WWII it was the major religious institutes, such as the French Sisters, the Italian Sisters and the Chinese Sisters of the Precious Blood, that were the main sponsors of social services. Later, lay Catholic associations, such as the St. Vincent de Paul Society, began to offer services but on a much smaller scale.

Immediately after the war, the refugees from the Mainland put great pressure on the territory which was already suffering from economic difficulties because of a Western embargo against China. Impromptu, church-run refugee settlement areas, such as those at Diamond Hill and King's Park, soon lead the way in offering relief and medical aid. These same centres were also used

Immediately after the Second World War, the Sisters of the Precious Blood, the Hong Kong Catholic Diocesan congregation sheltered the dislocated women and children of the Sham Shui Po district. Courtesy of the Archive Office of the Catholic Hong Kong Diocese.

In a building site it was posted that 'This is the site that the Catholic Social Service built refugee residents for the Hong Kong government'. Courtesy of the Archive Office of Catholic Hong Kong Diocese.

for Christian services. As the years passed, the number of centres grew. The government established resettlement zones and began massive housing projects (Ryan 1959, 243–58).

The Catholic social centres and schools, usually clustered around a Mass centre, were successful in part because of government financial assistance. In the early 1950s, on the land given them free (not at the discount price mentioned previously) by the government, the churches built most of the social centres. As the population increased in the 1960s, these centres became big parishes. The Churches' social service aid work was successful in converting great numbers of refugees. The Christian groups extended their religious activities by erecting big buildings, such as in Sham Shui Po, Wong Tai Sin, Cheung Sha Wan, Diamond Hill and King's Park in Kowloon, and Chai Wan and North Point on Hong Kong. Christian missionaries exiled from the Mainland almost exclusively served the Rennie's Mill refugee settlement.

Caritas-Hong Kong was established in 1953, although until 1961 it was known as the Catholic Social Welfare Conference. It was largely involved with co-coordinating and initiating Catholic welfare services, targeting the influx of refugees from China. In March 1955, it was affiliated with Caritas Internationalis, and in December 1957 became the official social welfare bureau of the Catholic Church in Hong Kong. In 1969 this organization was accepted as a member of the Community Chest.[32]

Caritas' services evolved over time. By 1968 it had begun to function as the social welfare arm of the Catholic Church offering extensive support services to the wider Hong Kong community. It became a pioneer in the field of social welfare, co-operating with the government and other agencies in developing new projects as funds and facilities became available.[33]

As the years passed, the colony became increasingly affluent and living standards improved. Accordingly, Caritas-Hong Kong branched into the Mainland, organizing exchange and training programmes and raising funds for relief projects.

Fundamental changes occurred in the 1960s as a result of the Second Vatican Council (Vatican II), 1963–65, which demanded that Catholics combine faith and daily life (Abbott 1966; Montemayor 1989). It altered the introverted nature of the Church and forced it to look outwards. Despite the changes, the co-operative relationship between the Church and the Hong Kong government remained as firm as ever. However, new social and internal church developments added a new dimension to the contractual relationship.

The Diocesan Convention was initiated and planned by Bishop Francis Hsu, the first Chinese bishop of Hong Kong. Its purpose, according to Hsu, following the changes introduced by Vatican II, was to evaluate the whole work of the Catholic Church in Hong Kong and plan for the future. In particular, he felt a need for the Church to attempt to understand the causes of, and to take stock of the social implications of the pro-China riot in 1967, and rapid economic growth in the early 1970s.[34] Eleven Catholic Church responsibilities were analysed and recommendations proposed. These were: evangelization, liturgy, religious education, general education, life of the laity, priestly life, religious life, the social mission of the Church, mass media, ecumenism and diocesan administration. In the first draft of the document, 'Social Outlook of the Church', discussed by delegates at the convention many of whom had Communist backgrounds and sought to disrupt the proceedings, it was recommended that:[35]

> The diocese set up a committee to explore the possibility of dialogue with the Communists, because the Pope himself had set an example by talking with Soviet officials on various occasions … because there is great possibility that our people could live under Communist rule in the future. It is far from proper that we are now adopting an attitude of antagonism and fear towards the Communists. We should adopt a more positive attitude to understand them and dialogue with them.[36]

This group continued its discussions over many months. The Hong Kong government accused the Catholic and Protestant churches of being too critical in this period.[37]

The idea of conducting dialogue with the Communists was almost unheard of in 1970, only three years after Hong Kong had been unsettled by a major pro-China riot ignited by a spillover from the Cultural Revolution still raging in China. The Hong Kong government was able to restore law and order, but immediately afterwards applied new measures to increase communication with the grassroots of society. The mass media severely criticized the Catholic Church, accusing it of betraying its religious roots by proposing dialogue with Communism.[38] Bishop Hsu gave in to public opinion and removed several key recommendations in the convention document such as the moving towards an initial understanding of the PRC, and holding dialogues with Communists in Hong Kong. The 'Social Outlook of the Church' Committee was renamed 'Social Mission of the Church' after a long discussion and heated debate among participants of the Convention.

Viewed from a different angle, the Catholic Church's relations with the British Hong Kong government looked different. Sir David Trench personally rebuked the Bar Association for demanding an end to the cozy conspiracy between the civil service and business elite in running the political system. He was downright rude to religious leaders: 'We are all familiar with — and often admire — people of strong religious conviction whose hearts are so full of love that it unfortunately impairs their judgment in practical situations. It is ethical, more than political, guidance that we all need from the churches; with great respect, church government does not have a very happy history and your cloth gives you no special expertise in the detailed solution of governmental problems' (Baird 1970a).

Bishop Francis Hsu, (1969–1973) an Oxford scholar and the first Chinese Catholic bishop of Hong Kong. Courtesy of the Archive Office of Catholic Hong Kong Diocese.

The Protestant and Catholic Bishops were initially offended when they realized what low priority the colonial administration accorded to welfare in 1968. The Catholic Church was even more alarmed when its first Chinese Bishop, Francis Hsu Cheng-pin, enlisted help from Irish Jesuits in the territory to prepare a document for public discussion on Hong Kong's political, economic and social situation. However, Trench's attack failed to dissuade the Catholic Church from pressing ahead with a series of public meetings to debate these issues.[39] This document was regarded as a menace to the established order because it called for dialogue with the CCP and 'indicts everything from lack of labour protection to the capitalist-orientated Legislative Council. One observer described its tone as more savage than even the effusions by local communists' (Baird 1970b). In reality, Bishop Hsu had no ambitions to incite political or social revolution but was simply responding to widespread resentment of social abuses, government corruption and official complacency.

The Catholic Church did not pursue the suggestion to hold dialogues with the Mainland Communists or establish a warmer relationship with Communists in Hong Kong. As a result the Catholic Church was not able to prepare itself for a future relationship with the PRC or find ways to solve fundamental ideological differences, in particular, Communism's atheistic roots. This lack of communication continued until the Sino-British Joint Declaration in 1984, which laid the foundations for the handover of Hong Kong to China.

In the end, the colonial administration overcame these critics by co-option rather than confrontation. Thus, by the time Bishop Hsu died in 1973, the colonial administration had co-opted the religious and philanthropic social service organizations. Moreover, the radical tendencies within his Church had ebbed, as they had in similar organizations. This process was not originally a deliberate strategy adopted by the colonial administration. It occurred as a result of institutional changes that reflected fundamental shifts in Hong Kong's social and economic characteristics.

In the 1970s the orientation of the Catholic Church's social services changed from meeting the immediate needs of refugees to offering services that would improve the quality of life for the population as a whole. The government remained passive in the face of changing needs though it tried to streamline the services. At the same time it encouraged various charitable organizations to carry a bigger share of the burden on its behalf. The Director of Social Services, in his *Annual Department Report of 1963–64,* noted, 'The public provision of social services is not a gratuitous act of charity, but a concomitant privilege of citizenship.' Thus the welfare services or relief services provided by the Catholic Church were diverted to target family and community needs largely through Caritas-Hong Kong. They were divided into three categories: child care, youth work, care for the elderly; and there was also its Family Life Education Service. Thus, under Catholic patronage, the Catholic Marriage Advisory Council was established to promote successful marriages, and the Birthright Society was launched to promote the value of life by providing hostel accommodation for unwed mothers. When Vietnamese refugees/boat-people arrived in the 1970s, Caritas offered counselling and educational programmes, medical aid and camp services (Baird 1970b, 8). Services for Filipino domestic workers were begun and a China Desk was set up to initiate and fund Caritas projects in China. Thus the Catholic Church was on contract to the government. It did not have any say over the kinds of social services provided, nor did it have resources for its most desired projects. Faced with this situation, the only answer was to agree to meaningful projects that it could operate according to Catholic principles. When social problems proliferated, the government stepped in, subsidized Caritas's pioneer projects and more involvement was encouraged.

Pax Romana leadership training in Hong Kong (1956) heralded the Catholic student movement and social concern in the Hong Kong Catholic Church. Courtesy of the Archive Office of the Catholic Hong Kong Diocese.

By co-operating with the government in providing education and social services, the Catholic Church received financial subsidies. As a result it was forced to sacrifice some of its independence in fulfilling its chief purpose, namely to be of service to mankind. The subsidies provided the government with a powerful tool with which to apply pressure and channel and implement its policies. Subsidies are a subtle means through which any government is able to control an organization and force it to do as it pleases. The Church's failure to establish a Catholic tertiary education institute in Hong Kong demonstrates this. By contracting education to the Catholic Church, the government was able to prevent the spread of Communism in the 1940s and '50s. At the same time by serving the government as a faithful contractor, the Catholic Church in return was given privileged access to the education sector, and able to use school buildings for religious services. It was also, as a result, able to obtain land at low prices for the building of churches or church centres.

Following the expulsion of foreign missionaries from China in the 1950s, the funds allocated by the New York-based Catholic Relief Service agency for its China projects were diverted to Hong Kong to be used for Chinese refugees. The fact that missionaries were chosen to distribute US relief aid (milk powder, flour and medicine) and fund refugee housing and medical projects, is evidence of a close connection between the American missionaries in Hong Kong and the US government. Moreover, the missionaries were involved in recommending and processing Catholic refugee immigrants to the US. Although their intentions were good, the American missionaries worked as de facto American agents in instituting the US government's refugee policy.

The US refugee policy had a hidden political agenda. Like the Marshall Plan in Europe (1948–1952), the US refugee policy in South-East Asia sought to block the spread of Communism (Dunbabin 1994, 479–509). Most of the American missionaries in Hong Kong were not aware of the political implications of their actions. They were not the only ones involved in the immigration service in the 1950s. The newly established Caritas-Hong Kong was also involved in so far as its orphan adoption and family reunion projects were concerned (Chang 1996). Project recipients have noted that US officials, when interviewing Chinese refugees, collected information about China.[40]

The contractual relationship between the Catholic Foreign Missionary Society of America (Maryknoll Fathers) and the US government was based on a common distrust of Communism. Thus the American missionaries re-enforced the existing anti-Communist attitude within the Hong Kong Catholic Church. Paradoxically, this anti-Communist sentiment would prove to be an important indicator of the kind of Church-State relationship that would prevail after the reversion of Hong Kong to Chinese rule on 1 July 1997.

Education and Social Services Offered by the Protestant Churches

As most of the British troops and civil servants were of the Protestant faith, there were already strong relations between many members of the Hong Kong government and the Protestant Churches even before they arrived in Hong Kong in the 1800s.

The business community, the Hong Kong government and *Sheng kung hui* (the Anglican Church of Hong Kong) discussed the territory's education problem in the early post-war years. The business community actually proposed that *Sheng kung hui* should assist in the development of primary education with minimal subsidies and administrative support from the government. *Sheng kung hui* consequently set up the Education Advancement Society on 1 September 1946. Primary schools were run in government-owned premises and privately owned buildings. Later, a school for workers' children was opened in Wanchai.[41]

Between 1851 and 1974, *Sheng kung hui* established 46 primary schools. Of these, 31 were established after 1950. Among the 31, 24 were subsidized schools and 7 were non-subsidized. Similarly, *Sheng kung hui* established 22 secondary schools between 1851 and 1974. Fourteen of these were established between 1950 and 1974 (Hong Kong Diocesan Office 1974, 16–21). The Church of Christ in China (CCC) was another fast-growing body in the 1950s and '60s in terms of the development of secondary and primary education. With the assistance of the Hong Kong government and the financial support of foreign churches, the CCC participated in the construction of 17 schools during a short span of seven years from 1957 to 1963, dedicating its efforts to secondary and primary education. In 1969, the CCC again accepted the invitation of the Education Department to run six secondary schools, located variously on Hong Kong Island, Kowloon and the New Territories. It also pioneered in the development of vocational schools. In 1960 and 1965, the CCC conducted two fund-raising programmes that helped raise over HK$1 million for the establishment of vocational and intermediate schools (Poon 2002, 13–5).

As the scope of social services required by the refugees from the Mainland began to prove a burden too heavy for the Hong Kong government with its limited resources, foreign Christian groups started to set up emergency relief groups. For example, the World Council of Churches (WCC) set up its Hong Kong Office of Migration Services in 1951. The Christian Welfare and Relief Council, the Church World Service's Hong Kong Office, and the Lutheran World Federation's Department of World Service were all founded in 1952. The Methodist Committee for Overseas Relief was founded the following year. The Presbyterian Mandarin Casework Centre was established in 1955, and the Lei Cheng Uk Friendly Centre of American Friends, in 1960. These organizations were mainly engaged in the provision of physical aid such as the supplying of clothes and food, mostly from the United States and to a lesser extent, Europe, Australia and New Zealand. With the assistance of overseas churches, local churches started to provide different forms of social services. *Sheng kung hui* established the St James Settlement in 1949 to serve its neighborhood. The Holy Carpenter Community Centre was set up in 1954 to provide youth services and vocational training. The Salvation Army set up an asylum for girls in 1948 and another one for boys in 1953. The Hong Kong Auxiliary of the Leprosy Mission founded a Rehabilitation Centre in 1950 and the British Christian Council set up a youth vocational school in 1960 (Webb 1977, 133–44).

In the 1960s and '70s the mainstream churches were influenced by new theological thought stemming from the ecumenical movement in Europe and North America and the World Council of Churches. The theology of ecumenism emphasizes that the Church should enter into society in order to realize the kingdom of God in this world. This mission to integrate faith and social reform was adopted by some clergy. For example: Reverend Kwok Nai-wang of the Church of Christ in China introduced the idea of 'local church', a concept suggesting that the Church should strengthen the solidarity of local people to fight for their rights, when he worked in the Shum Oi Church at Shek Kep Mei in 1966 (N.-w. Kwok 1993, 52–9). Bishop J. Gilbert H. Baker of the Anglican Church helped to establish the Neighborhood Advice-Action Council in 1967, an organization that provided services such as counselling, employment advice, legal aid, social welfare and family guidance. The Neighborhood Advice-Action Council expanded its services into the wider community in 1974 (Chow 1984, 203–4). Joe Leung, executive secretary of the Yang Memorial Service Centre of the Methodist Church, initiated social action such as the Blind Workers' Strike, the Relocation of the Yau Ma Tei Typhoon Boat Squatters and the Anti-dust and Blasting Campaigns in Tai Wan Shan from 1971 to 1972 (Yeung 1987, 64).

Impact of the Traditional Relations

The crucial role that the churches together had played in Hong Kong's development from the 1940s to the '60s seemed to be somewhat taken for granted by the Hong Kong government. The first white paper on social services, entitled 'The Objectives and Policies of Social Service Work in Hong Kong' was issued in 1965. Its focus was to explain why social services had not been fully implemented by the government, and to clarify government obligations in this area. Professor Nelson Chow of Hong Kong University was highly critical of the white paper's position, noting, '[Its] perception of the voluntary groups was rather negative. They were only seen as the tools of the government whose job it was to share the government's burden and fight for additional funds and resources on its behalf.' (Chow 1984, 50) The fact was that most of the voluntary groups referred to in the white paper were Christian groups, and it was these groups that had been the mainstay in Hong Kong's social services during the 1950s and '60s.

The second social welfare white paper and its supplement issued in 1973, entitled 'Plans for the Future Development of Hong Kong's Social Welfare' and the 'The Five Year Plan for Social Welfare Development in Hong Kong: 1973–1978', were greatly influenced by the Kowloon Riot Report (Hong Kong Government 1972, 1973). The Kowloon riot in 1966 prompted the government to appoint an independent commission to carry out investigations. The report indicated there was no distinct political motivation on the part of the young rioters. In order to prevent similar riots in the future, the report suggested that 'rigid measures be taken to amend the structural defects of the society' and that the government should try to 'provide better education and employment opportunities, improve the living conditions in Hong Kong, enhance welfare and recreational facilities and foster a sense of belonging among the youth by encouraging them to play a role in social affairs' (Hong Kong Government, Commission of Inquiry 1967).

In this paper, the government clearly defined the responsibilities and jurisdictions of the each of the various organizations providing social services for the first time. The contribution of voluntary groups was recognized and a pledge was made to increase subsidies for such groups. It confessed, though rather vaguely, that 'the government needed the assistance of voluntary groups'. In the 'Five Year Plan for Social Welfare Development in Hong Kong', goals and tasks for groups over the five years starting 1973 were set out in detail. At this point, an embryonic form of the Church-government partnership emerged (S.-h. Chan 1998a).

In terms of formal relations, the position of Hong Kong's Protestant churches was basically inherited from European and American churches. Due to the strong influence of American churches in Hong Kong, the American model for Church-State relations, namely the separation of the authority of the Church and the State, was predictably the model accepted by most Protestant churches in Hong Kong. According to this model, the Church and State should be independent of each other. For the Protestant churches in Hong Kong, the 'priest and prophet' model was also popular. The priestly role of the Church is to pray for the nation, while the prophetic role is to repudiate social injustice and insist that the government be just. The two roles are complementary rather than mutually exclusive. If the churches in Hong Kong are serious about these roles, they should bless the government when it does well and criticize it when it does not. As such, Protestant doctrines provide a clear ethical framework for Church-State relations, whether or not the authority of the two is separated. In other words, a church that holds on to the Church-State separation principle has a moral duty to monitor the authority and administration of the government.

As for substantive relations, when the churches in Hong Kong undertook work in education and social services in 'partnership' with the government, they gradually became the 'deputy' or 'contractor' for the government. This role reflects an informal social relationship between the Church and government, based upon unbalanced power. Many Protestant churchmen were aware of this state of imbalance.[42] A comment made by Reverend Alan Chan, a veteran *Sheng kung hui* clergyman epitomized the situation:

> Education and social service work were costly enterprises. Even with the assistance of foreign funds, the churches could only afford to start up schools and social service centres. Their ongoing operation had to rely on the government's support. The more the Church became involved, the more dependent it became on the financial support of the government. In order to maintain friendly working relations with the government, the Church often refrained from criticizing it. Over the years, the Church became dependent on the government and its prophetic voice grew weaker in the face of unjust government measures (A. Chan 1988).

Reverend Kwok Nai-wang, a veteran CCC clergyman, made the following remarks: 'The Church, government, and powerful businessmen were making use of each other and balancing against each other in such a way that the Church lost its position as a critic. As time lapsed, the Church was absorbed into this closely-bound hierarchy of power, obliging it to defend the position of the established order.' (N.-w. Kwok 1994, 79–80)

While the above comments reflect a churchman's point of view, they do reveal the substantive relationship of power between the Church and government evolving from the Church's role as a 'deputy' or 'contractor'. The concept of deputy or contractor is analogous to the model of a patron-client relationship discussed by Andrew G. Walder (1986, 22–5). According to his theory, the patron does not have to coerce his followers into loyalty by force. Rather, because of his power to own and distribute resources, the follower will pledge allegiance voluntarily in anticipation of getting a share of the resources. The patron-client relationship is built on two essential conditions: the patron's monopoly and manipulation of relevant resources and the mutual understanding between the patron and the client. This understanding may be implicit and not endorsed by any written contract, but the power relationship that exists upon it is effective. In the event that the patron no longer monopolizes the resources, the follower will disclaim allegiance in anticipation of the loss of such resources. The understanding will cease and the relationship will fall apart. In the case of the Church-State relationship in Hong Kong, when the Church became dependent on the government, it was rendered incapable of fulfilling its prophetic duties.

However, due to the diversity of the Protestant churches, the patron-client relationship does not fully explain the nature of the Church-State relations. In more specific terms, the patron-client model aptly describes the relationship between mainstream Protestant churches and the government. However, it cannot be used as successfully to describe the relationship between the evangelical churches and the government.

Generally speaking, the evangelical churches emphasize evangelism as the prime mission of the Church and are doubtful of the Church's involvement in social affairs, while the mainstream churches believe that the Church should be involved in social problems as well as evangelism. From the 1950s to the '70s, the evangelical and mainstream churches were constantly debating whether evangelism or social concern should come first. For most evangelical churches, involvement in education and social services ought ultimately to be aimed at evangelism. As a result of their understanding of the Christian mission and their principle of State-Church separation, the evangelical churches had never been strongly motivated to develop any relationship with the government. The evangelical leaders in Hong Kong had been used to keeping a distance from the government. However, because of their relative lack of initiative in social concern, the evangelicals had often been criticized for not fulfilling their prophetic role. Although both the evangelical and mainstream churches had been playing the role of deputies for the government, they obviously had different relations with the government.

Concluding Remarks

The contractual relationship between the Hong Kong government and Christian churches was in gestation before World War II, and began to take shape immediately thereafter. The British colonial administration had long realized that the churches could offer higher quality social and education services and at lower costs, than could the government. Thus the foundations for a long-term, co-operative relationship between the Church and State were laid, benefiting Hong Kong society through the decades.

After World War II, the relationship took on new dimensions. When Chinese refugees began to flow into Hong Kong, Catholic and Protestant churches took the initiative in offering education and relief services before the government could even begin to establish them. In response, the government granted more subsidies to the churches to assist in their efforts until the 1970s at which time there were far fewer church people available.

It is argued that the relationship was contractual, instead of a Church-State partnership. The word 'partnership' connotes equal status between the two parties involved especially in policy making and policy implementation, while 'contractual relationship' does not necessarily indicate equality between the two. It was indeed an unequal power relationship between the Christian churches and British government of Hong Kong. The Christian churches did not have any say in education, social and medical policy and could only offer the services on the government's terms.

Although the contractual relationship was formulated without prior planning by either side, the major force behind it was the common desire to maintain public order and prevent the spread of Communism. Moreover, the churches were able to mobilize foreign aid and did not pose a threat to the legitimacy of the colonial rule at a time when Hong Kong society was rocked by the political turbulence spilling over from the civil war in China, which eventually saw the Communist Party overthrow the Kuomintang government.

Their faithful performance as a government contractor provided Christian churches with both the opportunity and funds to expand services to Hong Kong society and directly strengthen evangelization work. However, the Catholic Church had to pay a price: firstly in that its involvement in education did not guarantee government funding or approval of the Catholic education policy, let alone the establishment of a Catholic tertiary education institute. Secondly, the church's fear of Communism and its relationship with the colonial government put it at odds with Communist China. This made future dialogue with Beijing difficult and increased the likelihood that co-operation with the future HKSAR government would not be easy.

Hong Kong Christian Churches Defend Religious Freedom and Choose Representation on the Selection Committee During the Transition Period (1984–1997)

The Basic Law of the HKSAR and Maintenance of Religious Freedom

At the beginning of the 1980s Church-State relations in Hong Kong were stable. However, the issuing of the Sino-British Joint Declaration in 1984 cast a shadow on this relationship. For Hong Kong Christians the preservation of religious freedom was the main concern. Religious 'freedom' includes the freedom to adopt a religious belief, freedom of the individual to worship in private and in public, freedom of giving and receiving religious instruction, freedom for religious communities to conduct religious activities, freedom to appoint and train personnel, freedom to erect and construct religious buildings and freedom to have connections with foreign religious believers and institutions abroad (Wu 1984).

Church leaders in Hong Kong wondered what would be the future government's policy towards the churches in Hong Kong and their religious activities, given the fact that the colonial government of Protestant England was to be replaced by a local government directly answerable to the atheist and socialist government of the People's Republic of China. They also wondered what would become of the thirty-year partnership in education and social services. Would it continue under the new regime after 1997?

The Christian community knew full well the actual extent of religious freedom in China and had good reason to suspect that after the handover, Hong Kong Church-State relations might change from the 'contractor' model to the 'political absorption of religion' model practiced in China.[1] The political ideology of China permits no claim of a religious leader to any authority of leadership, either moral or religious, over the citizens of the State. In fact, Beijing's religious policy has to be so if it to be consistent with 1) the atheism advocated by Marxism-Leninism; 2) the prevailing nationalism, which rejects anything that is not from China; and 3) anti-foreignism, stemming from the 'hundred years of humiliation' during the Qing Dynasty (B. Leung 1992a, chapter 2 and 4). In spite of the fact that in recent decades China has emerged as a major power in the international arena, the sensitive reactions of the Beijing authorities towards nationalism and anti-foreignism still pervade all their dealings in international affairs.

Throughout the political transition period, there was active political participation by a wide cross-section of Hong Kong society, including religious believers (Woodman 1997; Scott 1998; Vines 1998). The fear of losing religious freedom after the handover in 1997 united Catholics and Protestants. Together they issued various statements and expressed their views on religious freedom to the Chinese government.[2]

The Chinese and British governments began the process of negotiating issues relating to the handover, including the drafting and making of the Basic Law, which was to serve as the constitution by which the future Hong Kong was to be governed. The Basic Law Drafting Committee and Basic Law Consultative Committee were in charge of the drafting of the Basic Law and its consultative work.

Some church leaders sought ways to influence the drafting of the Basic Law and demanded that the pace of democracy be speeded up in Hong Kong. In the former, the demands were directed at the Chinese government, and in the latter, at the Hong Kong government. In pressing for political reform, they broadened their focus to political issues and gradually developed a political character that differed greatly from traditional church leaders. Opposed to the traditional role of 'contractor' played by the Christian churches in Hong Kong, some even became important figures in the democratic movement in the 1980s.

The Sino-British Agreement on the Future of Hong Kong promised there would be no change in Hong Kong during the fifty years following the handover to Chinese rule and that the 'one country two systems' model would be enforced. The Basic Law of the HKSAR pronounced that religious freedom would continue unchanged. Nevertheless, church leaders feared that the religious freedom they enjoyed under British rule would not be the same as that defined by the Chinese Communist Party (CCP).[3] While there was hardly any question that the CCP would not interfere with Hong Kong's economy, there was considerably less certainty that restrictions would not be put on political and ideological debate.

In July 1984, the Hong Kong government published the *Green Paper: Further Development of Representative Government in Hong Kong.* The paper suggested that the government intended 'to develop progressively a system of government the authority for which is firmly rooted in Hong Kong, which is able to represent authoritatively the views of the people of Hong Kong, and which is more directly accountable to the people of Hong Kong.'[4] The promises of the Sino-British Joint Declaration and *Green Paper* aroused the political expectations of the Christian community. Protestants and Catholics joined together in demanding political reform in line with the 1984 promises.

The Xin Weisi Article: Boundaries Between Politics and Religion?

In the mid-1980s, the increasing involvement of liberal Christian leaders and lay people in political and social issues in Hong Kong drew the attention of the Chinese government. The latter sent a warning to the Hong Kong churches. In December 1986, a 'social critic' name Xin Weisi who often conveyed the views of the Chinese government on social and political affairs wrote an article in *Ming Pao* entitled 'The Basic Law and Religious Freedom.' According to columnist Yu Kam-yin, Xin Weisi was not a person, but a group of writers at the New China News Agency (NCNA). Their articles served a variety of purposes (Yu 1986).

Before 1997 the Hong Kong Branch of the NCNA was the quasi-Chinese consulate in Hong Kong, and its director was the official representative of the PRC and CCP. In accordance with the United Front Policy, the NCNA staff collected information and tested the responses of every sector of Hong Kong society. The information was all transmitted to Beijing. Sometimes they conveyed messages from the Beijing government to the British government in London and Hong Kong. From 1980 cadres have been assigning contact persons to meet various Catholic and Protestant Church leaders periodically. In short, the Hong Kong Branch of the NCNA served a similar role to that of a foreign affairs office, though it could not be called a consulate.[5]

This article advocated a separation of Church and State and demanded that the Church demarcate clearly the boundary between politics and religion. It argued that the Church should not become involved in political issues or any affairs outside the realm of religion and was highly critical of Christian organizations. It went so far as to name names:

> Since the issue of 1997 appeared, the church-run organizations that were involved in social affairs have become gradually politicized. For example, the Hong Kong Christian Industrial Committee has been involved in workers' strikes, industrial actions and socio-political events. It has become a pressure group that crosses political, religious and industrial boundaries. On the other hand, the Hong Kong Christian Council (HKCC) and the Hong Kong Catholic Social Communications Office are always organizing meetings for Christians who are members of various councils, and have supported their political involvement ... In addition to supporting Christians' political involvement, clergy have openly commented on political matters. Church leaders played an important role in the anti-Daya Bay nuclear plant protests, which became an anti-Chinese Government political issue. On 2 November the Vicar-General of the Hong Kong Catholic Diocese and the General Secretary of HKCC made radical speeches on political reform at the Ko Shan mass rally. This shows that some church leaders wish the Church as a whole to participate in politics, and wish to mobilize the wider Christian population to participate in politics (Xin 1986, 1987b, 90–1).

The mentioning in this article of Catholic leaders in the 'anti-Daya Bay nuclear plant issue' and the 'Ko Shan mass rally' was originally aimed at the Catholic Church. Those cited included a progressive young priest Fr. Louis Ha, and the vicar General Fr. J. B. Tsang. Fr. Louis Ha by that time headed the Catholic Mass Communication Centre and was organizing two social movement groups including The Campaign Against the Anti-Daya Bay Nuclear Plant. The most important one was the Joint Meeting of the Catholic Bodies Concerned for the Development of the Hong Kong Government System in 1987. It collected a total of 765 signatures in August and September 1987 at various Catholic parishes to support the introduction of direct elections in 1988. Beijing suggested the holding of a direct election in 1991 after the formulation of the Basic Law, which governs the electoral system. The same Catholic group sent out 2,374 questionnaires to seek opinion on the introduction of direct elections in 1988. A total of 1,705 respondents favoured direct elections while 326 opposed them, and 342 had no opinion.[6] The Vicar General Fr. J. B. Tsang was not a social activist by nature and in the Ko Shan mass rally spoke for direct elections.

After the nuclear catastrophe in 1986 at Chernobyl, a mass opposition rally and signature campaign was held at the Daya Bay Nuclear Plant just outside of Hong Kong. There was strong objection in Hong Kong against the building of a nuclear plant so close to the territory. These rallies and the Chinese block on the 1988 direct election occurred at about the same time.

The Chinese government was embarrassed by the public demonstrations over these two issues. Xin's article, zeroing in on the Catholic political participation, was the first warning given to the Hong Kong Catholic Church. It had a long-term effect on Church-State relations and the Catholic Church's political participation during the later stages of the transitional period after 1989.[7]

The second part of Xin Weisi's article argued that the Church should comply with the principle of Church-State separation and that religious organizations should not participate in politics because politics is about government while religion is about morality and spirituality. Politics and religion are two separate and distinct entities with different views that may be in conflict with each other, it said, warning that this could threaten social stability:

> Now that Hong Kong has entered into a transitional period, the politicization of some groups in the Catholic and Protestant churches is not a good thing for Hong Kong's economic prosperity and social stability. We know that in the world today countries where religious organizations possess strong political power, such as in Ireland, Poland, Iran and the Philippines, are seldom socially stable and not economically prosperous. If the purpose of the Church in Hong Kong is to gain political power, I am concerned that Hong Kong might not be able to bear the consequences of the [resulting] Church-State conflict. Therefore, I hold that the protection of religious freedom in the Basic Law should limit such freedom to religious activity and not allow the Church to become involved in activities outside religion. The protection of the Basic Law should not include activities that obstruct the Chinese government's 'freedom' to exercise her sovereignty (Xin 1986, 1987b, 92–3).

The third part of the article stressed that religious organizations in Hong Kong and the Mainland ought to comply with the 'Three Principles of mutual non-subordination, mutual non-interference and mutual respect'. In this matter, Xin Weisi did not openly give evidence to support his accusation. However, the bridging efforts of the Christian churches beginning in 1980 with Deng Xiaoping's open door policy angered the CCP, whose latent religious policy as stipulated by Ye Xiaowen, director of the Religious Affairs Bureau, was to eliminate the influence of religion in the socialist China (Ye 1996). Nevertheless, these efforts steadily expanded due to generous foreign assistance. In 1983, there were 500 Catholic churches in China and 2,100 by 1987, 3,900 in 1992, and 4,600 by 1998. The Catholic population is estimated to have increased from 3.3 million in 1986 to 12 million in 2000. Of the 12 million, 5 million belonged to the open (government sanctioned) sector of the Catholic Church while the rest belonged to the underground (non-government sanctioned) sector.[8] As the growth of the underground Catholic population had exceeded that of the open church, the Chinese government became increasingly alarmed because most of the foreign assistance to the Chinese Catholics had gone through Hong Kong. Xin's article said:

> When we demand that the Chinese Government should not apply its religious policies in Hong Kong (after 1997), and this is to be stated in the Basic Law, we should also understand that we cannot demand the Chinese Government apply the religious policies of Hong Kong in mainland China (Xin 1986, 1987b, 94).

Liberal Protestants were quick to criticize the arguments made in the article, which they called untenable (Sung 1986; Kei 1986; Po 1986; Law 1986). The Catholics in Hong Kong did not rebut Xin Weisi, and the bridging efforts continued, as shown in the above statistical figures.

In response to the Protestant Church's arguments, 'Xin Weisi' wrote a second article in February 1987 reiterating the view that religious organizations and religious personnel should not participate in politics and suggested that clergy could participate in politics as individuals. It cited Bishop Peter Kwong of the Anglican Church as a good example:

> There is a difference between clergy who participate in politics in their religious capacity and those who participate as individuals. The former can easily be misunderstood as representing the will or view of the whole religious organization, the latter is clearly seen to be representing only him or herself. Although the six religious representatives and Peter Kwong in the [Basic Law] Consultative Committee are leaders of their religious organizations, they

participate in the committee as individuals and yet reflect the views of their respective religions. This is the way it should be (Xin 1987a, 1987b, 125).

This article went further, arguing that some Christians who participate in politics do so because they desire to reconstruct a form of Medieval 'Christendom':

> Some clergy believe that the Church's participation in politics is not for material interest but merely an attempt to build a just, equal and loving society in the spirit of Christ. Frankly speaking, this was also the goal of Christendom in Medieval Europe, which sought to unify the Church and State (Xin 1987a, 1987b, 125).

The reason for embracing this opinion was fear of the ability of religious organizations to promote, in the name of religion, a particular political view. Using a tactic developed from the Bolshevik tradition, the CCP sought to use non-governmental organizations as a weapon to secure State control (Selznick 1960; Schurmann 1968; Saich 1997). Also the CCP was well aware that the Catholic Church in Hong Kong is an organization opposed to the spread of Communism. Therefore the CCP was determined to limit the Catholic Church to purely religious activities, and to terminate its involvement in local politics (B. Leung 2001).

In response, the Christian Sentinels for Hong Kong wrote an article in *Ming Pao*, entitled *Church-State Separation: Misunderstanding and Clarification* in February 1987 (Christian Sentinels for Hong Kong 1987, 96–99). It outlined four different kinds of Church-State relations in order to highlight the weaknesses in Xin's argument. The article differentiates the concepts of *zheng* from *zheng-fu* (literally, 'government') and *zheng-zhi* (literally, 'politics') and *jiao* from *jiao-hui* (literally, 'church') and *zong-jiao* (literally, 'religion') in Chinese. So the word *zhen* could refer to a political institution or political activity, and *jiao* could refer to a religious institution or religious activity. Hence, *zheng-jiao* (literally, 'State-Church') relations can be divided into four different types: politics and religion, politics and the Church, government and religion and government and the Church.

The Christian Sentinels stated that the power bases of the State and Church were derived from different sources and their personnel and distribution of resources were independent of each other. Therefore they should be separated in both organization and institution. Regarding the relationship between political activity and religious faith, it was pointed out that the Christian faith is concerned about people and society as a whole. In Christian theology, God the creator shares a common ground with human beings, so Christians in the world have to take part in the human destiny in history. The article argued that when Christians say that their goal of political participation is 'to build a just, equal and loving society that is in the spirit of Christ', it can be understood as a spontaneous expression of faith. The principle of Church-State separation, therefore, does not apply at this level.

Apropos the relationship between the Church and politics, the Christian Sentinels stressed that the Church needs and has the right to participate in politics. In the former, the content and mission of the Christian faith includes concern about and involvement in politics. In the latter, the Church as a civic organization has the right to participate in any political activity *de jure*. Therefore, the principle of Church-State separation does not apply as well at this level. As for the relationship between the State and religion, the Christian Sentinels stated that as long as the religious doctrine and activity of a religion does not violate the law, the government does not have the right to interfere with that religion. The principle of Church-State separation does apply at this level. The fundamental point was that the political participation of the churches and Christians is both justified and needed and that their actions have a theological and legal basis.

The same article also pointed out that there were several errors in arguments of 'Xin Weisi' on Church-State separation, and that many were unclear. For example, Xin argued that politics and religion have different focuses, with religion focused on questions of morality and spirituality. From a Christian perspective, the Christian faith relates to all forms of human behaviour, not only human morality or spirituality. Moreover, the assertion that Christians who took part in politics were aiming to reconstruct a Medieval Christian State, mixed up two sets of concepts, namely, religious activity and the Church on the one hand, and political activity and the government on the other.

The Church-State Controversy Surrounding the Establishment of the Selection Committee

In 1996, in accordance with the time schedule laid out in the Basic Law, the HKSAR Preparatory Committee, commissioned by the Chinese government, began to set up the Selection Committee (SC).[9] The initial function of the SC was to elect the first SAR Chief Executive to replace the British Governor at the time of the handover. The first SC was made up of 400 permanent residents of Hong Kong. The Basic Law specified that the SC must include people from four sectors: 100 from the industrial, commercial and financial sectors; 100 professionals; 100 labour, grass-roots, religious and other sectors; and 100 representatives made up of existing Legislative Council members, Hong Kong deputies to the National People's Congress and representatives of Hong Kong members of the National Committee of the Chinese People's Political and Consultative Conference. Due to a breakdown in negotiations between Beijing and London over political reform in Hong Kong, the Chinese government decided to abolish the pre-handover Executive Council, Legislative Council, Urban Council and District Council on the day of the handover, 30 June 1997. The SC was ordered by Beijing to select 60 members of a 'Provisional Legislature', which would run Hong Kong until elections for a new Legislative Council could be held.

According to the Basic Law a number of seats on the SC were reserved for religion. As a result the HKSAR Preparatory Committee held a consultative meeting for religious representatives on 14 April 1996. Protestant, Catholic, Buddhist, Taoist, Confucianist and Muslim representatives attended the meeting and discussed how they would participate in the SC.

The Protestant response

Five representatives from the Protestant churches attended the consultative meeting for religious representatives: Elder Simon Sit Pun-kei and Reverend Lo Lung-kwong of the HKCC, Stephen Liu Chi-kan of the Hong Kong Chinese Christian Church Union (HKCCCU), Reverend Paul Ng Chun-chi of the Church of Christ in China (CCC), and Reverend Lam Chun-wai of the Anglican Church. After the meeting, the HKCC called a meeting among the Protestant churches to inform other church workers on the matters concerning the SC and to seek their views on how to elect Protestant representatives to sit on the SC. It sent out more than 200 invitation letters but only about 30 people attended the meeting. To resolve the question over whether Protestants should send representatives to sit on the SC, the HKCC called for a meeting of its Executive Committee on 22 April 1996 and a special General Meeting of all members on 17 May 1996. It was agreed at the General Meeting that the HKCC should nominate Protestant representatives to take part in the SC.

The participants at the General Meeting suggested that the churches adhere to certain broad principles when taking part in the SC. They decided that a joint nomination committee be set up by the HKCC and other Christian organizations in order to find possible Protestant representatives; the Protestant representatives should not represent any church but participate as individuals in the election of the Chief Executive; the Protestant representatives should not be involved in choosing members of the Provisional Legislature; the nomination committee should play the role of consultant and advisor to the Protestant representatives, as well as to monitor their work; and finally, the committee be dissolved after the Chief Executive was elected.

Two of the above principles merit particular attention. Firstly, that the Protestant representatives only take part in the election of the Chief Executive and not the Provisional Legislature was a sign that the HKCC wished to set conditions on the participation of Protestant representatives. Simon Sit told the press that the Provisional Legislature did not comply with the Basic Law and that it was therefore the HKCC's position that the Protestant representatives should not be involved in electing the Provisional Legislature. Secondly, to uphold the principle of Church-State separation, the Protestant representatives should take part in the SC as individuals, not as church representatives. Simon Sit stressed that although the HKCC would help organize the nomination committee, tasked with finding suitable Protestant representatives for the SC, it was indirect participation in politics. By following the above rules, the churches could participate in the election of the Chief Executive, as stipulated by law, and yet maintain the principle of Church-State separation. However, it later proved difficult to monitor the Protestant participants to make sure that they acted not as official church representatives but as individuals. To deal with this problem, Reverend Lo Lung-kwong suggested that the nomination committee issue a statement to condemn the participants if they violated the principles set forth by the committee.[10]

The HKCC's decision drew the attention of some Christian social concern groups and the latter started to organize protest action against the involvement of the churches in the SC. On 28 April 1996, nine Christian groups jointly organized a 'Hong Kong Christian Sharing Meeting' to discuss whether the churches should be involved in the SC.[11] About 80 people attended the meeting and views for and against were presented, although by the end of the meeting most of the participants were opposed to the churches sending representatives to the SC. Those in support of involvement in the SC argued that: by being involved in the SC the churches could create a channel of communication with the Chinese government; the Protestant representatives could take part as individuals and therefore their involvement would not affect the status of the churches; the representatives could restrict their involvement solely to electing the Chief Executive; and finally, involvement in the SC was the duty of a citizen. The arguments made by those opposed to participation were that:

opposition to the SC did not imply rejecting communication with the Chinese government but there were many ways to communicate, official and unofficial; the churches should not take part in any government bodies or 'power games' but merely monitor the operation of the government; the argument that the Protestant representatives would participate as individuals did not stand because there was no way for the Christian community to guarantee this; the election of SC members lacked the basis of public support; and the SC formed by 400 people did not represent true democracy and deprived Hong Kong citizens of the right to elect their own leaders.[12]

After the meeting the Christian groups published an extra of a newsletter in which they briefly recorded the details of the discussion. In it, the organizers of the meeting wrote a short essay entitled 'Refused to be a Silent Lamb' expressing their position on Church-State relations:

> The political system situation of political system has exposed Church-State relations in Hong Kong. Where should we stand and make our views known? The powerful or the powerless?
>
> As Christians, we should look at the question of church involvement in the SC from the perspective of Christian faith and church witness. The Chinese government has clearly pointed out that any person who becomes a member of the SC must support the Provisional Legislature and that means that they have to support an executive body which is *de facto* commissioned by the State and will replace another body that is more democratic.
>
> From the Christian perspective, the SC basically deprives every citizen of the right to equal political participation and shows that some people enjoy privileges. This is against our faith. We believe that in the eyes of our God everyone is equal. If a system provides privileges to some and not to others, that system should be criticized by Christians.
>
> From the perspective of church witness, if the churches know the limitations of the SC and still take part, they cannot play the role of 'prophet'. By insisting on taking part in the SC the churches will convey a negative message, that the churches think only about their own interests and neglect the interests of Hong Kong people as a whole. If the churches join a regime that deprives the rights of people, the witness of the churches will then be destroyed in Hong Kong.
>
> As Christians, we must care about the well-being and rights of Hong Kong people. We hope that the Church will be a lamp [in the darkness] and that in times of difficulty she will shine light on

the way of truth to suffering people and stand with the people. In this way the Church will fulfil her mission. Hence, we call for all Christians to say 'no' to the involvement of the churches in the SC.[13]

To show their opposition to the SC, eight Christian groups and 178 individuals published a statement entitled, 'Joint Statement of Christians Opposing the Churches' Participation in the Selection Committee' in *Ming Pao* on 17 May 1996.[14] Seven of the Christian groups organized a protest to express their views at the venue where the Special Meeting of the HKCC took place.[15] The statement had five main points:

1. To safeguard the independent status of the Church, the churches should not take part in any government body. Therefore, we oppose the churches choosing any representatives by whatever means to take part in the Selection Committee.

2. As the election of the members of the SC is based on sector, the nature of the election rules out the status of individual representatives. So the Protestant representatives cannot claim that they take part in the SC as individuals and thereby escape from the fact that they are accountable to the Protestant churches.

3. The SC violates the spirit of 'high autonomy, Hong Kong people ruling Hong Kong' as stated in the Sino-British Joint Declaration. This method of election is *de facto* a system of commission which produces a Chief Executive and executive body, and this is a regression of democracy in Hong Kong.

4. The Provisional Legislature, which is *de facto* produced through a system of commission, cannot represent public opinion. There is no channel for citizens to monitor these representatives and therefore the interest of citizens will be damaged.

5. The mission of the Church is to safeguard basic human rights, promote the development of human rights and protect the vulnerable victimized by the system. In the case of the SC, it is obvious that Hong Kong people cannot express their opinion. If the churches take part in the SC it means that they are also undermining the rights of Hong Kong people.[16]

At the Special Meeting of the HKCC, Reverend Chu Yiu-ming, chairman of the Hong Kong Industrial Committee, cast his vote against sending Protestant representatives as individuals to take part in the SC. Later, Chu and Reverend Lo Lung-kwong debated the issue and criticized each other's arguments through the media. According to Chu, although the Protestant representatives would participate in the SC as individuals, the HKCC and other Christian churches or organizations nominated them. This was in conflict with the principle of Church-State separation. For Lo, the reality was not so clearly black and white. A willingness to communicate with Beijing did not imply acceptance of Beijing's views.[17] In preparation for the 1997 handover, the churches should become more active in political issues. He criticized his opponents for refusing to deal with the Chinese and HKSAR government in the name of Church-State separation.[18] Other members of the HKCC believed that by taking part in the SC, the churches could act as a 'candle in the darkness'. For example, the Protestant representatives could refuse to take part in work related to the Provisional Legislature and even cast their votes against the motion.[19]

When the HKCC endorsed the proposal to nominate Protestant representatives to the SC, some Christian social groups published an article in *Ming Pao* on 24 May 1996, publicly questioning its position (Christian Social Groups 1996). The first criticism was that at the Special Meeting of the HKCC, less than 50 per cent of the membership was in attendance. The small number of attendants showed that the decision made at the meeting was not representative. Secondly, they questioned the argument made by the HKCC that to take part in the SC was 'to do the duty of citizens'. Since the SC deprived Hong Kong citizens of the right to participate in politics the argument did not stand, the opponents said. Another criticism was that the HKCC had no mechanism to monitor their elected representatives. The opponents slated the HKCC's argument that the Protestant representatives would not take part in the vote for the Provisional Legislature. The opponents argued that the very participation of Protestant representatives was already a gesture of support for the undemocratic political system. Finally, the Christian social groups accused the HKCC of breaking the principle of Church-State separation. The article stressed that what it called 'indirect participation' was deceptive:

> The spokesmen emphasized that the principle of Church-State separation means Christians should not take part in any political or governmental body in the name of the Church. But at the same time the Council set up a nomination committee, which in their eyes has comprehensive representation, and they use it to elect Protestant representatives to join the SC. These Protestant representatives do not represent the HKCC, but will be produced by the Council. Once elected, the representatives can 'directly take part' as individuals

in the SC without any restrictions. This complicated structure reflects the fact that the churches are contradicting themselves in regards to Church-State separation by ungracefully joining a game organized by the Chinese government (Christian Social Groups 1996).

Disregarding the strong protests from Christian social groups, the HKCC continued to organize the nomination committee, consisting of 20 members mainly from the Council itself, the Lutheran Church and the Baptist Church.[20] However, the Secretariat of the HKSAR Preparatory Committee announced in August 1996 that those who intended to compete for seats on the SC needed only verification of status from their respective sectors. Nomination was not therefore necessary. Hence, the Council's nomination committee was dissolved. In October 1996, the secretariat of the Preparatory Committee announced the names of the candidates who competed for the seats of the SC. In the Protestant sector there were 14 people, including Anglican Bishop Peter Kwong and Simon Sit Pun-kei of the HKCC. Most of the names were either clergy of the Anglican Church or had Anglican roots.[21]

The media's attention was drawn to the election of the Protestant representatives after Bishop Peter Kwong and Shi Jiao-guang, Chairman of the Hong Kong Buddhist Association, both members of HKSAR Government Preparatory Committee, sent a private letter to all the members of the Preparatory Committee on 4 October 1996. The letter listed the names of the representatives of the six religions in Hong Kong to be elected into the SC, and asked the members of the Preparatory Committee to choose their preferred candidates. Most of the Protestant representatives were clergy of the Anglican Church.[22] Some critics complained that the letter was an attempt to deal underhandedly. Other critics commented that the letter was an attempt by the religious leaders to organize political faction.[23] A letter sent to *Christian Times Weekly* criticized Bishop Peter Kwong for opposing the will of Hong Kong people, for siding with the future political regime, for publicly supporting an Anglican member who was affiliated to a pro-Chinese government political party, and as a result dividing the churches.[24]

In November 1996, the Secretariat of the Preparatory Committee announced the membership list of the SC. On the list of Protestant representatives were three names: Bishop Peter Kwong, Simon Sit Pun-kei and Alice Yuk Tak-fun, general secretary of the Hong Kong YWCA. Just before the election of the Chief Executive and Provisional Legislature, some Christians issued an open letter entitled: 'To Bishop Peter Kwong, Elder Simon P. K. Sit,

Alice Yuk Tak-fun and Christians in the Selection Committee' in the name of 'A Group of Christian University Students and Graduates'. The letter was published in *Ming Pao* on 11 December 1996 and signed by 90 concerned Christians. The open letter listed some normative conditions for electing a good Chief Executive, and demanded that the Protestant representatives not cast their votes or take part in any activity related to electing the Provisional Legislature.[25]

However, Sit and Yuk told the media that they would participate in the election of the Provisional Legislature.[26] The position of Sit soon aroused the attention of the Protestant community. Raymond Fung, deputy chairman of the HKCIC, wrote an article in *Christian Times Weekly* criticizing Simon Sit. He said he had lost his integrity by agreeing to take part in the election of the Provisional Legislature, and demanded that Sit resign as chairman of the HKCC. Fung's demand was based on the previously stated opposition of the Council to Protestant members of the SC participating in any work related to the Provisional Legislature. Since, however, the Protestant representatives were in fact participating in the SC as individuals it was impossible for the Council to constrain their actions. Fung made the following criticism:

> Regarding Simon Sit, when he decided to take part in the election of the Provisional Legislature, he was free to do so and his involvement does not violate the rules of procedure. But he violates the clear position of the Council. On moral grounds, he has failed in his duty as chairman of the Council. If he resigns from the post, he could regain a small amount of integrity (R. Fung 1996d).

Sit did not resign from the post and the HKCC did not issue any statement condemning him.[27]

The Catholic response

Although the Sino-British Agreement on the Future of Hong Kong (1984) promised 'one country two systems' and the Basic Law of the Hong Kong SAR guarantees that religious freedom will continue unchanged after the handover to Chinese rule, Hong Kong Catholics were concerned that the definition of religious freedom used by the British would not be the same as that used by the Chinese Communist Party.[28]

Chinese interference has been increasingly felt in political and ideological matters. China denounced the semi-democratic 1995 (Legco) election, and after the handover did not allow the elected councillors to retain their seats. Against the provisions of the Basic Law, Beijing decided to establish a temporary legislative body immediately following the transfer of sovereignty. Religious freedom is an important indicator of social freedom, and is closely linked with the degree of ideological and political freedom. Hong Kong Catholics, aware of the hardships endured by Catholics in the Mainland, and with freedom of the press already under threat, many feared that after the handover, Church-State relations in Hong Kong would change from the 'contractor' model to the 'political absorption of religion' model practised in China (Chan 1995).

The deep concern of the Catholic Church in Hong Kong over its future stemmed from the recognition that Christianity presents a world view irreconcilable with the ideology of Marxism-Leninism. The CCP has shown no intention of allowing any religious belief, including Christianity under its reign. The CCP leadership has displayed little positive inclination towards Christianity because they consider it an element of cultural imperialism. As nationalists, the CCP leaders do not support Christianity because they believe it to be a foreign religion (Chan and Leung 2000).

The fear and anxiety of the Hong Kong Catholic Church is reflected in the action of its bishop, Cardinal Wu. After consulting with his advisers, he issued a manifesto in which he specified the type of religious freedom which the Hong Kong Catholics had been enjoying and emphasized the point that Catholics needed to be united with the universal church through union with the Pope (appendix 1). His statement on religious freedom was as follows:

> Religious freedom as we enjoy it in Hong Kong includes the following rights:
>
> 1. The right to have, or to adopt a religion or belief of one's choice, and to manifest it in worship, observance, practice and teaching.
> 2. The right of the individual to worship in private and public, alone and with fellow-believers.
> 3. The right to make one's religion known to others, and to instruct those who are interested in this religion and the spoken and written word.
> 4. The right of parents to provide religious instruction in bringing up their children.
> 5. The right of religious communities and associations to hold meetings and to promote educational, cultural, charitable and social activities.
> 6. The right to appoint personnel, and to train and send them abroad for specialized studies, and at the same time the right to utilize, if and when necessary, the services of personnel from abroad.

7. The right to erect and/or use buildings for religious purposes and to acquire such property if necessary.
8. The right for Catholics in particular, to maintain their existing links and existing unity with the universal church, through union with the Pope and also with the Bishops and Catholic communities in other parts of the world. This unity is basic to the Catholic Church's outlook (Wu 1984).

Due to his personal background, Cardinal Wu knew very well that the religious freedom Hong Kong Catholics enjoyed was quite different from that permitted in China. He was born in Wuhua, Guangdong Province. After ordination in Hong Kong in 1952, he could not return to work in his own diocese of Meixian, Guangdong. He first worked in the United States, then in Taiwan. In 1975 he was appointed to the bishopship of Hong Kong, and in 1988 became Cardinal Bishop. His family remained in Wuhua. His elevation to the Cardinalate took place during the transition period (1984–1997). Beijing was very sensitive to this move and suspected that the Vatican tried to take the lead in appointing the man of its choice, Bishop Wu, to be the Prince of the Church stationed in Hong Kong. As Cardinal Wu would be the head of the Church in China after the handover, the Chinese government believed Wu would ultimately indirectly oversee the Church in China.[29]

Cardinal Wu wrote to the British Foreign Secretary, Sir Geoffrey Howe, and to Cardinal Hume of England, to express his concern over the future of Hong Kong. He appealed to Sir Geoffrey to provide a clear legal guarantee in the Sino-British agreement for 'full and effective recognition to all the rights and freedom hitherto enjoyed by all religious associations and their members in Hong Kong and to preserve all such rights and freedoms beyond 1997'. The news was not reported in Hong Kong but in a Catholic magazine in Britain.[30] His letter aroused some criticism among progressive Catholic leaders who considered it, given the repeated assurances made by the Chinese authorities, to have an over-suspicious tone. This was especially true after the deputy director of *Xinhua* held a luncheon for Italian Senator Vittro Colombo, one of the contacts between the Vatican and China. On this occasion the China representative in Hong Kong assured Hong Kong Catholics they would enjoy the same amount of freedom after 1997 as before.[31]

Pro-China clergy and Catholics did not like the fact that the Cardinal approached the British side to show his concern for future religious freedom and did not trust China. However, the criticism was restricted to the inner circle of the Catholic Church. No outsiders were informed of the disagreement because the Catholic authorities held to the principle that unity among Catholics was of first priority.[32] The Catholic prelate of Hong Kong was aware that the 'divide and rule' technique was commonly used in political struggles.

'March into the Bright Decade': Cardinal Wu Prepares the Church for Post-1997 Hong Kong

Cardinal Wu's 'March Into the Bright Decade' pastoral letter (exhortation) was launched in October 1989 after two years of consultation and formulation. A working committee consisting of senior clergy, religious men and women, professionals and scholars including a leading political scientist, Professor Kuan Hsin-chi of Hong Kong Chinese University was established to work on it. Public opinion was also sought. It was regarded as the blueprint plan for the Catholic community in preparation for the handover. Ironically, it was issued on 7 October 1989 when Hong Kong society was in deep shock and despair following the violent crushing of the pro-democratic movement at Tiananmen Square in June that year.

The exhortation recommended a two-pronged strategy for responding to political change in Hong Kong after 1997 and listed seven main themes that needed particular attention: 1) the formation of the laity, 2) small faith communities, 3) on-going formation of priests, brothers and sisters, 4) mass communications, 5) education, 6) social services, and 7) relations between the Diocese and China and the Church in China (J. Wu 1989, 8). The strategy aimed first to encourage the Church guided by Christian principles, to become more involved in Hong Kong's socio-political affairs, and second to strengthen the Christian community through the deepening of religious beliefs. It was intended that through sermons, preaching and catechising at the parish level, the social teaching of the Church would spread to grassroots Catholics.

A 'Committee for Promoting the Cardinal's Pastoral Exhortation' was established for the continual monitoring of the implementation of the pastoral letter. It enjoyed high legal status as a constant diocese commission chaired by the Vicar General with eight members chosen by the Cardinal including reputed priests, nuns, and laity who held high positions with in the Catholic hierarchy.[33] Item 7 'on relations between the Diocese and China and the Church in China', referred to the bridging efforts between Hong Kong and China. In spite of the warning through Xin Weisi's writings, the Hong Kong Catholic Diocese was determined to go ahead with these efforts to revive the Catholic Church in China. It implied that the Catholic Church in Hong Kong would carry

In a rally supporting the pro-democratic movement in Tiananmen Square 1989, the Catholics joined under the banner 'Catholic Groups Supporting the Democratic Movement in China'. Courtesy of the Archive Office of Catholic Hong Kong Diocese.

(From left to right) Protestant Rev. Lee Ching-chee, Rev. Chu Yiu-ming and Catholic priests Fr. Louis Ha and Fr. Ferdinand Lok jointly appealed to the public for donations in a campaign for the relief of Eastern China flood victims in July 1991. Courtesy of the Archive Office of the Catholic Hong Kong Diocese.

on with its own agenda regardless of what Beijing said or did. In the drafting of the HKSAR Basic Law, Beijing, through its selection of religious members to the Drafting Committee, exposed its relationships with the various religious organizations in the territory, including its cool relations with Hong Kong Catholic Church.

Neither Cardinal Wu, nor any other Catholic clergy were invited to participate in the formulation of the Basic Law of the HKSAR. The Anglican Archbishop of Hong Kong, Bishop Peter Kwong, and the top leader of Hong Kong Buddhist 'church' were, however, asked to join the Basic Law Drafting Committee.

The prelate of the Hong Kong Catholic Church actually has a higher position and more prestige in the Catholic Church hierarchy than does the bishop of Macau; in terms of the strength of church life, compared to Macau, Hong Kong has the greater number of clergy, followers and church institutions. However, in 1988 when the Drafting Committee for the Basic Law of Macau was recruiting local prominent religious people, the young and progressive Fr. Peter Chung of the Diocese of Macau, who had been trained in Hong Kong, was recruited in the Consultative Committee, while the Catholic bishop of Macau, Domingos Lam, was in the Drafting Committee. They were the only religious representatives from the religious sector. The Church authorities in Hong Kong saw this appointment as a deliberate snub.

On Preparing Catholic Leadership: The Cardinal and His Two New Bishops

The Bishop of Hong Kong, John Baptist Wu, was consecrated as a Cardinal on 28 June 1988. The ceremony was officiated by the Pope in Rome after the Sino-British Agreement on the Future of Hong Kong had been signed. On the surface, Bishop Wu's elevation to the cardinalate had nothing to do with politics. Untypically, the British had not interfered with the activities of the Catholic Church in Hong Kong. However, the year of his elevation (1988) occurred during the transitional period and China was beginning to pay more attention to the religious activities in Hong Kong. Moreover, following the row between China and the Vatican over the elevation of Dominic Deng Yiming to Archbishop of Guangzhou in 1982, China had been suspicious of all that the Catholic Church in Hong Kong did.[34] By tradition, Bishop John Wu, as cardinal, will be the Prince of the Church, and the consultant of the Holy Father on important issues. China expressed its dislike through the remarks of Bishop Aloysius Jin Luxian of Shanghai who said that the Vatican had long term plans to put its own man at the head the Catholic Church in China. When Hong Kong returned to Chinese rule after 1997 Cardinal Wu would rank highest among all the Chinese bishops. It was a move to have the Vatican's man in Hong Kong aiming at heading the Church in China in the long run.[35] Neither the Vatican nor the Hong Kong Church reacted to the remark.

Born in 1925, Cardinal Wu would reach 70 in 1995, and beginning in the early 1990s, a search had been going on for his successor. In October 1996 it was announced that Fr. Joseph Zen and Fr. John Tong would be the coadjutor bishop and auxiliary bishop, respectively.[36] The coadjutor is meant to be the successor of Cardinal Wu as the prelate of Hong Kong. Neither Zen nor Tong had pastoral experience, but both had two decades of experience in dealing with China. In 1980 Bishop Tong was transferred from his theological professorship in the seminary to a new China-focused centre, the Holy Spirit Study Centre. He was regarded as the most well-informed person in the Catholic Church about China. Zen had spent at least six months of each year from 1989 to 1996 in China, teaching in seminaries. A resident of Shanghai, Zen had a thorough understanding of the Catholic Church in that part of country. However, he was chosen as the successor of Cardinal Wu to lead the Hong Kong Catholic Church.

In the Catholic Church, at least three bishops are needed for a bishop's consecration: the principal Ordaining Bishop, and two or more other Ordaining Bishops. In this case, the Principal Ordaining Bishop was automatically Cardinal Wu, the prelate of Hong Kong. The public was unaware that the selection of the Ordaining Bishops had posed some thorny problems for the Hong Kong Diocese. Doctrinally, the bishops in the open sector of the Chinese Catholic church were illegitimate but their consecration was valid. In other words, their union with the universal church is not yet completed. They cannot be the Ordaining Bishops due to their defective status in the church hierarchy. On the other hand, the government would not allow the underground Chinese bishops to come for this occasion either. The Hong Kong Diocese felt very awkward in this political dilemma, so it was suggested that the consecration be held in Rome. However, this idea was rejected because some Hong Kong Catholics believed that the consecration of their religious leaders ought to occur at home, not thousands of miles away.

Without inviting bishops from the Mainland, Hong Kong feared that the arrival of the seven Taiwanese bishops would irritate Beijing. Thus Zen went to Taiwan to explain the difficulties to the hierarchy there. Only the president of Taiwan Bishops, Cardinal Paul Shan Kuo-hsi, Bishop of Kaohsiung was invited to serve as one of the eight Ordaining Bishops. The other seven were all related to Tong and Zen or were specially related to the diocese. One was Archbishop Charles Schleck, representative of the Rome-based Congregation for the Evangelization of Peoples, and another was Bishop Franz Vorrath, Auxiliary Bishop of Essen, Germany, the sister diocese of Hong Kong. Cardinal Peter Seiichi Shirayanagi of Tokyo, was a personal friend of John Tong, and Bishop of Macau Domingos Lam is the godfather of Tong. Bishop Leo Drona of San Jose, Philippines, Bishop Michael Chaicharoen, of Surat Thani, Thailand, and Bishop John Chang Yik of Chun Cheon of South Korea were all personal friends and classmates of Zen. The eight bishops constituted an international team for this occasion. However, the NCNA contact person expressed displeasure after the ceremony.

The ordination ceremony was held on 9 December 1996. The Hong Kong Diocese decided to keep it as a religious service and did not invite any officials, diplomats and dignitaries to take part. Chris Patten, the governor, and a practising Catholic asked for an invitation and a special seat was duly reserved for him. Some leaders of other Christian churches were invited, but there were no guests from Islamic, Buddhist, or Daoist groups. However, on the next day, a cocktail party was given by the Hong Kong Catholic Diocese to introduce the two new bishops to the public. Hong Kong officials, diplomats, dignitaries and Chinese officials from the NCNA Hong Kong Branch, were all invited to attend.[37]

This event, just before the handover demonstrated the Hong Kong Catholic Church's desire not to compromise on doctrinal matters even at the expense of sacrificing its own interests in future Church-State relations. It was later revealed to one of the authors that Beijing, through NCNA, wanted Mainland bishops to be invited and to hold a concelebration Holy Mass with other bishops to legitimize the position of the government-chosen bishops. Beijing was disappointed by the snub.[38]

The Catholic Church Distances Itself From the Electoral Committee

In 1994, when the HKSAR Preparatory Committee was established, Fr. J. B. Tsang, the assistant director of Caritas-Hong Kong, was appointed as a consultant on Hong Kong Affairs. However, by then the consultancy role was minimal because China had already fixed its agenda regarding the role of religion, and the transition preparations were in their final stages. In the midst of Chris Patten's work towards political reform in 1995, church leaders from mainland China, whenever they had an opportunity to meet, tried to dissuade Hong Kong Catholics from supporting the Governor, himself a devoted Catholic.[39] Actually, the Chinese Catholic leaders, such as the bishops in Shanghai, Sichuan, and Shaanxi had little knowledge of the complexity of Hong Kong politics in the transitional period. Thus, it is reasonable to wonder if these Chinese Catholic leaders spoke their mind or were merely propaganda instruments of the Beijing government in the row over Chris Patten's political reform.

Five liberal and pro-democratic Catholic associations including the DCJP openly dissuaded the Catholic authorities from sending a Catholic candidate to the SC from which Provisional Legco members would be elected.[40] They gave the reason that the SC was being manipulated and went against the principle of justice.[41] Within the Catholic Church there were long debates over this issue.

Opinions were very much divided. Some Catholic clergy believed that the Catholic Church should listen to Beijing. The progressive, middle-class laity professionals hoped the Catholic Church would act as the conscience of society. They believed the Catholic Church, by distancing itself from SC, would be in a better position to call for moral integrity. Espousing democracy, and supporting the autonomy of Hong Kong as a means of preserving religious freedom, they did not support the Provisional Legco, and in fact deemed it illegal. On the other hand, Democratic Party leader Martin Lee, also a devoted Catholic, persuaded many Catholic middle class people to vote for democrats.

The Catholic Church was expected by democrats to take the lead in opposing Mainland interference in Hong Kong politics.[42] Pro-China priests such as Fr. Luke Tsui, the director of the Catholic Institute for Religion and Society, did not all agree. They felt that Catholic participation in the SC's activities was not only civic duty, but also regarded their support of the government as following the Holy Father's advocation that good Christians ought to be good citizens.[43] Sending Catholic candidates was seen as a gesture of willingness to cooperate with the future HKSAR government.

On the same issue of joining the Electoral Committee, there were also fiery debates and strong disagreements within the Protestant Church. Two publicly opposing Protestant groups emerged. The Catholic Church, however, was determined to remain united and decided to confine its disagreements within the church circle and prevent the heated discussions from leaking into the hands of the media.

In an attempt to break the stalemate, the Cardinal and his two new assistants, Bishops Joseph Zen and John Tong decided to hold an unprecedented consultation, permitting all levels of the church circle, including priests, religious men and women, as well as laity express the pros and cons of sending Catholic candidates to the SC. Participants attended in the name of the associations they represented. These associations were major organizations of priests, sisters, brothers and laity constituting the backbone of the Catholic church in Hong Kong: the Board of Diocesan Consulters, Diocesan personal Commission, Council of Priests, Diocesan Pastoral Council, Association of Major Superiors of Religious Men in Hong Kong, Association of Major Superior of Religious Women in Hong Kong, Hong Kong Diocesan Pastoral Sisters Association, and Hong Kong Council of Catholic Laity. The vote held after the discussions yielded the following results:[44]

Table 3   Catholic Consultation Results on Sending Selection Committee Candidates (%)

Do not participate in SC	18.88
Participate in SC (perform 2 functions)*	35.44
Participate in SC (elect only Chief Executive)	45.68
No clergy should be recommended (only laity are recommended)	29.55
Clergy can be recommended	70.45

* *perform 2 functions* means to elect the Chief Executive as well as members of the Provisional Legco.

With such results, the Catholic Diocese could neither follow the Democrats' wish to boycott the SC, nor could it oppose the mainly laity's wishes to uphold its moral leadership by not supporting it. The compromise was to endorse Catholic candidates' participation in the SC as their right as individuals, but to make it clear that they were not representatives of the Church. These Catholic candidates could elect the Chief Executive only. As the Catholic authorities believed that the SC lacked legitimacy, it was left to the Catholic candidates themselves to elect Provisional Legco members.[45] However, the compromise position of the Catholic Diocese pleased no one within or outside the Church. It was taken as a sign of weakness and lack of courage to voice the truth.

The Justice and Peace Commission of the Hong Kong Catholic Diocese (DJPC) took the lead both within the church circle and outside it to advocate that the Catholic Church should not cooperate with the SC and questioned the legitimacy of the Provision Legislative Council. Together with other Christian institutes and democratic groups, the DJPC launched signature campaigns on the street, convened seminars and placed public statements (supported with signatures) in newspapers to advocate their democratic stance. The DJPC was one of eight Christian groups and 178 individuals that published a statement entitled, 'Joint Statement of Christians Opposing the Churches' Participation in the Selection Committee' in *Ming Pao* on 17 May 1996.[46] The compromise made by the Catholic authorities disappointed the leaders of the DJPC, and the fact that the authorities sought their cooperation and understanding and asked them not to voice disagreement with the Catholic decision was very difficult for the DJPC. However, it had to follow the Catholic tradition of keeping silent on this issue, obeying the teaching authority, and respecting the final decisions of the top leaders. It was paramount to maintain a sense of unity within the church especially when the future was uncertain, possibly even hostile.[47]

Concluding Remarks

Due to the ideological incompatibility between dialectic materialism and religion, the PRC adopted atheist dialectic materialism as its official ideology. China's 'religious freedom policy' with its own dialectic interpretation allows no other ideologies except that of Marxism-Leninism and Mao Zedong Thought. In practice, China's current Church-State relations follow the 'political absorption of religion' model which caused great anxiety to Hong Kong Christians in the 1980s at the time of the Sino-British negotiations on the future of Hong Kong, and subsequently when the 1984 Sino-British Joint Declaration announced the return of Hong Kong to the Chinese rule in 1997. For Hong Kong Christians, religious freedom was key because the Mainland had continually violated religious freedom for forty years in the PRC. Both Catholics and Protestants cherished the hope that political autonomy promised by the 'one country two systems' would protect religious freedom and other important values in Hong Kong. This hope motivated Hong Kong Christians to participate in the political process, namely in the anti-Daya Bay Nuclear Plant protest, and in promotion of the 1988 Direct Election in the Legislative Council.

The articles of Xin Weisi in the pro-China paper were an indication of Beijing's disapproval of the Hong Kong Christians' political participation, and not long afterwards a stiffer stance was taken towards Hong Kong religious groups. The authorities in China sought separation of religion and State in the Basic Law and laid down three basic rules after Hong Kong's transfer to Chinese rule: 1) contractorship in education and social service could continue, 2) assistance in reviving the Catholic Church in China should be eliminated, and 3) all political participation by church members and clergy should stop.

The nomination of religious representatives to the Selection Committee in 1996 created considerable controversy among the Protestant churches. The Hong Kong Christian Council, representing mostly the Protestant churches, was willing to elect Protestant representatives to take part as individuals indirectly in the Selection Committee. It was argued that if the church leaders were to take part as individuals and not as church representatives the principle of Church-State separation would be upheld. However, some Christian social concern groups protested against the involvement of the churches in the Selection Committee. They argued that such 'indirect participation' was a deception and violated the principle of Church-State separation. The Selection Committee incident revealed a split in the political orientation between church leaders and social concern groups in the Protestant community.

On the Catholic side, no church leader was invited to sit on the Drafting Committee of the Basic Law, though there were Buddhists and Protestants present. Macau Catholic Bishop Domingos Lam was the only religious representative invited to contribute to drafting of the Basic Law of Macau. On the other hand, the Catholic Church's reluctance and ambiguous position with respect to joining the Selection Committee belied a lack of preparation in dealing with the future SAR government in transitional period. Immediately following the handover, the Hong Kong Catholic Church seemed caught in dilemma. It compromised when offering support for the Provisional legislature whose legitimacy was highly questionable (S.-h. Lo 1998; Copithorne 1998). It was also very reluctant to withdraw its assistance to the Catholic Church in China because the help rendered was by order of the Holy See.

CHAPTER FIVE

Non-traditional Relations Between the Hong Kong Government and Christian Churches

Non-traditional Relations Between the Hong Kong Government and Progressive Catholics

The Second Vatican Council, or Vatican II, was a watershed in the development of the universal Catholic Church. The Council Fathers advocated the integration of the Church into the modern, secular world and new methods in theological teaching. In 1967, Pope Paul VI established the Pontifical Commission of Justice and Peace as an office in the Roman Curia. It was his intention that the Church do more in promoting justice and global peace.[1] The Justice and Peace Commission of the Hong Kong Catholic Diocese (DCJP) is one of many local commissions of the Pontifical Commission of Justice and Peace, and aims to promote social justice and foster development in developing nations.[2] Promoting world justice is considered an essential element of spreading the gospel message. It is believed that existing social systems need structural change and that all Christians must participate in the work of promoting world justice by standing on the side of the poor and opposed. In the 1980s the role of the DCJP was to:[3]

1)   advise the Bishop and Catholic Diocese on plans and projects for the promotion of social justice.

2) provide the Church with relevant information and source material for the training of personnel in the work of promoting social justice, and the better education of Catholics in this area of work.

3) obtain collective opinions on social issues through exchanges of views and consultation with all segments of the Catholic community, and to channel such information to the Diocese for reference in matters of policy and decision making.

4) organize and implement action plans for the promotion of social justice.

5) take timely and appropriate steps in response to any unjust occurrence in society.

The Hong Kong Catholic authorities did not condone any political activity that might disrupt British rule in Hong Kong, fearing it could backfire on the Church. The Catholic Church could not afford to offend the government because it relied on continued government subsidies to operate its education and social services. In the 1970s, before the signing of the Sino-British Agreement on the future of Hong Kong, the Hong Kong Catholic authorities were only half-heartedly implementing Catholic social teaching.[4] However, when the British government in Hong Kong itself began to promote democracy in the final stages of its rule, the Church did not worry that its advocacy of democracy would embarrass the British.

Due to the ideological incompatibility between religion and atheist Communism, as well as the ongoing dispute between Chinese Catholics and the communist Chinese regime, Hong Kong Catholics sought democracy and political participation as means to keep the autonomy as promised by the 'one country two systems' policy. By doing so, they intended to protect themselves and their Chinese counterparts from persecution and the loss of religious freedoms (Chan and Leung 1996).

In its early stages the DCJP merely promoted the Church's concern for social and political affairs but it later issued many public statements and petitions (Abbott 1996, 199–308). Committees of Justice and Peace were established in local parishes to introduce this aspect of Catholic social teaching at the grassroots level. These Committees were then combined with the Major Superior Religious Men and Women Associations of Hong Kong, educating the nuns and priests about the need for social justice, and preparing them to be serious in promoting justice and peace in the Christian context.[5] With their dedication, it was expected that they would make a great impact. Allied with other like-minded church and non-church associations, they studied local social, political, and economic issues such as poverty, housing, unemployment and human rights.[6] Publication of a monthly bulletin entitled *Sharing (Fan sheng)* began in 1981.[7] Ad hoc committees were set up to study current issues such as the Sino-British negotiations on the future of Hong Kong, the Basic Law on the future of the HKSAR, the Repatriation of the Vietnamese Boat People, the 'cage dwellers' and the issue of church leaders helping women from China who were married to Hong Kong men but did not have the right to reside in Hong Kong.[8] Generally, these committees and groups were successful in obtaining improved treatment for the underprivileged. The colonial government tolerated these Catholic social movements because they did not jeopardize its rule. In fact, the government's granting of assistance to underprivileged people, following pressure by the Church, served to give the impression to the rest of the world that Hong Kong was a place where peaceful lobbying and demonstrations were not only tolerated, but considered legitimate.

DCJP committees produced various socio-political pamphlets for mass education. For example, at the time of the Legislative Council (Legco) Elections in 1991 and 1995, the Justice and Peace Commission sent pamphlets to parishes encouraging them to exercise their civil right to vote and giving guidance on how to choose candidates. The Union of Hong Kong Catholic Organizations in Support of the Patriotic and Democratic Movement in China, an offshoot of the DCJP, enjoyed flexibility in responding to the development of the pro-democratic movement in China.

The establishment in 1984 of the Catholic Institute for Religion and Society (CIRS) was aimed at training Christian leaders, on the basis of the gospels, to participate in socio-political issues. Through research and study programmes it underscored real political situations often unknown to the laity as well as to some church personnel. The CIRS cooperated with the local tertiary institutes and well-known thinkers and writers in advocating direct elections in the Legislative Council in 1988. When the Draft of the Basic Law of the HKSAR was available for public input, the CIRS commented on the protection of human rights. Other topics studied included the role of Catholic women in society, and emigration problems within the Church.

In the later stages of the transitional period, the focus of work centred on promoting a general understanding between Mainland and Hong Kong Catholics. Short training programmes for church personnel were held annually. Catholics in the Mainland were instructed about Hong Kong, and Hong Kong congregations visited churches in China. In December 1995 the institute organized a conference on Church-State relations. It was able to attract a Chinese delegation composed of 22 members including high-ranking religious researchers, religious cadres, Catholic bishops, priests and sisters. Liu Bainian, deputy president of the Chinese Patriotic Association and leader of the Chinese religious delegation, was very positive about the conference because it was an opportunity for both sides to present their views and clear up misunderstandings.[9] The institute was very careful to screen out anti-Communist participants and censor the papers of the Hong Kong participants, so as to avoid upsetting the Chinese government. It must be pointed out that the pro-China voice from Hong Kong presented a less than accurate picture. At the same time the official delegates from the Mainland also gave only a partial picture of the Catholic Church in China. From a political perspective, China's continued restrictions on religion were partly the result of the unresolved problem of conflicting authority between Beijing and the Vatican (B. Leung 1998).

After the Cultural Revolution and before Deng Xiaoping launched the 'open-door' policy in 1979, the Catholic Church in China did not have sufficient time to revive itself after the almost complete annihilation of all religious activity. Immediately following Deng's policy announcement, informal Sino-Vatican contacts were proposed with the eventual aim of rapprochement. However, even before a dialogue could take place, the whole process experienced a setback in 1981 due to the controversial issue of the appointment by the Holy See of Deng Yiming as Archbishop of Guangzhou without the consent of Beijing (B. Leung 1992a, chapter 7).[10] After this failure to build a channel for official contact, in 1982 Pope John Paul II changed his strategy and called upon overseas Chinese Catholics to build a bridge of reconciliation between the Church in China and the universal church (B. Leung 1991).

The Catholic Church in Hong Kong, in meeting local needs as well as serving as a bridge, found itself acting as a focal point in a triangular relationship between China, the Vatican and Hong Kong. The dynamics of the socio-political development of China and Hong Kong unavoidably shaped Church-State development. In other words, the triangular relations of the Church in Hong Kong gave it added momentum in the formulation of its own policies during the transition period. Through their 'bridging' work Hong Kong Catholics gained opportunities for contact with the Chinese government and Chinese Catholics.

The Catholic prelate, Bishop John Wu (elevated to Cardinal in 1988) released a public statement, 'Statement on the Catholic Church and the Future of Hong Kong' immediately after the issuing of the Sino-British Joint Declaration (Wu 1984). While supporting in principle the return of Hong Kong to Chinese sovereignty, he listed in detail the various types of religious freedom prevailing in Hong Kong and expressed his hope that these would all be recognized and respected in accordance with the Sino-British Joint Declaration.[11]

The possibility of drastic change after the handover led Cardinal Wu to issue in 1989 a pastoral exhortation entitled 'March into the Bright Decade' (Wu 1989). In it, he suggested a strategy for responding to political change after 1997. In terms of external relations, Wu advocated that the Church expand its teaching with the community, that is, to demonstrate the role of Christian principles in social and political affairs. As for internal relations, he sought to strengthen the Christian community through internalization of religious belief and faith. His goal was for the social teachings of the Church, through sermons, preaching and catechizing at the parish level, to be spread to the Catholic grassroots. The role of the 'bridge' was the concluding theme of the document.

The 'March into the Bright Decade' exhortation by Cardinal Wu became the blueprint for Catholic policy after 1997. As early as February 1987, *Xinhua,* as well as the CCP Committee on Work in Hong Kong and Macau, expressed through *Wen Wei Po* the official Chinese view that the Chinese government was concerned about the participation of Christians, both Catholic and Protestant, in politics. In fact, even before the spectacular scene of Catholics marching behind the banner 'Catholic Committee in Concern for and Support of the Pro-Democratic Movement in China' in rallies held in May and June 1989, China began to make definitive statements. When discussing religious freedom in the context of the Basic Law of the HKSAR, *Xinhua* reiterated that there should be a separation of religion and politics (Xin 1987b, 89–94, 121–31). Christian involvement in political issues was openly criticized. The Chinese government frowned upon senior clergymen who were active in political issues, such as the vicar general of the Catholic Diocese who spoke out about constitutional reform and against the building of the Daya Bay nuclear plant on the north of the Hong Kong border. The Chinese government regarded these speeches as provocative. The lead that other clergymen took in supporting political reform in Hong Kong and preparing the formation of a political group also unnerved Mainland authorities. They argued that political involvement represented a diversion from what were supposed to be the Church's true purposes, namely, to preach Christian doctrine and carry out Christian deeds (Xin 1987b, 89–92). *Xinhua* repeatedly called for the separation of Church and State, saying:

> In the name of God the Church has great means to promote its political views. This is unfair to believers and in the long run is also harmful to the Church. Church personnel should refrain from

politics. They are as equally manipulative as ambitious politicians
(Xin 1987b, 121–31).

The visit to Hong Kong of Ye Xiaowen, head of the Religious Affairs
Bureau, one year before the handover, was used by the Chinese government
to delineate the boundaries of religious activities in the territory. Ye also
indirectly set limits for the 'bridging' efforts.[12]

Although the Basic Law assured the continuous operation of Catholic
education and social services, from various statements and actions it was clear
that the Chinese government wanted the Catholic Church in Hong Kong to
continue to be a 'contractor' of social services and education with the HKSAR
government. There was to be no more political involvement, and no more
'bridging' work.

The Interim Evaluation of the Pastoral Exhortation: 'March Into the Bright Decade'

The Pastoral Exhortation, 'March into the Bright Decade' aimed at setting the
direction and objectives for the next decade (1989–99) to cope with the political
transition of Hong Kong. The Catholic authorities requested all sectors of the
diocese to set policy and strategies at the time when it was launched. A section
of it reads:

> We hope that the whole People of God in Hong Kong will with one
> heart make every effort to follow this pastoral commitment in the
> coming ten years. In 1994 we shall carry out an evaluation and bring
> to a conclusion the five years of implementation, in order to make
> a more practical adjustment of direction and pace for the following
> five years (J. Wu 1989).

The Committee for Promoting the Cardinal's Pastoral Exhortation was
responsible for monitoring its implementation. After five years of monitoring,
the Committee decided to carry out a formal evaluation and appointed the
Catholic Institute for Religion and Society to devise consultation and surveying
methods including a questionnaire, and to collate the information and write a
report. A total of 744 questionnaires were sent to various communities and
organizations in the diocese. It was formulated according to the seven themes
listed in the exhortation. These were: the formation of the laity; small faith
communities; on-going formation of priests; on-going formation of brothers

and sisters; mass communications; education; social services; and relations between the diocese and China and the Church in China (J. Wu 1995). A report was written based on the responses made in the 377 returned questionnaires. Also, 2,035 self-administered questionnaires were sent to churchgoers at twelve parishes and the Mass Centre. In all, 1,752 (86.1 per cent) valid questionnaires were collected.

The purpose was to evaluate the work done in the last five years. According to the interim report, in the area of the formation of laity, there were five essential aspects to be cultivated: a deep faith, a sense of Church, love for Hong Kong, concern for China and the mission of evangelization (J. Wu 1995, 6). Though the orientation was towards the laity, it set a tone for the whole diocese. The love for Hong Kong and concern for China were to encourage more socio-political participation in Hong Kong and more assistance to the Catholic Church in China. Given the possible change in educational policy after the handover, it was proposed that there be a strengthening of contact, co-ordination and co-operation among various educational institutions of the Catholic Church (16).

Changes in the Hong Kong SAR immediately following the handover did affect the Catholic Church, however, the Church has yet to formulate a policy to respond to the change.[13] In the area of social services, the interim report emphasized the 'servant role' and 'prophetic role' of Catholic social services. Therefore it was proposed that support for parish social concern groups be given to reactivate the parish Justice and Peace groups. The call to fulfill the 'servant' and 'prophet' role led Caritas to initiate services for new Chinese immigrants and family services for women who discovered their husbands had mistresses in China (19–25). Lastly, the Hong Kong diocese confirmed that it would continue its contact with the Catholic Church in China despite the Mainland government's request that the 'bridging efforts' be eliminated (24–5).

Catholic Voting Behaviour in the Legislative Council Elections

The support for democratization in Hong Kong began as early as 1987. Before the 1988 Legco election, the Hong Kong Catholic diocese had asked priests, sisters and other church personnel to encourage Catholics to cast their votes in order to fulfill their duty as citizens. Catholic parishes, schools and diocesan institutes were permitted to be open to election activities but were not to promote individual candidates.[14] Fervent Catholic support for the Legco election started in 1991. In 1990–91, the diocese celebrated its 150th anniversary with the motto 'to walk with the people'. Priests and pastoral workers were instructed by the Church authorities to encourage Catholics to cast their ballots. Cardinal Wu, in March 1991, six months before the Legco election issued a pastoral letter reminding the congregation to participate actively in the election. Sermons from the pulpit became a channel for the Church's social teachings (appendix 2).[15] The prelate's pastoral letters were reprinted in the parishes. Outlines of sermons and prayers for the faithful were distributed by the Diocesan Liturgical Committee to the Catholic parishes encouraging Catholic participation in the elections and praying for the success of the elections.

A smaller electoral study was conducted in four parishes (North Point, Tze Wan Shan, Shun Lee Estate, and Tai Koo Shing) and the Mass Centre amounting in all to a sample size of 1,120 (B. Leung 1992b). For the electoral study on the 1995 Legco election, a sample of 1,335 was drawn by means of multi-stage cluster techniques. It divided the eighteen districts into four clusters. The sample size of each district was made proportionate to the district's Catholic population and the samples were evenly distributed among sampled services in each district. The electoral study in 1995 was more sophisticated than its pilot study in 1991. However, the outcome was more or less the same with very minor differences. A main characteristic of Catholic voting behaviour was very high turnout rate, 86.6 percent (Catholic community) versus 39.1 (public as a whole) in 1991, and 81.5 percent (Catholic) versus 35.8 (public) in 1995. In the 1995 election, it was apparent that Catholic voters, as compared with the general electorate, were more likely to have a party preference (78.3 percent versus 52.5). The Democratic Party (DP) was obviously the most popular political party among Hong Kong voters. Catholics were more inclined to choose the DP than the public (78.3 per cent versus 52.5). On the other hand, Catholics were less supportive than the general public of the pro-China Democratic Alliance for the Betterment of Hong Kong (DAB) Party (4.3 percent versus 5.0) (Chan and Leung 1996).

The high Catholic voting turnout was more a result of group mobilization than individual motivation. It was discovered that Hong Kong Christians, including Catholic voters, were more influenced by the China factor and their church than factors of individual disposition when they decided whether to vote or not in the Legco election. Also, Catholics were more influenced by church teachings in their political participation (Chan and Leung 2000). Hong Kong Catholics were concerned that the Church-State relationship after 1997 might change from the 'contractor' model to the 'political absorption of religion' model. Their belief was that a democratic government was more likely to protect the Church from possible oppression.

Involvement and Support for the Pro-democratic Movement

When the pro-democratic movement was gaining momentum between April and June 1989, the people of Hong Kong watched and waited in alarm. Some Catholic organizations joined the Hong Kong Alliance in Support of the Democratic and Patriotic Movements of China to commemorate the June 4 Tiananmen Incident. The Union of Hong Kong Catholic Organizations in Support of the Patriotic and Democratic Movement in China arose from the joint involvement of a dozen grassroots Catholic associations led by the DCJP and all concerned about democratic freedom. The Diocesan Centre next to the Cathedral, in which many Catholic associations and the Bishop's Office were located, became a meeting place for the Catholic pro-democratic movement. Hundreds of volunteers worked round the clock to plan the logistics of major rallies (a total of four in Hong Kong before and after the military crackdown on 4 June 1989). Priests and nuns in full religious habit marched under Catholic banners chanting religious songs. Some superiors even re-scheduled religious celebrations to maximize the nuns' participation.[16] Fr. Louis Ha, a diocesan priest became deeply involved in the Alliance of Hong Kong Citizens in Support of the Democratic and Patriotic Movement in China (Alliance), which was headed by leading democrats such as Szeto Wah and Martin Lee. He was the key figure in communicating with the Catholic Union and Alliance throughout the Tiananmen Incident, and at the Alliance's annual election held in 1989, he received the highest number of votes ever as a member of the steering committee. The Catholic Church, through him, had great potential to promote democracy if it chose to do so.

The Church's involvement and support for the pro-democratic movement in China could not escape the attention of Beijing.[17] Although the Catholic authorities refused to admit they were under pressure from China, they instructed the Catholic social communication office, headed by Fr. Louis Ha, to withdraw its membership from the Alliance. Fr. Ha wanted to remain on the Steering Committee as an individual, but the Church did not grant him permission to do so and asked him to leave the directorship of the Catholic Social Communication Centre to do historical research on church history. This was meant to be a demotion as well as a means to prevent him from engaging in further political activity.

Although Fr. Ha appeared to yield to the demands of the Beijing authorities, his involvement in Hong Kong politics did not end until the 1995 the Legco election. When the Catholic Church in Hong Kong in 1991 celebrated the 150th anniversary of its inauguration, the Central Council of Catholic Laity took the lead in preparing the celebrations. The theme 'hand in hand towards the future' was chosen to signify the close relationship between the Church and Hong Kong society.

As it turned out, the political participation of Hong Kong Catholics, in terms of voting in the 1991 and 1995 Legislative Council Elections, was much higher than the voting rate of the general public (86.5 percent versus 39.5 percent in 1991; and 81.5 percent versus 35.8 percent in 1995). Research revealed that both the 'social-economic status of Catholics' and the 'China factor' were influential in both voter turnout and party preference. Most Catholics were from the middle class and supported the Democratic Party (Chan and Leung 1996). The Hong Kong Catholic authorities reduced their promotion activities in 1995 and this is reflected in the slightly lower voting rate in 1991.

The Catholic Supervision of Legco Councilors Committee was established in 1992. Occasional reports on the performance of Legco councillors as well as on their attitudes towards the social issues debated in the Legco were published.[18] The DCJP also published books and booklets to promote the election and guide Catholics in their choice of candidates.[19]

Bridging Work and the Triangular Relations Among the PRC, Vatican and Hong Kong

The Hong Kong Catholic Church responded to the call of Pope John Paul II in 1981 to establish an informal relationship with China. Formal relations between China had ended in 1951 with the expulsion of the papal nuncio (B. Leung 1992a, 189–256). The revival of the Catholic Church in China from the late 1980s was partly due to Deng Xiaoping's open door policy, and partly due to material and spiritual support provided by overseas Chinese Catholics and the Church in Hong Kong. Caritas-Hong Kong's China Desk, overseeing the services on the Mainland, is part of a Church endeavour to facilitate a rapprochement in Sino-Vatican relations. Difficult problems between China and the Vatican were somewhat eased by the working of a triangular relationship between China, the Vatican and Hong Kong. Over the course of two decades, various forms of assistance were provided to the Church in China (both the open and underground branches), in the form of training church personnel, the provision of religious literature and financial aid to church-related enterprises in rural and urban areas. Most was funded by foreign Catholic communities but channelled through Hong Kong with the blessing of the Vatican (Lam 1997, 94–112).

Caritas, working as a non-governmental organisation, began in 1983 to offer social services mainly in rural China, initially in Guangdong province and then later in more remote areas of the country. By 1997, both in terms of quality and quantity, Caritas's services had spread widely, due to its agreement to act as a distribution agency for various European Catholic social welfare institutes. Funding for China projects from international bodies such as Caritas Internationalis, Caritas-Germany and Caritas-Switzerland was entrusted to Caritas-Hong Kong.

Hong Kong Catholic laity began to join the clergy and religious teaching teams, travelling to remote areas to teach the Bible and doctrines to seminarians and novices. This helped the Church make up for lost time since 1957 in conducting pastoral service to Chinese Catholics and in evangelizing non-believers (B. Leung 2000). Caritas-Hong Kong, however, was careful to keep its China account separate from its Hong Kong account in order to reassure the Hong Kong public that its services in China would not be at the expense of Hong Kong's underprivileged.

The Vatican hopes to prevent the Catholic Church in China from becoming completely separate from the leadership of the Holy See, as did the Church of England during the reign of Henry VIII.[20] Caritas-Hong Kong, through its China services, has been helping the Vatican build a bridge of reconciliation, although it is only one partner in a multi-faceted plan. The assistance to the Church in China can be divided into two main categories: church-related projects and non-church related projects. The Chinese government welcomes church-funded social services such as vocational training, medical and relief work because these do not involve any proselytizing. China is prepared, even keen, to accept Catholic social service aid but not the Catholic religion. By agreeing to provide social services without strings attached, however, Caritas is not evangelizing, the ultimate purpose of the Catholic faith.[21]

In 1989 the Chinese government issued a document calling for an end to Catholic aid to China.[22] The CCP was resolute in its intention to eradicate the influence of religion in socialist China, for it was suffering from a crisis of its own making (Ye 1996). Since the launching of the economic reforms, support among the general population for communism had been evaporating (Document Centre of Party Central and Policy Section of Religious Affairs Bureau 1995, 177). The late Chen Yun, paramount leader next to Deng Xiaoping, ordered Jiang Zemin to take actions to curb the spread of Christianity, especially among the Chinese youth:

Dear Comrade Zemin,

I am deeply troubled after reading reports of the ever-increasing infiltration of religion, especially those concerning the distribution of anti-revolutionary materials under the cloak of religion. It has been a customary technique employed by our class enemies, both within and outside the country, to use religion to snatch away our youth. There is a painful lesson to be learned from other Communist States that lost political power this way. Now is the right time for the CCP to grasp this important issue firmly. It is important not to allow it to become a new element contributing to social instability. You may have already seen all these documents and reports, but I am sending some back to you for a second reading.

Chen Yun, 4 April 1990.

When Ye Xiaowen visited Hong Kong twelve months before Hong Kong's reversion to Chinese rule, he told Hong Kong Catholics that since the Mainland was not intending to make Hong Kong people conform to the Mainland's ideas, they should not attempt to influence the thinking of Mainlanders. He also cited the principles of 'mutual non-subordination, mutual non-interference and mutual respect' as stipulated in the Basic Law.[23]

The 'Civil Liberties and Social Order Consultation Document'

The Catholic Commission of Peace and Justice openly expressed its view on social issues, and indirectly criticized the Hong Kong government's handling of the repatriation of Vietnamese boat people and illegal child immigrants, as well as labour and social insurance issues. Catholics and Protestants often formed joint *ad hoc* lobbying groups and did manage to influence government policy to a certain degree. However, they were among only a few groups to ask for a meeting with the Secretary of Justice-designate, Elsie Leung Oi-sie. They wanted the 'Civil Liberties and Social Order Consultation Document' to be withdrawn. It had been issued by the office of the Chief Executive-designate, Tung Chee-hwa, on 9 April 1997 for a three-week consultation, and proposed the barring of local political organizations from soliciting or accepting cash or loans from foreign organizations, or from affiliating with foreign political organizations.[24]

Non-traditional Relations Between the Hong Kong Government and Progressive Protestants

Three Protestant statements

Throughout the 1980s and '90s, the 'question of 1997' became the dominant issue facing Hong Kong society. In response, a group of liberal Protestants, including church leaders and lay Christians, chose to take a lead in the reform process ahead of Hong Kong becoming a Special Administrative Region of China. The concept of Church-State relations held by these liberal Christians differed greatly from that of more conservative church leaders. Although the impact of this group on Church-State relations was limited, their presence and activities had significant implications.

Three important statements were drafted and published by the Protestant churches in 1984: 'Proposed Statement of Faith for Hong Kong Christians in the Face of Social and Political Change', the 'Statement on Religious Freedom by the Protestant Churches of Hong Kong' and the 'Opinions of the Hong Kong Protestant Delegation to Beijing on the Future of Hong Kong'.[25] Set in the social context of the early 1980s, these documents all had significant implications on Church-State relations, and reveal the extent of Protestant concern about the future of religious freedom in Hong Kong.

On 12 March 1984, a group of evangelical church leaders met to discuss the future of Hong Kong society and the role of the Church in Hong Kong. The church leaders came to the conclusion that they should write a 'Statement of Faith' to express the Church's position on the issue of 1997 and the churches' mission in the territory. Five leaders, Jonathan Chao, Chin Pak-tau, Carver Yu Tat-sum, Anthony Leung Wing-tai and Timothy Lau Siu-Hong, formed an action group to draft the 'Statement of Faith' (C. Yu 1984). On 16 April the church leaders organized a conference at which more than 80 clergy, leaders of church organizations, and theologians from various denominations discussed the Statement. The conference participants declared the 'Statement of Faith' a formal document representing their position.[26] The main points included: to express views and principles on social and political change from a Christian perspective; to stress the nature and mission of the Church; to affirm Christians' responsibility in Hong Kong and China; to affirm the relationship between the Church in Hong Kong and churches overseas; to express Christians' views on Church-State relations; to stress that the Church should renew its organizational model; and stress solidarity, unity and faithfulness (see appendix 3).

The 'Statement of Faith' has undeniable significance in that the Protestant church leaders pronounced their faith in the future of Hong Kong and called on Christians to commit themselves to Hong Kong society. Secondly, the Statement reflected a change of attitude among these leaders towards Christian social responsibility. Before the 1980s they often narrowly focused their attention on evangelism and were largely detached from Hong Kong society. It suggested that the churches should become active in society and play a role in building relations between Hong Kong and China. Thirdly, although it was written for Christians, the document called on China to respect religious freedom in general and human rights for all. Articles 4 and 5 of the ten-point statement declared: 'We expect that after 1997 Hong Kong will continue to experience a high degree of autonomy and that its people will still enjoy the human rights and freedoms bestowed by God, including freedom of speech, press, association, assembly, travel and religion, etc., to the extent that Hong Kong might contribute positively to the modernization and democratization of China as a whole.'; and 'We look forward to the Chinese people at large being able to share the human rights and freedoms bestowed by God, to the extent that China will become a nation where people live in prosperity and where justice is upheld.' The seventh point was on Church-State relations:

> We believe that the authority of the government comes from God and that we should obey the government on matters that fall within the scope of its due authority. However, if the government requires what God forbids we should submit to God's will. The authority of the government has a definite scope. God endows the government with the duty of maintaining law and order and the stability of the society so that people are protected. On this basis, the government should be accountable to the people under the constitution. Christians should assume a prophetic role in society and actively encourage the government to do justice and work towards the well being of the people.

In other words, the 'Statement of Faith' expressed implicitly that Christians accept the rule of government with certain conditions. If the rule of government violates the values or principles of Christian faith, Christians are free to oppose the government.

In June 1984, church leaders from the ecumenical and evangelical circles drafted a joint 'Statement on Religious Freedom', which expressed the views of Protestants regarding the future of Hong Kong after 1997. Initiated by 84 church leaders, this statement (see appendix 4) was supported by 12 denominations, more than 200 local churches, 4 seminaries, and 44 church organizations. It was presented to China's Premier Zhao Ziyang as well as to Britain's Foreign and Commonwealth Office of State and demanded that London and Beijing ensure in their drafting of the Basic Law that religious freedom, as enjoyed by religious organizations in Hong Kong before the handover, be continued after 1997.[27] In the introduction, the position of the Church on religious freedom was clearly outlined:

> The measure of religious freedom is closely related to the openness of a society, and religious freedom is evidence of progress in a society. We affirm that genuine religious freedom is based on human rights. Human rights are the birthrights of all men and women granted by God. Therefore, all governments have the responsibility to safeguard human rights. The protection of religious freedom hinges upon respect for human rights by society as a whole. Human rights are specifically expressed in the freedoms of thought, speech, press, organization, assembly and action. We believe that genuine freedom for religious faith and activities is only possible in a society that respects human rights.

The second part of the statement explained the content and details of religious freedom for the individual, family, church and the religious ministry as protected by law. The conclusion stressed that religious freedom and human rights are inseparable and that Christians have a responsibility to commit themselves to 'maintaining and developing a society that respects human rights'. In sum, this statement is a position paper in which the Protestant churches as a whole express clearly and fully their views on religious freedom.

In September 1984, a group of 21 Hong Kong church representatives, led by Bishop Peter Kwong of the Anglican Church, Reverend Kwok Nai-wang of the Hong Kong Christian Council (HKCC) and Reverend Lincoln Leung Lam-hoi of the Hong Kong Methodist Church, travelled to Beijing to present their views on religious freedom directly to the Chinese government.[28] Apart from reiterating the positions expressed in the 'Statement of Faith' and 'Statement on Religious Freedom', the 'Beijing Delegation Statement' (see appendix 5) also gave a detailed description of the partnership between the Protestant churches and the Hong Kong government in the second section of the paper headed 'Views on the Hong Kong Church'. An implicit request was made to the Chinese government for the continuation of the Church-government relationship, namely for the Church to remain in the role of a government deputy or contractor in education and social services. The relevant paragraphs are as follows:

Press Conference of the Hong Kong Protestant Delegation to Beijing, 1984. (From left to right) Lincoln Leung Lam-hoi, Kwok Nai-wang, Philemon Choi Yuen-wan, Lo Lung-kwong and John Hsu Tao-leung. Courtesy of the Hong Kong Christian Council.

Bishop Peter Kwong, 1986. Courtesy of the Hong Kong Christian Council.

3. Although Christians in Hong Kong (excluding the Catholics) account for only 5% of the total population, they are undertaking a significant share of the responsibility in medical care, education and social welfare. The churches currently run 200 kindergartens, 175 primary schools, 120 secondary schools, 15 theological seminaries, 3 schools for the deaf, 5 hospitals and numerous social service centres, such as homes for the elderly, youth centres and elderly centres. The churches' undertaking is inspired by their faith and driven by a genuine desire to help meet the needs of society. The churches have been shouldering this responsibility since the early years of Hong Kong's development, when the government was unable to provide sufficient education opportunities and social services. Because of their rigorous attitude and their emphasis on moral education and the cultivation of virtues, they have won the trust and support of the people of Hong Kong. In fact, the churches have been pioneers in Hong Kong's education and social service sectors. We believe that the churches should continue to make contributions in this regard so as to improve and advance society in terms of morality and spirituality.

4. Currently the responsibilty of funding developments in education and social services is largely taken up by the Hong Kong government, which grants subsidizes to schools and social services managed by religious groups on a full or partial basis. The government shows respect for and trusts the religious groups and allows them to run their schools and social services according to their own principles and objectives. We believe that the future government of Hong Kong should continue to adhere to this policy.

With respect to the Church in Hong Kong, it also emphasized the principles of religious freedom:

1. The future Hong Kong should not only maintain its freedom and openness in economic activities: it should also maintain the same freedom in ideology and religion, so that the Hong Kong Church will be able to continue to make a contribution to society.

2. Religious freedom has a broad scope that includes freedom of personal belief, public worship, preaching, religious education, assembly, speech and the press. In this connection, a 'Statement on Religious Freedom by the Protestant Churches

of Hong Kong' has been submitted to the Chinese authority
by a group of Christians. We propose the detailed incorporation
of the current scope of religious freedom enjoyed by Hong
Kong citizens in the Basic Law.

Referring to the Mainland's religious policy, which stipulates that the churches
should comply with the principles of self-governance, self-support and self-
evangelism and thereby have no connection with overseas religious
organizations, this statement expressed the wish that the churches in Hong Kong
be allowed to maintain their relationships with overseas churches after 1997:

> 5. Although the churches in Hong Kong are deeply rooted in
> Hong Kong society, the catholic and ecumenical character of
> the churches means that they have an intimate fellowship with
> Christians and churches all over the world, sharing in Christ's
> hardships as well as happiness with each other. As a member
> of the global Church, we shall share the work and hope of
> Hong Kong people with people in other nations through the
> international church, so that they may come to respect Hong
> Kong and deal with us on an equal basis.
>
> 6. While most churches in Hong Kong are independent and
> autonomous, they are closely related to their denominational
> affiliates in other parts of the world in terms of tradition and
> history. This is a relationship that we ardently treasure. We
> hope that the churches will be able to interact with churches
> and Christians of other countries in mutual respect after 1997.

Ji Pengfei, Director of the Hong Kong and Macau Affairs Office, who
promised that religious freedom would be maintained after 1997, and that the
Hong Kong churches would be able to continue their education and social
welfare work, received the Delegation. He also said that the Religious Affairs
Bureau would not set up any sub-office in Hong Kong.[29] To a certain extent,
Ji's promises seemed to have relieved the Protestant churches of their worries.

The Consultative Committee and Hong Kong Lutheran Church Controversies

In the mid-1980s certain mainline church leaders became more closely
associated with the Chinese government than before, one of the more distinctive
examples of whom was Bishop Kwong, Bishop of the Anglican Church *(Sheng*

Kung Hui). As Anglican Christianity had been the official religion of England, *Sheng Kung Hui* also enjoyed a unique status in Hong Kong. Before 25 October 1998, the Hong Kong and Macau Diocese was placed under the direct supervision of the Canterbury Primate of England, and the Anglican bishop of Hong Kong had always been from Britain.[30] The Anglican Church in Hong Kong occupied a symbolic position in the Hong Kong Government, and its bishop ranked fifth on the government's protocol list, following only the governor, Chief Justice, Chief Secretary and Commander-General. The Anglican bishop also had numerous channels for non-official communication with the Governor (Paton 1985, 188–9). The Anglican bishop had thus been closely related to England and the Hong Kong government until Kwong became bishop in 1981, when changes occurred in both sides of this Church-State relationship.

Kwong himself had been a controversial figure in the Protestant community. In each of a number of disputes in the 1980s, including the re-election of standing members for the Basic Law Consultative Committee in 1985, the HKCC incident in 1986 and the Fung Chi-wood incident in 1988 (all to be described in this chapter), he took a pro-China stance.

The re-election of standing members for the Basic Law Consultative Committee was one of the events that highlighted the changing Church-State relations. As an eminent religious leader, Kwong was invited to sit on both the Basic Law Drafting Committee and the Basic Law Consultative Committee. On 6 December 1985, the Basic Law Consultative Committee held a preparatory meeting to elect 19 standing members from a list of 32. According to the rules, the 19 members should, upon their election, hold a further election among themselves to fill the required posts in the Standing Committee. However, upon the proposal of certain members of the Drafting Committee, it turned out that appointments to the posts were made according to the Drafting Committee's recommendations. When the public learned this through the media, they generally felt that the Consultative Committee members had violated the rules. In response to public criticism that the appointments to the Standing Committee were a sham, Kwong openly defended the election by recommendation and maintained that the procedure had been appropriate.

The Protestant community was less than pleased with his comments. In January 1986, under the name 'Sixty Christian Professionals', a group of Christians wrote a letter to both the Chinese and English newspapers, criticizing the election procedure of the Consultative Committee by stating it 'ignored' the rule of law and justice. They also claimed that Kwong's remarks in no way represented the Church's position. The letter accused Kwong of giving up fundamental principles in order to please the Chinese government:

> From the opinion stated by you in public, we find that you always play the role of a 'reconciliator' and the emphasis you put on the spirit of trust and forgiveness ... However, we must state clearly that trust and forgiveness must not displace the necessity of objective and rational critique. Of course, we should tackle problems in a calm manner and should seek unity in diversity, but at the same time, we must use reason and objectivity as our yardsticks while facing problems. If the latter are to be forsaken, peace-making is in no way different from the recent prevailing behaviour of 'following suit' and 'sitting on the fence'. If the circumstances were so, the image of the Church would be severely hampered.[31]

The Ninth World Lutheran Assembly was held in Hong Kong in July 1997. Towards its closing, the members debated a proposed statement to be issued by the Assembly, criticizing China's record on human rights. The following accusations in the proposed statement led to great contention: 'There are, however, a number of aspects of the situation in China which cause us, as churches, serious and legitimate concern. Such aspects include the treatment and imprisonment of dissidents, the expanded application of the death penalty, the lack of due process in criminal prosecutions, and the continued use of administrative forms of detention.'[32] The representatives from Hong Kong were the first to object to a statement criticizing the Chinese government. Reverend Kin-son Pong, pastor of the Hong Kong Synod of the Chinese Rhenish Church queried: 'Why single out China, why not America, why not Britain?'[33] and Reverend Josephine Tso Shui-wan, president of the Evangelical Lutheran Church in Hong Kong, was of the opinion that 'this [declaration] is a great insult to China. Why don't you be more general? Why just China?'[34] The arguments of Pong and Tso were less than convincing. First of all, if the statement also included the United States or Britain in its criticism, would the representatives of these countries not demand that other countries be included as well? It would have to include all countries if it were to satisfy all the delegates. The condemnation set off a chain reaction. If China did have a record of violating human rights, the Church had a moral obligation to criticize the Chinese government so that it would seek improvement. This is the prophetic duty of the Church. If the Church deliberately downplayed China's abuse of human rights and diverted public attention from the issue because it feared the criticism would humiliate China, there would be no motivation for China to improve, and the Church would have failed to fulfil its goal.

On the other hand, there were also voices in favour of criticizing China. The representatives from Brazil, who had hosted the previous World Lutheran

Assembly, pointed out that the Brazilian administration had undergone criticism for misgovernment at that assembly. Dr Lam Tak-ho, Dean of the Hong Kong Lutheran Seminary, also supported the inclusion of the above remarks. Ultimately, the statement was passed without the above sentences, with 159 representatives voting in favour of the deletion and 106 against it. There were 29 abstainees. Anneli Janhonen, Director of Communications of the World Lutheran Alliance, explained that out of respect for the position of the Hong Kong representatives the deletion was passed.[35]

The position of the bishop of *Sheng Kung Hui* in the re-election of standing members of the Basic Law Consultative Committee, and the Lutheran Assembly's decision to delete critical remarks in its statement illustrate the changing relationship between the Church and State in Hong Kong caused by the shift in political power during the transition period prior to the handover. Put in the context of the patron-client relationship mentioned earlier, the implications of the change become clear. These incidents may justifiably be interpreted as follows: the Chinese government would replace the British government as the legitimate sovereign government of Hong Kong after 1997, and would possess the monopolistic power to control and apply the territory's resources. Groups that were formerly followers of the British government switched their pledge of allegiance to develop a new patron-client understanding with the Chinese government when they came to appreciate the latter's position. Understood from this perspective, the transition of political power in 1997 might have altered the position of power in the Church-State relationship in Hong Kong, but the power relation remained largely unchanged. It was still a Church-State relationship underpinned by the role of the Protestant churches as the 'deputies' or 'contractors' for the government.

The Work of the HKCC and Other Christian Organizations

The HKCC in the 1970s and '80s, with Reverend Kwok Nai-wang as General Secretary, took a lead in Protestant social action. It provided a gathering place for Protestants who were ecumenically minded and a base for Christian social consultation and deliberation. During that period, the HKCC expressed opinions on various social policies and issues, promoted social concern and urged the government to face and deal with social problems.[36] For example, in November 1980, it called for a 'Consultation on the Mission of the Churches in the 1980s'. Two leading bus companies on Hong Kong Island and Kowloon demanded a fare rise as high as 100 per cent during the 1980s. With the support of the conference participants who represented various churches and Christian organizations, the HKCC issued a statement protesting the fare rise and demanding that the bus companies consult public opinion before making any increase in fares. It called on the government to explain to citizens the criteria and proper procedures behind calculating fare increases. Later, more than 200 organizations joined the 'Anti-rise in Bus Fares Movement' initiated by the HKCC.

Thereafter, the HKCC and various Christian and non-governmental groups involved in the protest became allies, supporting each other and acting as pressure groups in subsequent years. In September 1981, the electricity companies in Kowloon and on Hong Kong Island demanded an increase in charges. This would have been the third increase in two years. More than 40 NGOs immediately formed an alliance: 'Joint Committee for Monitoring of the Two Electricity Companies', and demanded that the charges be frozen. The members of the Committee came from trade unions and the religious, social work and education sectors.[37] As a result of the attempt by the bus and electricity companies to increase charges, many social groups decided that it was necessary to monitor public utility companies in Hong Kong. In May 1982, 16 NGOs joined together to form a 'Joint Committee for Monitoring of Public Utilities'.[38] The HKCC had participated in the campaigns against the bus and electricity companies and once again joined the Committee to monitor public utility companies.

In the 1980s the Commission on Public Policy (CPP) of the HKCC was active in speaking out on social issues and calling for reform in Hong Kong. For example, the committee suggested that the tax system be reviewed. It proposed that the level of tax exemption on individuals and couples with two children be raised and that the tax assessment of couples be separated. Moreover, it called on the government to tax the profits earned from selling property.[39]

In April 1982, the HKCC organized a theological forum on 'Hong Kong's Future and Hong Kong Society'. It was one of the first activities held on the issue of 1997 among the Protestant community.[40] In February 1984, Reverend Jonathan Chao, Director of the Chinese Church Research Centre, openly expressed concern about the articles on religion to be included in the Basic Law, the mini-constitution under which Hong Kong would be governed after the handover, in an open lecture on 'China and the Church'. He urged Protestants to express their opinion on the formulation process in order to safeguard religious freedom and human rights in Hong Kong.[41]

On 2 March 1984, Christian Communications Limited organized a seminar entitled, 'The Three "Selfs" and Prospects of the Church in Hong Kong'. The speeches and discussions reflected the thoughts and concerns of many Christians at the time (Christian Communication Ltd 1984). The intent of the seminar was to discuss the history and nature of 'independent' Protestantism in China and its implications for the churches in Hong Kong after the handover. The seminar had three sessions. The theme of the first was, 'The History of the Self-governance, Self-support and Self-evangelism Movement of the Protestant Church in China and its Biblical Basis', which examined the history of nationalistic Protestantism in China in the nineteenth and twentieth centuries. The theme of the second session was, 'The Development, Position and Policy of the "Committee of the Christian Three-self Patriotic Movement" in China', which discussed Communist China's religious policies and the history and development of the Three-self Patriotic Movement in China after 1950. The theme of the third session was, 'The Self-governance, Self-support and Self-Evangelism of the Hong Kong Churches and the Year 2000', which explored the future prospects of the churches in Hong Kong. At the third session, Theodore Hsueh, General Secretary of Christian Communications Limited, expressed his views on the future of the churches in Hong Kong:

> In December 1983, *Wide Angle* magazine disclosed the Chinese government's principles in handling religion. The New China News Agency considers these principles to be important and reliable, so every Protestant leader should read them:
> 1. The Chinese government will not send anyone to oversee the churches in Hong Kong, that is, the 'Three-Self Movement' will not be set up in Hong Kong.
> 2. Hong Kong people will enjoy religious freedom.
> 3. [The Chinese government] will not establish any official 'Three-Self Movement', but Hong Kong people are free to organize a 'Three-Self Movement' on a voluntary basis.
> 4. Church property will be protected.
> 5. Religious people may not use religion to launch anti-government activities; as to whether religious organizations will be allowed to continue to offer social services will be decided by the Hong Kong Special Administration Region government.
> 6. Religious freedom is to be one of many policies to be implemented by the Chinese government in Hong Kong. These policies are to be implemented in accordance with the foreign policy of the Chinese government in achieving the aim of the modernization in four areas.

The religious policy to be implemented in Hong Kong appeared similar to the religious policy of the Mainland. When the [*Wide Angle*] article discussed the Mainland, it said 'the policy of religious freedom has been resumed and implemented', and 'to believe in or not to believe in [any religion] is decided by oneself'. But, in reality this is far from the case. On the Mainland, Christian leaders are being arrested and religious books and tapes confiscated by government officials. When overseas Christians visit churches on the Mainland the meetings are prearranged by the 'Three-Self Movement'. Sometimes overseas Christians are accused of being spies attempting to collect information that could be used against the interests of China and Chinese people. The implementation of religious policy means that the Church may only work within specific boundaries. The government appoints officials to deal with church affairs, which is quite different in reality from our understanding of the spirit of the 'Three-Self' Movement (Christian Communication Ltd 1984, 63–4).

To put it simply, Hsueh believed that although religious freedom was an official policy guaranteed in the laws of the Mainland, in reality officials did not comply with it. He suggested that the churches prepare for the 1997 handover by putting more emphasis on teaching their disciples to strengthen their spiritual lives and become responsible members of society. The churches should also, Hsueh said, make their views known to the Chinese government:

> Although part of the policy decisions have been announced, China still knows little about Christianity. One pastor who works for the 'Three-Self' Church in mainland China once commented: Even today, the Communist Party does not understand Christianity. The officials who drew up the policy on religion contacted some church-related people, but these people did not represent all the denominations and churches ... So I very much agree with Reverend Jonathan Chao who is calling for the churches in Hong Kong to be united. They should express their opinions to the Chinese government on the issue of religious freedom and make their demands, seek clarification and explain clearly what kind of religious freedom they are struggling for before July this year [1984] (Christian Communication Ltd 1984, 68).

Hsueh's views to a large extent reflected the general feeling of Protestants in the early 1980s. Another indication of Protestant concern about the handover was the number of clergy and lay Christians applying to immigrate overseas. In 1983 large numbers of Protestants began to immigrate. At first individuals applied quietly but as the years passed, and the numbers grew, immigration became an open and collective action. But it was not until 1987 that the churches felt the need to face the phenomenon and discuss the pastoral issues related to immigration in the Church.[42]

In September 1984, the Commission on Public Policy (CPP) of the HKCC issued a paper on political reform, and presented it to the members of the Legislative and Executive Councils. The paper opposed the idea of setting up functional constituencies. It demanded that 25 per cent of the seats in the Legislative Council be directly elected in 1988, 33 per cent of the seats in the Executive Council be elected by members of the Legislative Assembly and all seats in the Legislative Council be directly elected by 1997.

A Christian NGO active in promoting political reform was the Christian Sentinels for Hong Kong, established by a group of evangelical Christian professionals in June 1985. Every week from 1986 to March 1988 they submitted articles to various Hong Kong newspapers criticizing China's record on human rights and commenting on social and political issues in Hong Kong. Of the five categories of articles — political issues or issues related to the political system; the Basic Law or related problems; economic issues; issues related to the legal system; and educational issues — political issues and issues related to the Basic Law tended to dominate.[43] The members of Christian Sentinels constantly issued statements on political reform, organized press conferences and expressed their views to Hong Kong government officials and the Chinese government via the Hong Kong and Macau Affairs Office during 1986 and 1987 (Chui 1992, 32–3).

In January 1985, with the support of the HKCC, a group of church leaders and lay Christians formed a 'Committee of the Hong Kong Christians Concerned for the Basic Law'. The core members included solicitor Iris Tsang Yin-ling, Reverend Lincoln Leung Lam-hoi of the Methodist Church, Reverend Chu Yiu-ming of Chai Wan Baptist Church and Joseph Chan Cho-wai of Hong Kong Baptist College. The Committee formed six working groups to discuss important topics including: politics, law, religious freedom, human rights, education and society, economics, and the Basic Law. In January 1986, it completed a report on the Basic Law and sent it to more than 600 churches of various denominations and approximately 1,000 church leaders across Hong Kong. It called for an assembly to discuss and endorse the report on 27 January.

Later, the Committee presented the report to the Chinese government via Lu Ping, Secretary of the Hong Kong and Macau Affairs Office.[44] The report had two parts. Part one stated the 'basic idea' of the report while part two made suggestions on 'the normative structure of the Basic Law and the principles for drafting various sections'. These suggestions focused on the relationship between China and Hong Kong and the distribution of power; the function and power of the executive, legislative and judiciary bodies in Hong Kong; human rights and freedom and the right of interpretation and of the Basic Law.[45] The content of the report was comprehensive and ambitious, as Articles 5 and 6 pertaining to the right of political participation and the need for a system of checks and balances shows:

5. As written in Article 2 of the general structure in the Chinese constitution, power belongs to the people. We believe that social and political institutions should be based on the power of the people. Power derived from the people must be effectively and concretely expressed in political institutions. Therefore, the government must be accountable to the people. People of all social strata should have an equal right to political participation. All strata should have an equal right to elect their representatives to enter the executive body and participate in the process of policy making. No single class should monopolize the power of managing the government.

6. The government must have ultimate authority. However, it is our concern that any government can potentially abuse or misuse power. Therefore any political institution should have a system of checks and balances. The exercise of power should be monitored. Hence, no matter whether it is the legislative or executive body, the core of power in the HKSAR government should comply with statements written in the Sino-British Joint Declaration: 'The legislative body should be accountable to the executive body.' Accordingly, the legislative body of the HKSAR government should be accountable to the executive body. The meaning of accountability is that the government should rule Hong Kong in accordance with the policy made by the executive body and report to the executive body about the condition and result of governance and to accept the monitoring of the executive body. If the legislative body makes a mistake, it should be questioned and even impeached and recalled by the executive body.

On 6 October 1986, the CPP issued a 'Preliminary Proposal on Future Development of Representative Government in Hong Kong'. The report demanded that 18 of the 60 seats in the Legislative Council be directly elected in 1988; and in 1997, all the appointed and official members in the Legislative Council be cancelled. Of the 60 Legco seats, 36 should be directly elected, 15 should be chosen by functional constituencies and 9 by electoral college. As for the election of the Chief Executive of the HKSAR, who would replace the British-appointed Governor, it was proposed that he or she be nominated by five members of the Legislative Assembly and be directly elected by the population of Hong Kong through 'one person, one vote' (Chui 1992, 28, 31). On 2 December 1986, the JCPDG organized a mass rally at the Ko Shan Theatre in Hung Hom. The CPP was a member of the JCPDG and its general secretary, Reverend Kwok Nai-wang, openly supported political reform in his speech at the Ko Shan mass rally.

On 18 June 1987, 10 Christian groups attempted to organize a 'Joint Committee of Christians Concerned for the Review of Representative Government'. The Christian bodies included: the Social Concern Group of the Society of Religion at the Chinese University of Hong Kong, the Community Church in Kwun Tong, the Community Church in West Kowloon, the Church Workers Association, the Fellowship of Shum Oi Church, the Fellowship of Theological Graduands, the Society of Chung Chi Theological Students, the Tsuen Kwai Christian Fellowship on Social Concern, the Fellowship of Baptist Students, and the Christian Study Centre on Chinese Religion and Culture. Although the plan to form a 'Christian Joint Committee' did not succeed, most of the groups issued a 'Joint Statement of Christians Concerned on the *Green Paper: The 1987 Review of Developments in Representative Government*'. The Statement demanded that 25 per cent of the seats in the Legislative Council be directly elected in 1988, the official and appointed members in the Council be reduced gradually, all the seats in the Legislative Council be elected by direct election in 1997, and that the age for voting be lowered to 18.[46]

In April 1988, the Basic Law Consultative Committee released the *Draft of the Basic Law* for public consultation. A group of 28 Christians called for a 'Seminar on Church Workers in Response to the Basic Law' and again to organize the 'Committee of the Christians Concerned About the Basic Law'. They encouraged Christians to think about, discuss and respond to the draft of the Basic Law. Later, the committee wrote a 'Position Paper of Church Workers on the *Draft of the Basic Law*', and a group of 63 Christians from various denominations launched a signature campaign in support of the statement. The number of Christians joining the campaign increased to 303 later.

The representatives of the Committee of Hong Kong Christians Concerned for the Basic Law then presented their position paper to the members of the Basic Law Drafting Committee from the Mainland. The demands of the position paper were that: the two treaties on human rights be included into the Hong Kong judiciary system; mainland China's 'Three-Self Principles'[47] religious policy not be included in the Basic Law; the political system should move towards full democratization; concrete checks and balances be introduced to monitor the political system; the power between the Beijing government and the Chief Executive be clearly divided; the Court of Final Appeal in Hong Kong have the power to interpret the Basic Law and investigate matters related to the violation of the mini-constitution; and there should be an independent judiciary (Chui 1992, 44).[48]

As can be seen from above, the Protestant churches became more active in Hong Kong's social affairs in the 1960s. During the 1970s and '80s the Protestant churches and other social groups worked together to launch movements in response to various social and economic issues in the territory. In the 1980s, however, the 1997 handover of Hong Kong to the Mainland became a disturbing matter that finally drove liberal Protestant church leaders to delve into political issues. In particular, the Protestant churches began to call for greater democracy in the political system and as a result became prominent players in the territory's democratic movement.

The HKCC and Fung Chi-wood Incidents

The message of the Chinese government through the Xin Weisi article (see chapter 4) to the Hong Kong Christian Community was clear, and a series of unusual events later occurred in the Protestant churches. From 1986 to 1988, a power struggle emerged in the HKCC, and the conflict was widely reported by the media.[49] In 1986, the progressive young delegates who had been chosen by their churches to represent these churches in the executive committee of the HKCC were replaced by conservative people. The HKCC was formed by 19 mainstream churches and church organizations, and the churches and church organizations sent their delegates to different committees of the HKCC to take part in policy and decision making. The change of personnel implied that some of the churches and church organizations were exercising control over political involvement of HKCC by replacing the more progressive delegates (Lee 1987).

In 1987, the executive committee members of the HKCC, including Anglican Bishop Kwong, Lutheran Reverend John Tse and Reverend Yung Kok-kwong of the Church of Christ in China, amended the organization's constitution. They introduced a regulation stipulating that the CPP should have the approval of the executive committee before they initiate social actions or issue statements.[50] Thereafter, the monthly meeting of the executive committee became a mechanism to silence the voice of the CPP and soon the committee disappeared from the platform of Hong Kong politics. Reverend Kwok Nai-wang resigned from the HKCC and founded a new organization called the Hong Kong Christian Institute in September 1988 and continued his mission of social and political participation in Hong Kong.[51]

(From left to right) Kwok Nai-wang, Szeto Wah, Carver Yu Tat-sum, Rose Wu and Luk Fai at the inauguration ceremony of the Hong Kong Christian Institute, 1988. Courtesy of the Hong Kong Christian Institute.

Another liberal church leader, Reverend Fung Chi-wood of the Anglican Church was also under pressure from traditional church leaders. Reverend Fung was spokesperson of the Joint Conference for Shelving the Daya Bay Nuclear Plant, and one of the Protestant representatives criticized by Xin Weisi. In April 1986, the Chernobyl nuclear plant disaster in the former USSR triggered fear among Hong Kong people about the plan of the Chinese Government to construct a nuclear plant at Daya Bay in Shenzhen, 50 kilometres away from Hong Kong. Two months after the disaster, 37 NGO groups in Hong Kong formed a 'Joint Conference for Shelving the Daya Bay Nuclear Plant', and elected Reverend Fung Chi-wood of the Anglican Church as the spokesperson of the committee. The Daya Bay committee collected approximately one million signatures from Hong Kong citizens who wanted to prevent the construction of the nuclear plant. Soon the action turned into a protest movement against the Chinese government, which was accused of ignoring the will of the Hong Kong people.

In December 1987, the Church of England Trustees and Bishop Kwong instructed Fung to stop commenting on 'secular issues', and suggested that Fung go to study in the United Kingdom for two years. Fung refused. He remained in Hong Kong and became a member of the Legislative Council in 1988. The media in Hong Kong reported that Fung had been pressured by the Church.[52] It was reported that Bishop Kwong had said the Anglican Church did not force the clergy to take a different position on political issues due to pressure from the Beijing government. However, he emphasized at the same time that the Church as a whole should not participate in political activities, saying that if it did so, it would become a political party. A church should be separate from a political party. Nonetheless, individual Christians can put what they have learned from church into practice in their everyday lives and political concern (Lam 1987). In response to Bishop Kwong, Fung stressed that he had been participating in the anti-nuclear protests in his own name and as a result his political involvement was not in conflict with the regulations of the Anglican Church. Fung publicly admitted that he had been under pressure from the Church. He said the Church had become nervous about its members' social and political activities and did not want its members making critical comments about the Hong Kong or Chinese government (Lau 1987, 24).

In theory, Bishop Kwong's remarks are questionable. A church that participates in politics does not necessarily become a political party. A church can express its political concerns in regard to every day life and still maintain its status as a church. Secondly, relationships between churches and political parties can take many forms. If a church agrees with a party on some social issues, a church can support that party's position but strictly separate itself from the party in terms of organization. To put Bishop Kwong's remarks in the context of Church-State relations, we can note that Kwong's position is in conflict with the statement of the Christian Sentinels for Hong Kong but consistent with the position of Xin Weisi.

Conflict between conservative and liberal church leaders regarding Church-State relations can be clearly observed from the HKCC and Fung Chi-wood incidents. By this time Reverend Kwok Nai-wang had assumed the role of a 'prophet'. He continued to urge the churches to become concerned about Hong

Kong's social and political affairs through the Hong Kong Christian Institute. He retired in August 2000 and his mission was taken over by the new general secretary Rose Wu. In his article entitled, 'The Role and Task of Christianity in the Social Development of Hong Kong' in 1994, Kwok reflected on the problems caused by the Church acting as a government 'deputy' or 'contractor':

> In the 1950s and '60s, the cost of establishing and maintaining aid, medical, welfare and education services were almost completely covered by overseas churches or the government. In the 1970s, foreign assistance declined due to Hong Kong's economic development. However, the social services run by the churches in Hong Kong had expanded so greatly that there was no way they could be cut back. Since the Church could not depend on donations from church members, she had to rely on local business tycoons or charity funds (including the fund sponsored by the Hong Kong Jockey Club) and the government. In reverse, the government too had to rely on the assistance of the churches to provide ample and reliable social services, while the business tycoons needed the Church to enhance their reputation and image. A relationship of mutual benefit between the Church, the government and business tycoons made it impossible for the Church to act as a social critic. As time past, the Church became so dependent on this relationship that it even defended the establishment (N.-w. Kwok 1994, 79–80).

Referring to Church-State relations, Kwok suggested that:

> Churches in Hong Kong still need to be concerned about the overall and long-term development of Hong Kong society. They should not fall short of providing services for the needy, but also have the courage to question the Government and the business tycoons who influence Hong Kong's politics, economics and culture. As a conscience of society, the Church should uphold democracy, human rights, and the rule of law and oppose corruption, monitor those who hold power and make them serve the people faithfully in years to come (N.-w. Kwok 1994, 92).

Concluding Remarks

In both the Catholic and Protestant churches there were progressive Christians who advocated social justice and were concerned for the poor and oppressed.

During the transitional handover period, an increasing number of Catholic and Protestant clergy and lay Christians took part in social activist movements and began to urge democratic reform in the face of major social and political change.

In the spirit of the Vatican II, the Justice and Peace Commission of the Hong Kong Catholic Diocese was established in 1970 to promote social justice. However, the Catholic authorities did not condone any political activity that might disrupt British rule in Hong Kong out of fear that it could backfire on the Church. The Catholic Church could not afford to offend the Hong Kong government because it relied on government subsidies to operate its education and social services. Before the signing of the Sino-British Joint Declaration on the future of Hong Kong, the diocesan authorities only half-heartedly implemented Catholic social teaching.

The Catholic Church's political involvement in the transitional period was complicated by the triangular relationship between China, the Vatican and Hong Kong. The possibility of drastic change after 1997 handover led Cardinal John Baptist Wu to issue his 1989 pastoral exhortation 'March into the Bright Decade', which suggested a strategy for responding to political change after 1997. Apart from the Union of Hong Kong Catholic Organizations in Support of the Patriotic and Democratic Movement in China, the Hong Kong Catholic diocese asked priests, sisters and other church personnel to encourage Catholics to vote in the Legislative Council elections in 1991.

The Chinese government frowned upon the participation of the Catholic Church in politics, both in terms of the its attempts to act as a bridge between the Church in China and the universal church and in terms of its effort to promote democracy in Hong Kong. As discussed in chapter 4, the Chinese government was also displeased with the consecration of two new Hong Kong Bishops because it was held before the handover, and Chinese bishops from the official sector of the Catholic Church in the Mainland were not invited.

Among the Protestant churches, three public statements were issued in 1984 in response to the handover of Hong Kong to mainland China. The 'Proposed Statement of Faith for Hong Kong Christians in the Face of Social and Political Change' expressed the churches' position on the issue of 1997 and their mission in Hong Kong. The 'Statement on Religious Freedom by the Protestant Churches of Hong Kong' was a position paper that expressed the concerns of Protestants about religious freedom after 1997. The 'Opinions of the Hong Kong Protestant Delegation to Beijing on the future of Hong Kong' sought assurances from Beijing that there would be a continuation of Church-State relations after 1997.

During the transitional period, progressive Protestants called for greater democratization and political reform. Prominent examples are the 'Committee of the Hong Kong Christians Concerned for the Basic Law', which in 1985 expressed the views of Protestants on politics, law, religious freedom, human rights, education, society, economics and the Basic Law. Some progressive clergy and lay Christians took part in a mass rally at the Ko Shan Theatre in Hung Hom in 1986 organized by the JCPDG to urge democratic reform. The 'Committee of Christians Concerned about the Basic Law' encouraged Protestants to discuss and respond to the draft of the Basic Law. The committee issued a 'Position Paper of Church Workers on the Draft of the Basic Law' in 1988.

The conflict between conservative and the liberal church leaders also revealed the difference in their political orientation. For example, Anglican Bishop Peter Kwong was criticized for giving up fundamental principles in order to please the Chinese government in 1986. The conservative church leaders of the Hong Kong Christian Council exerted their power in an attempt to silence the voice of General Secretary Kwok Nai-wang on social and political issues. An Anglican priest, Reverend Fung Chi-wood, was asked by his denomination to stop commenting of 'secular issues' in 1987. Criticism of China's record on human rights was deleted in the Ninth World Lutheran Assembly in 1997 due to the objection of the Hong Kong representatives from the Rhenish Church and Evangelical Lutheran Church.

Progressive Catholics and Protestants had a different attitude towards Church-State relations. Contrary to the 'contractual' relationship with the government, which was supported by traditional church leaders, progressive Christians advocated a 'prophetic' role or a critical stance towards the government and supported Christian participation in urging social and political reform in Hong Kong.

CHAPTER SIX

The Hong Kong SAR Government and the Catholic Church

The Church's Response to the Mother Tongue Teaching Policy (December 1998)

At the time of the reversion of Hong Kong to Chinese rule, the Chief Executive, Mr Tung Chee-hwa, presented his vision for the future of Hong Kong in the context of the 'one country, two systems' policy. He formulated it as follows: 'a society proud of its national identity and cultural heritage; a stable, equitable, free, democratic, compassionate society with a clear sense of direction; an affluent society with improved quality of life for all; a decent society with a level playing field and fair competition under the rule of law; a window for exchanges between China and the rest of the world; a renowned international financial, trading, transportation and communication centre; a world class cultural, education and scientific research centre' (Tung 1997a, 3).

In October 1997 Mr Tung Chee-hwa gave his first policy speech dealing with education, the caring of the aged, and housing. He believed that the most important goal of the HKSAR government was to enhance Hong Kong's economic vitality and growth, and that education was the main means to accomplish this (Tung 1997b). Outlining a mission for educators, he stated that the education system must cater to Hong Kong's needs, contribute to the country, and adopt an international outlook (Tung 1997a, 5). Among other things, he called for the expansion of mother tongue teaching (Tung 1997b). In December 1997, the Education Department announced its instruction medium guidelines, which allowed 100 of the 400 secondary schools to teach in English with the rest in Chinese. Subsequently fourteen schools' applications for appeal were honoured, making the number of English-medium schools increase to 114. While the school administrators, teachers, students and their families at the 114 privileged schools were pleased, their counterparts were not. Of the 114 schools, more than a third were Catholic schools.[1]

From a public policy analyst's long-run perspective, the mother tongue teaching policy is highly problematic because it will greatly reduce Hong Kong's capacity to maintain its competitive position in the Greater China region and in the world as a whole.[2] The labour force's knowledge of English has been one of, if not the most important factor in Hong Kong's business edge in Asia, helping to facilitate the immediate absorption of information from around the world.

The Hong Kong Education Department did not bother to examine in depth the experiences of other countries. A thorough investigation was not carried out to determine the precise causes of learning barriers and deficiencies, such as learning and entertainment habits, changing cultural values, peer influence, school-family co-operation and so on. Rather it copped out and forced most high school students to be educated in Chinese. The government was in fact giving up on this generation of students, blaming their poor English skills on inadequate training during their primary school years. The administrators of Catholic schools also saw the problem and also, unfortunately, did not fully analyse the relative impact of each of the above-mentioned social factors.[3]

The Catholic Church did not carry out a serious study of its education policy during the 1960s, 70s and 80s, instead relying upon political expediency and co-operation with the colonial government under the 'contractor relationship'. In theory, it is the goal of Catholic education to promote Christian transformation of the world and to contribute to the good of society as a whole (Abbott 1966, 637–51).

In the 1970s, for nationalistic reasons, some Chinese priests supported the mother tongue teaching policy. Cardinal Wu, in his exhortation 'March Into the Bright Decade' (1989) suggested mother tongue teaching, and the Catholic Board of Education of the Hong Kong Catholic Diocese also supported it in principle (Wu 1989, 7).

This policy is highly regressive because the effective use of English is fundamental to maintaining Hong Kong's competitiveness especially vis-à-vis China and Taiwan. The new policy will deprive a substantial percentage of

Hong Kong youngsters the opportunity to master English at an early age, the stage at which human cognitive capacity for learning a second language is greatest. More importantly, as youngsters in the Mainland are catching up fast in their usage of English, Hong Kong students many soon fall behind. Thus this policy clearly contradicts Tung's calling for the education system 'to cater to Hong Kong's needs' (Tung 1997a, 5).

Catholic schools in Hong Kong can be divided into two groups, those run by the Catholic diocese of Hong Kong, and those by missionary societies called mission schools. In terms of quality and historical significance it is the latter which contribute the most to local education. The Catholic Bishop's representative, Mr Lo Kong-kai, a former principal of Diocesan School, openly supported the government's mother tongue policy, whereas he got no support from Catholic mission schools. The failure of the Catholic Church to form one voice in dealing with the government's policy may become a time bomb waiting to explode.

Hong Kong Bishops at the Special Asian Synod (April-May 1998)

A Special Asian Synod, held in Rome 19 April to 14 May 1998, was attended by more than 250 prelates from over 30 countries in Asia and related areas.[4] Its theme was 'Jesus Christ, the Savior and his Mission of Love and Service in Asia'.[5] The fact that two bishops in China, Bishop Mathias Duan Yinmin, and his auxiliary, Bishop Xu Zhixuan of Sichuan Province, were not permitted to attend, though they had been openly invited by the Pope, caused quite a stir.

The coadjutor bishop of Hong Kong, Joseph Zen and the auxiliary bishop, John Tong, were invited to make presentations at the Synod. They emphasized that the focus of their work was not just Hong Kong but the Catholic Church in China as well.[6] Despite the fact that they could potentially face problems from the Mainland government, the two bishops did not discuss the Church in Hong Kong, but rather talked about the Catholic Church in mainland China. Zen remarked that the Church needs to 'proclaim the truth' and 'work towards reconciliation'. In exploring these two themes the hardships of the Mainland churches were indirectly exposed.[7] Bishop John Tong remarked, 'Originally the Communist Party, being atheistic, had no place for religion in its ideology. However, it was confronted by the fact that religion exists and cannot be eradicated. The Party had to develop a way to make use of religion in order to serve the government's aims.'[8] His candidness was very unusual, for Tong had long been noted for his mild manner when dealing with conflict. Before the handover, the Hong Kong Catholic Church repeatedly received messages from Beijing requesting that the bridging efforts be curtailed. However, it was plain from the behaviour of the two Hong Kong bishops at the Asian Synod that they did not take these messages seriously when they ignored the Beijing's request.

The speeches of Hong Kong Bishops Zen and Tong were somewhat exploratory. From the Chinese perspective, they violated Article 148 of the HKSAR Basic Law that clearly states that the relationship between the HKSAR's religious organizations and their counterparts in China should be based on the principle of non-subordination, non-interference, and mutual respect. However, these two bishops had both spent over ten years assisting mainland Chinese Catholics. They regarded their presentations at the Synod as the sharing of experiences with their ecclesiastical brothers in the Church. The Chinese government did not openly denounce the presentations. However, when Bishop Zen attempted to continue his visits and assistance to Mainland seminaries, he was firmly but gently forbidden to do so.[9] Ye Xiaowen, Head of the Religious Affairs Bureau, asked him to meet him in Shenzhen. There he received the message that Beijing was happy neither with Zen's speech at the Synod nor the Catholic Church's bridging efforts within China.

This was the first contact between the Hong Kong Catholic Church and the Chinese government after the handover. The reaction to the bishops' words at the Synod could be regarded as interference in Hong Kong. The Catholic Church is a transnational actor in international politics and the local Catholic Church must serve the interests of the headquarters, the Vatican (Vallier 1971, 479–94). The Holy See is keen to assist the growth of the Church in China. However, the bridging efforts with China are very much against the interests of the CCP, and Hong Kong as the focal point for the bridging efforts is expected to come increasingly into direct conflict with the Mainland government.[10] Resolving this conflict will require skilful and tactful discussion and demonstration of tolerance by each of the three parties — Beijing, the Vatican, and the Hong Kong Catholic Church.

God Is Love: The Catholic Stance on the Right of Abode Issue (June 1999)

Hong Kong's Court of Final Appeal on 29 January 1999 ruled that under the Basic Law all Mainland children born of Hong Kong permanent residents are entitled to live in the HKSAR. Before this verdict, only legitimate children born after at least one parent had become a Hong Kong permanent resident were admitted. However, the HKSAR government did not like the Final Appeal Court's verdict, and tried to appeal. The result was a battle between the administration and the rule of law striking at the heart of Hong Kong's autonomy. The government tried to alarm the general public by reporting that over one million newcomers would put intolerable pressure on housing, employment and public health (Ching 1999, 18). For example, the Secretary for Security, Regina Yip, stated in the Legislative Council on 28 April 1999 that 'the number of people to be absorbed by Hong Kong as a result of the judgment, that is some 1.6 million people, is likely to pose a very heavy — and even unbearable burden on Hong Kong.' The Hong Kong Policy Research Institute was asked to conduct a survey and found that 83.8 per cent of respondents were opposed to the ruling of the Final Court of Appeal. This survey was one of many actions taken to inflame negative public opinion and demonstrate the Hong Kong government's unwillingness to accept the ruling of the Final Court of Appeal. Some scholars and human rights groups accused the government of producing dubious statistics to instill fear in the public and give the impression that the only possible solution would be to have the judgment effectively overturned (Ching 1999, 18).

In his pastoral letter titled 'God is Love', Cardinal Wu sharply criticized the government's stance on the right of abode (appendix 6). The following was his main argument:

> A large number of adult Hong Kong residents came from the Mainland to settle here in the 1950s and 1960s. Hong Kong at that time was not blessed with a strong economy or firm social structure. Nevertheless, when faced with a continuous flood of refugees, there was no hesitation and doors were opened to welcome them. At present, the economic outlook is not nearly as bright. Yet compared with the rest of the world, Hong Kong is still the envy of many. Based on the belief that 'blood is thicker than water' and that 'all within the four seas are one family', the Chinese people have always shown kindness to others and taken delight in sharing. Faced today with the question of children born to Hong Kong parents in the Motherland, how can we harden our hearts, look on with indifference and a lack of humanity, and use 'interpretation' to deny them hope? ... (J. Wu 1999)

Arguing from a humanitarian point of view, he put the government's stance to shame, saying, 'Now you are getting rich. How can you refuse others who seek to move to Hong Kong as you did only a few decades ago? He offered the opinion that:

> ... Given sufficient time, and provided with adequate information and proper arrangements, Hong Kong's zealous people, philanthropists, voluntary bodies and church communities could deal with the present right of abode crisis. United in hand and in heart, these groups could respond to the challenge, and grasp the opportunity to develop a spirit of love and create a new miracle. Let it be seen that Hong Kong society is loving and caring ...
> (J. Wu 1999)

The Cardinal was exceptionally blunt in criticizing the government for asking the National Peoples Congress to re-interpret the Basic Law:

> ... It (the government) seeks the long term prosperity of Hong Kong by requesting the Standing Committee of the NPC to re-interpret the Basic Law in order to limit the right of abode of children born in the Mainland to Hong Kong parents. This fosters a certain resistance on the part of Hong Kong residents towards Mainland people, with lamentable consequences ... It is extremely important that the Basic Law and government be maintained in all their integrity. Solving the question of right of abode is a Hong Kong matter. The SAR should itself give its own interpretation, but this has not been done. Asking for a re-interpretation by the Standing Committee of the NPC cannot help but damage the foundation of the autonomy of the SAR, shake the foundations of the Hong Kong family, raise doubts in people's minds about the central government's promise of 'one country, two systems with a high degree of autonomy', and undermine the confidence of the international community towards Hong Kong. Who can be sure how far-reaching the effects will be?

The pastoral letter's voicing the conscience of Hong Kong society pleased political commentators and the general public. The Catholic Church was the first organization to denounce the government's policy on the right of abode.[11] The public immediately condemned the HKSAR government and Beijing.[12] The archbishop of the Hong Kong Anglican Church *(Sheng Kung Hui),* Archbishop Peter Kwong, who is also a member of the NPC and the Chinese People's Political Consultative Conference, openly supported the Cardinal's letter based on the fundamental Christian social teaching that God is love, and all human beings are brothers and sisters.[13] Christians and Catholic progressive groups such as the Justice and Peace Commission of the Hong Kong Catholic Diocese, and the Hong Kong Catholic Commission for Labour Affairs also allied themselves with Protestant groups to carry out a signature campaign, issue announcements, and hold public conferences and seminars to show their support for the Cardinal's views.[14] Inspired by the official stance of the Catholic Church, hundreds of individual Christians and 23 Protestant groups signed a full page notice in *Ming Pao* on 17 June 1999 outlining the reasons why they opposed the government's handling of the right of abode issue.[15] In an unprecedented act, the Secretary of Security, Regina Yip, on 17 June 1999 wrote a long letter to the Cardinal defending the government's position. However, the Justice and Peace Commission published a statement in the newspaper rebutting Yip's claim.[16]

The Church risked offending the HKSAR government and Beijing by openly opposing the controversial 'right of abode' policy. It was the first prominent social issue in which the Catholic Church expressed its concern, knowing very well that its stance would set the Church against the State.[17] Cardinal Wu's landmark pastoral letter undoubtedly launched a new era for the Catholic Church in Hong Kong.

The Diocese Decides to Practise Passive Compliance in the Legco Elections (July 1999)

Before the last Legco elections in 1998, the Catholic Diocese repeatedly made known that it did not wish to participate in a body it considered 'undemocratic', 'unfair' and 'against the principle of fairness and openness of an election'.[18] The Diocese sought the government's permission to withdraw from the Election Committee but the request received no reply. In the end, due to legal requirements, it agreed to offer 'passive co-operation' and allowed Catholic candidates to be chosen to sit on the Election Committee. However, new legislation governing the selection of religious participants for the Election Committee, which was passed by Legco on 15 July 1999, provided a loophole through which the Catholic Church could withdraw from nominating Catholic representatives for the Election Committee.

After lengthy negotiations with the Constitutional Affairs Bureau, both sides agreed to compromise in order to resolve the stalemate. The Church agreed that it would only verify the Catholic identity of the candidate, while the Constitutional Affairs Bureau would make arrangements for choosing seven participants from the candidates. In practice, if Catholics wish to participate in the Election Committee, the Catholic authorities will verify the only identity of Catholic candidates who are not representatives of the Catholic Church. If a large number of candidates apply for the seven seats open to Catholics, the diocese will make it known that the Constitutional Affairs Bureau, the organizer of the election, must draw lots to choose the winning candidates.[19]

Reactivating the Parish Catholic Social Concern Groups (July 1999)

The diocesan level of the Justice and Peace Commission was established under the instruction of the Vatican in 1970. However, the Catholic clergy as a whole hesitated in responding. It feared that social criticism would embarrass the colonial rulers.[20]

Among the 59 Catholic parishes of the Hong Kong diocese, 16 have social concern groups. The establishment of these groups is a manifestation of Catholic social teaching at the grassroots level. However, the degree of activism depends on the diocesan support for socio-political participation and the relative conservatism of the various parish priests. In the last two decades, apart from the massive Catholic support given at the rallies commemorating the victims of 4 June 1989 Tiananmen Square Incident, the social concern activities have been rather inactive. Some even became dormant.

In reactivating the social concern groups at the parish level, the Hong Kong Catholic Church seemed to be taking its prophetic role as the conscience of society quite seriously. The Catholic authorities gave front-page coverage of the issue in the *Catholic Chinese Weekly* with an interview heralding its main architect, Bishop Joseph Zen, and providing a detailed report on the plan for reactivation of the social concern groups. In the following issue of the same newspaper an instruction was issued, and on the next Sunday all priests delivered sermons on this theme.[21]

According to Zen, 'social concern' and 'evangelization' are equally important. In fact these are the two arms of the Catholic Church.[22] He admitted that social concern would lead unavoidably to political participation. If the Church wished to take up the role of witness, political participation was necessary to ensure human rights and the good of the majority.[23]

The reactivation of social concern groups has very far-reaching consequences and serious implications in future Church-State relations. From the start of the transition period beginning in 1984, it had not been the wish of the Chinese government to see religious organizations in Hong Kong play a political role.[24] It had already expressed, on several occasions, its intentions for religious organizations in Hong Kong, including the Catholic Church.[25]

Rejection of a Proposed Papal Visit to the HKSAR (August 1999)

The Holy Father, Pope John Paul II, had planned a trip to Asia in late 1999 to announce the results of the previous year's Special Synod for Asia. The Vatican hoped to secure him a visit to Hong Kong in order that he could realize his dream of preaching on Chinese soil before his death. However, the Vatican's diplomatic campaign to secure an invitation for the Pope was rejected. The Chinese government refused to allow him to visit because the Vatican would not accept the condition that the Beijing authorities alone must manage the trip. An official in the Chinese Foreign Ministry added: 'It would not be appropriate for the Pope to visit Hong Kong as the Vatican still maintains diplomatic relations with Taiwan'.[26] The unwillingness to allow the papal visit concerned both Catholics and non-Catholics because it again challenged Hong Kong's autonomy and the promise of 'one country, two systems'. The HKSAR government issued a statement on 9 August 1999 saying that 'it would be appropriate to discuss the proposed visit only after the [Chinese] central government and the Vatican have resolved the relevant issue.[27] The news was given full coverage by foreign media and was heavily critical of the HKSAR government.[28] A leading political critic in Hong Kong noted:

> The Pope has been warmly welcomed everywhere he goes, including the bastion of Communism, Cuba. During the 21 years of his reign he has visited 120 nations, including Iraq, which he shall visit in 2000. The Pope is the personification of the world's conscience, justice, and mercy. He fought for workers' rights and opposed the arms race in the Cold War period. He ordered the governments of the countries involved in the Persian Gulf War and Kosovo War to resolve their conflicts by negotiation, not war. Allowing the Pope to visit Hong Kong would demonstrate the flexibility of China's foreign policy. More importantly, the visit would crystallize the promised non-interference in Hong Kong's internal matters. Not only Catholics, but all citizens in Hong Kong were disappointed. The HKSAR government's following of the will of Beijing is not in the interests of Hong Kong (Lin 1999).[29]

The Catholic authorities did not make any formal negative statement towards the HKSAR government on this issue. The news about rejecting the papal visit to Hong Kong was first known upon Bishop Zen's return from his visit to the Vatican in July 1999. It was then disseminated by the Catholic official papers, *Kung Kao Po* and *Sunday Examiner*.[30] The *South China Morning Post* on 9 and 10 August 1999 discussed the various views given in the Catholic papers. Although the public expressed outrage at the news, the Catholic authorities kept a low profile, with Bishop Joseph Zen and the Diocesan Chancellor, Lawrence Lee, understating that the Hong Kong Catholics would be disappointed. Unlike the Executive Secretary of Justice of Peace Commission, who voiced very strong words against the decision, they did not denounce Beijing.[31]

The contrast between the sharp criticism from the Hong Kong public and the silence of the Hong Kong Catholic authorities caused embarrassment to the Mainland government. Hong Kong Catholics knew very well that the purpose of the papal visit to Hong Kong was to speak to the Chinese Church in China, as was the case when Pope Paul VI came to Hong Kong on 4 December 1970 (B. Leung 1992, 193–6). Given the strong reaction towards Tibet, Muslim unrest in Xinjiang, and the Falun Gong Movement, Hong Kong Catholic leaders realized that it was not a good time to propose a papal visit to China.[32] However, the Vatican had been anxious to test the water and therefore proposed this visit at the Asian Synod.

Division Over the Canonization of Chinese Saints (October 2000)

On 1 October 2000, Pope John Paul II canonized 122 men and women in the Church to be saints. Among these, 120 were martyrs in China (1648–1930). Canonization is a part of the Catholic tradition, and these were the first saints from China. Among the 120 martyrs in China, 87 were Chinese and 33 were foreign missionaries. Their martyrdom occurred as a result of the expulsion of foreign religion in Kangxi and Chenglung period stemming from the Controversy of Chinese Rites, and the Boxer Rebellion, which took place in late Qing Dynasty. The Chinese government staged a confrontation with the Vatican on this issue, saying that the canonization of those missionaries who committed monstrous crimes in China was a severe provocation and insult to 1.2 billion Chinese people. In the official mouthpiece, the *Renmin Ribao,* it argued that 'the canonization laid bare the Vatican's scheme of trying to resume control over the Chinese Catholic Church and to encourage Chinese Catholics to oppose the socialist system'.[33] For China, the Vatican's canonization was equivalent to 'cutting open the historical scars' of the Chinese people.[34]

The Chinese government then recruited Bishop Michael Fu Tieshan, Chairman of the China Catholic Patriotic Association, together with a group of religious women (sisters) and priests in religious attire to attend the Chinese National Day flag-raising ceremony at Tiananmen Square to show the Catholic community's allegiances. Bishop Fu was even openly critical of the canonization, saying that it was an insult and humiliation against Chinese Catholic adherents.[35] One week before and after the canonization, the Chinese media was filled with statements such as 'the martyred saints were criminals with perverse and vicious acts'. The Catholic Patriotic Association and the Bishops College of the People's Republic of China were summoned to Beijing to hold a seminar on 2 October 2000 to pronounce a critical statement criticizing the Holy See and denouncing the canonization. After that, various religious sects were forced to hold meetings in which they supported the Catholic denunciations.[36] The international mass media was perplexed by the great variation in interpretation of the word 'saint'.[37] Overseas Catholics were distressed to hear Bishop Fu openly criticize the Pope's decision about the canonization. A Catholic bishop openly criticizing the Holy See on religious matters was unprecedented and shocking.[38]

However, the Hong Kong Adjunct Bishop, Joseph Zen, on 5 October 2000 published a strong article in *Ming Pao*, not only defending the canonization, but responding to the political behaviour of Beijing. Deliberately using a provocative tone, Bishop Zen overtly doubted the authenticity of the denunciation of the Chinese Bishops College. He noted it was a well-known Communist tactic for the government to put words into the mouths of the bishops. He affirmed that the canonized saints could not be robbers, murderers and rapists as claimed by China, because the investigation of each martyr was thorough, and a system of 'devil's advocate' was used to expose any possible scandal. He claimed that there was no way such 'enormous crimes' could pass undetected.[39] However, the article aroused great public attention because firstly the Catholic Church had gone out its own way to write to the public news media instead of its own weekly, *Kung Kao Po*. By approaching *Ming Pao*, he indicated that he wanted his message to be known to the general public, not just limited to the Catholic circle.[40] Secondly, the Bishop revealed that the Chinese Liaison Office in Hong Kong had requested that the Catholic Diocese on 18 September 2000, keep its canonization celebrations low-key.[41] He loudly divulged the message of the Liaison Office, causing embarrassment to both Beijing and the HKSAR. The assistant director of the Chinese Liaison office in Hong Kong, Wang Fengqiao, declined to comment on Zen's accusations, while Lam Wun-kwong, the Secretary of Civil Affairs of the HKSAR, immediately declared that religious freedom in the HKSAR had been prevailing without disturbance.[42] Lam's political gesture was an attempt to defend Hong Kong when the public was beginning to doubt there would be continued religious freedom after the handover. The doubts over Hong Kong's freedoms had already begun to take hold after an incident of alleged erosion of academic freedom concerning the University of Hong Kong earlier that year.[43] Bishop Zen's strong reaction drew public attention to the violation of religious freedom, instead of the canonization. It also drew a halt to Beijing's continuous accusations, but cast a pall on the HKSAR's Catholic Church and government relations.

This was proved to be true in the official visit of Li Ruihuan, Chairman of Chinese People's Political Consultative Conference, to Hong Kong in November 2000. It was the first official visit made by a high-ranking Chinese official after the handover. The HKSAR government arranged a social gathering to give a cross-section of civil and political leaders an opportunity to meet Li. The head of the Democratic Party, leading political dissidents such as Martin Lee, and the leader of the Hong Kong Catholic Church were all not invited.[44] It seemed that the Beijing authorities found the Catholic Church leaders as odious as political dissidents.

The Chinese denunciation of the canonization was a political move associated with the Sino-Vatican negotiations. An internally circulated document called upon Chinese officials to prepare for the Sino-Vatican rapprochement to ensure that the Party would win the Party-Catholic struggle for organizational control after the normalization of the Sino-Vatican diplomatic relations.[45] The economic reforms had unleashed social forces, which before Deng Xiaoping came to power, had been exclusively in the hands of the Party. Now the Party's capacity for exercising control over society, including the religious sector, had been greatly reduced (Kang 1999). Several incidents revealed that the Party was experiencing difficulties in monitoring the official sector of the Chinese Catholic Church. For example, six Chinese bishops were consecrated without the prior approval of the Vatican. Among twelve designated bishop candidates, only six accepted the State consecration. The others, not wanting to antagonize the Vatican, declined the government's offer.[46] Many bishops gave their own excuses to be absent from the consecration ceremony. Even seminarians in the national seminary collectively refused to be present at the ceremony. Party officials at this stage realized that even after monitoring the official sector of the Church, using united front tactics for many years, could not yield the results the Party expected. While the official Chinese Catholic Church paid only lip service to the State, the underground Church continued its rejection of the Party leadership.

The Falun Gong Dilemma (2000)

Falun Gong is an indigenous movement whose organization, discipline and beliefs are drawn from Buddhism and Taoism. Besides calming the spirit, it is also considered in China to be a practical health care alternative for those unable to afford the higher costs, following the economic reforms, of conventional medical treatment. The movement attracted people from the fringes of society including retired and semi-retired cadres who had not benefited from the economic reforms, and had therefore become disillusioned with the CCP.

In 2000, the Falun Gong Movement was seriously undermining the ideology of the State by persistently demanding freedom of assembly, which was something the Party could not tolerate. China condemned it as a cult and launched a campaign to wipe it out. However, repression of the 100 million strong membership was difficult.[47]

The Falun Gong was registered in the HKSAR as an organization and held international conferences in 1999 and 2000. Beijing's labelling of the Falun Gong as a cult put the HKSAR government in a very awkward position. The Chief Executive and Minister of Security were all very negative towards it. However, more than ten Christian organizations including the Catholics believed that, on the basis of religious freedom, the movement ought to be allowed to have a chapter in the SAR.[48] They stood by the Falun Gong in the name of religious freedom. Christian organizations were not necessarily sympathetic to movement's beliefs, but they were highly sensitive to any potential erosion in the religious freedom they had enjoyed in Hong Kong over past several decades, and were therefore willing to regard the Falun Gong as a new religion. An editorial in the *Kung Kao Po* expressed the Catholic authorities' grave concern about the possible suppression of the movement because it could be the first step towards the end of religious freedom in the SAR.[49]

The movement put the HKSAR in a dilemma. However, according to the principle of 'one country, two systems' policy, the Falun Gong ought to be able to continue to exist in Hong Kong so long as it observes the Basic Law. At the time of this writing the HKSAR government has not made a final decision on how to handle it. In this manner, the Falun Gong is a critical testing ground for the HKSAR.

Schooling for Abode-Seeking Children (November 2001)

This issue was the continuation of the issue of Mainlanders seeking right-of-abode in Hong Kong. After re-interpretation of the NPC Steering Committee, there were 187 abode-seeking children from the Mainland who had been granted a letter permitting temporary stay while awaiting the results of their right-of-abode applications. However, they were barred from studying in Hong Kong. Bishop Joseph Zen wrote to the principals of all 300 Catholic schools in Hong Kong requesting them to take the children if they had room, or at least let them sit in on classes. The government took a hard-line and warned that schools that by admitting these children without approval from the Education and Immigration Department they could be committing a crime.[50] This move immediately caught the attention of human right activists, including the director of the Society for Community Organization, Ho Hei-wah, Margaret Ng Ngoi-yee, and democratic legislators such as Cheung Man-kwong and Ho Sau-lan, who criticized the government for shamelessly depriving children of their right to an education (Ng 2001). Professionals, especially legal professionals supported Zen's humanitarian move, deeming the government's position bewilderingly cold-blooded. Writing in the *Ming Pao* Daily News, Ronny Tong, SC, former chairman of the Bar, pointed out that though the government's stance was firm, its legal basis was weak (S. Lee 2001; M. Ng 2001). Bishop Joseph Zen decided to fight for the children to the end even if it meant employing civil disobedience.[51]

Public opinion sided with the Catholic bishop, and the government had no choice but to soften its stance: the children were allowed to attend classes. Credit for resolving the matter was due to the Bishop who stood up to the Education, Immigration and Legal Departments.

Joseph Zen's Accession to the Catholic Leadership and Article 23 of the Basic Law

When Cardinal Wu died on 23 September 2002, Coadjutor Bishop Joseph Zen Ze-kiun automatically became the prelate of Hong Kong Catholic Diocese and leader of 260,000 Hong Kong Catholics. Speculation on the future of Church-State relations under Zen was given unusually extensive coverage by secular media as well as church media.[52] The *South China Morning Post* had reported on 21 September, during the final stages of Cardinal Wu's illness, that Zen was critical of the SAR government's newly launched 'Ministerial

Responsibility System' and was skeptical about the prevailing political culture, which in his view was without integrity.[53] People were already asking whether Zen would continue to be so critical over socio-political issues after he assumed the leadership of the Catholic Church in Hong Kong. Although he was honoured as the conscience of Hong Kong, an atmosphere of confrontation had developed between Zen and the SAR government.[54]

At the Cardinal's funeral, Hong Kong's Chief Executive went to the Immaculate Conception Cathedral to offer his condolences in person. At the Vigil Mass (27 September) Auxiliary Bishop John Tong stated that the Catholic Diocese would like to have more communication with the HKSAR government. Shortly after the funeral, on 30 September, Zen and Tong held a press conference in which Zen stated that he would continue to follow the social teaching of the Church to stand with the poor and oppressed. However, Zen emphasized that he would present his message in a more reconciliatory manner.[55] At his Inauguration Mass, Zen reiterated the same message, that he would hold to the principle of the separation of Church and State but that he would continue to be a voice for the underprivileged as guided by Catholic social teaching.[56]

The most recent events concerning the proposed implementation of Article 23 of the Basic Law has put Bishop Zen's comments to test. Article 23 requires Hong Kong to legislate to prohibit acts of secession, subversion, treason, theft of state secrets, sedition and links between local and foreign political organizations.[57] The proposed anti-subversion laws in the consultation paper aroused strong opposition from legal professionals, academics, pro-democratic groups and Christians who deemed that the expression of civic freedom would be greatly curbed, and the rule of law would be shaken. The Chairman of the Bar Association, Alan Leong Kah-kit, held the opinion that the proposals were alarming and too vague, and that a draft bill should be published to clear up doubts. Bishop Zen shared the views of the democrats and legal professionals, and openly expressed his worries on the issue. He stood with the opposition was attacked by pro-government legislators.[58] The issue, which split society, was not yet resolved at the time of the publication of this book. Bishop Zen is definitely a dissenting voice and he looks set to be as outspoken on socio-political issues as before.

Discussion: Where Is the Hong Kong Catholic Church Going?

Before the handover, the Hong Kong Catholic Church knew very well that due to ideological incompatibility, it was virtually impossible to establish a warm relationship with the Mainland and future SAR government. It therefore watched closely how and when Beijing would replace the 'contractor relationship' with 'political absorption of religion'.[59]

The first hint was 'the Mother Tongue Teaching Policy' in 1998 that heralded a series of SAR government education reforms. The Catholic Bishop's delegate for education supported this weak policy in the hope of gaining government appreciation, but the government never acknowledged it. Bishop Joseph Zen actually believed that the government was gradually distancing itself from the Catholic Church in terms of social policy and education.[60] Though a major provider of social services, the Catholic Caritas did not have a representative on the Elderly Service Committee headed by Tam Yiu-chung, the pro-China Executive Councilor tasked with formulating policies for the elderly. On the other hand, the Catholic Church also interpreted the administrative reforms in education as unfavourable towards the Church. The Hong Kong Catholic Church, by adding outsiders — non-church related people who may not be Catholics — to the Catholic School Board of Directors, might find it difficult to implement Catholic education principle in its schools.

During the colonial period, the Catholic Church avoided embarrassing the government lest it jeopardize the 'contractor relationship'. The Second Vatican Council (1963–66) promoted Christian social teachings, emphasizing social justice in early 1970s, but Hong Kong Catholic political participation did not take place until the 1980s when all of Hong Kong society had been politicized. Catholics had supported the British Hong Kong government in promoting democracy during the last stages of its rule.

The prophetic role of the Catholic Church had to give way to the 'contractor relationship' for the sake of traditional evangelization in schools and social services. These services had been receiving 80 per cent of their funding from the government. A by-product of the SAR's education and social service reforms would be the weakening of the Catholic presence in education and social services.

After the handover, the Catholic Church realized the new government was less tolerant of Christian activities and expected to lose the societal and economic favours it had enjoyed under colonial rule. Thus it was decided there was nothing to lose if it had to embarrass the government. This explains why after two years of readjusting itself to the new SAR government, the Catholic Church, under the leadership of its coadjutor bishop Joseph Zen, adopted a 'prophetic' or 'dissident' role, voicing strong opinions on socio-political issues such as right-of-abode, schooling for children of abode seekers, as well as the

Article 23 of the Basic Law issue, and passive compliance in the Legislative Council Elections, while firmly continuing the 'bridging' work with Mainland churches.

Religious ideas often provide the means of expressing socio-political protest against secular regimes. Religious movements may come to be regarded as the vanguard in the struggle for cult autonomy, even political freedom (Turner 1991, xxi). The dissident voice of the Catholic Church won support from a silent public and the 'bridging' sandwiched Hong Kong between the Vatican and Beijing (B. Leung 1997). The Hong Kong public lauded Bishop Zen for his firm stance on the right-of-abode and the Article 23 of the Basic Law issues. Hong Kong liberal intellectuals regarded him as the conscience of the society, and invited him to give public talks at the University of Hong Kong and the Hong Kong Democratic Foundation, where he could share with the public his struggle for the weak in the name of justice and love.[61] However, many diocesan priests did not share his conviction on implementing Christian teaching at the grassroots. Though Zen spoke of love and compassion according to the teaching of the Gospel, there were a few who openly disagreed with him.[62]

A recent survey illustrates the priorities of Hong Kong Catholics by asking what type of pastoral work was most important. The top ten responses were: 1) pastoral care in family life, 2) study of the Bible, 3) more understanding of Sunday Mass, 4) caring for the weak, 5) application of electronic media, 6) developing the relationship with the Church in China, 7) strengthening the continuous education of clergy and pastoral workers, 8) working on non-practicing Catholics, 9) pastoral work by laity, and 10) cultivating the attitude of faith in adversity.[63] Apart from the fourth and the sixth, this list is inward looking, and the socio-political concern and promotion of Christian social teaching were not on the list at all. Thus it seems Bishop Joseph Zen must nurture the Church's role of servant and prophet among Catholic laity. The Church must be outward looking or it will be pushed to the margins of society.

Concluding Remarks

The sudden surge in political participation by Hong Kong Catholics is seen by some as a reaction to 'the right-of-abode' and the Article 23 of the Basic Law issues. Bishop Joseph Zen persuaded the Cardinal to make candid statements on relations with the SAR government. Indeed, the second right-of-abode wave in December 2001, and the schooling problems of the children who awaited their fate, led to open confrontation with Regina Yip, Secretary for Security. This exacerbated relations between the Catholic Church and SAR government.

In the new division of labour plan in the Catholic bishop's office, Bishop Zen led the controversial Justice and Peace Commission, and invited the progressive priest, Fr. Louis Ha to resume general editorship of the two Catholic weekly papers (both the English and Chinese versions).[64] Fr. Louis Ha's dismissal from that post ten years earlier was due to his deep involvement in support of the pro-democratic June Fourth Movement in 1989 in China. His return to office with the persistence of Zen; this is more evidence that Zen will lead the Hong Kong Catholic Church in a different direction in the coming years. It is clear that he will not heed Beijing's request to end the 'bridging'. It is also plain that the education reforms in Hong Kong mean an end to the 'contractor relationship'. The outlook for the Catholic Church's social work is not good either. Under Bishop Zen's leadership, the Catholic Church will most certainly be in conflict with the SAR government and Beijing.

Before the handover, the Hong Kong Catholic Church was eager to try to maintain the traditional relationship with the SAR government, and continue its services as usual. When it became apparent that this relationship had ended, it no longer attempted to avoid openly confronting the SAR government.

The Church's response to the mother tongue teaching policy in 1998 served as the touchstone for Catholic-government relations. It was hoped that by offering support, favour with the government could be regained. However, the lack of a positive response on the part of the government was very disappointing, and in the years following the handover, issues such as the right-of-abode (June 1999), reactivation of the parish Catholic social concern groups (July 1999), schooling of abode seekers' children (November 2001) and the Catholic Diocese decision to practice passive compliance in the Legco elections (July 1999), put the Hong Kong Catholic Diocese at odds with the SAR Government. The Bishop's discussion on the Church in China at the special Asian Synod (April-May 1998), and Zen's open letter on the Canonization of Chinese Saints (October 2000), showed that Hong Kong Catholics would defy Beijing by continuing the 'bridging' efforts. This was like rubbing salt in the wounded Catholic-SAR government relations. Zen's joining with the dissent to oppose the implementation of Article 23 of the Basic Law put the Catholic Church on the opposing camp to the Hong Kong SAR government.

CHAPTER SEVEN

The Hong Kong SAR Government and Protestant Churches

In the mid-1990s, Hong Kong was in the final stages of transition from a British colony to an integrated part of China. Faced with the political reality that the Chinese Government would rule Hong Kong after 1997, a group of church leaders attempted to find a third form of Church-State relations; a middle line between being a state 'contractor' or a critical 'prophet'. From 1996 to 1998, three controversial issues affected the churches, namely, the establishment of the Selection of Committee (see chapter 4), the National Day celebration service and the Election Committee. In this chapter, we shall examine the controversies surrounding the issue, and the political attitude of church leaders and comment on the prospects of the emergence of a third form of Church-State relations.

The National Day Celebration Service

In November 1995, some Protestant church leaders (sponsors) discussed the idea of hosting a National Day service in 1996.[1] The sponsors argued that it was necessary to organize an alternative Christian National Day celebration before the handover so that they could more easily refuse to take part in the official, government-organized celebrations after 1997 (R. Fung 1996c).

Secondly, the church leaders hoped to inject a Christian element into the National Day celebrations.[2] They planned to invite officials of *Xinhua* to attend the proposed service as guests. They hoped that the service would neutralize the political backdrop of the official National Day celebration (R. Fung 1996b). By March 1996, the sponsors behind the proposed service had increased to 47. The sponsors planned to hold two open forums in an attempt to persuade members of the clergy and lay Christians to take part in the service. On 8 May 1996, *Ming Pao* printed a story on the proposed service under a front-page headline, 'Lo Lung-kwong calls for National Day and reunification celebration and refuses to evade the issue'.[3] The story immediately drew wide public attention.

On 24 May 1996, the sponsors hosted the first 'Road to Reunification' forum. More than 250 Protestant clergy and church personnel attended. Lo Lung-kwong, one of the core members, issued a challenge: should the Church accept growing restraints on Christian activities or should it fight to maintain its independent status? 'I want to celebrate the National Day, too,' he declared. 'If they [the Chinese government] have their interpretation [about how to celebrate the event], do we not have ours? Can we not have our own way of celebrating?'[4] Carver Yu Tat-sum, another speaker at the forum, said that political leaders and regimes would come and go, but that expressing solidarity with the nation and celebrating China's history together with 1.2 billion Chinese compatriots was perfectly correct. The sponsors conducted a poll during the forum to collect views from the clergy and church workers. They openly stated that the proposed service and other related activities would not be held if the polls from the two forums showed that the clergy and lay Christians did not support the idea. Clergy and church workers attending the forum held different views and a consensus of opinion was not found. The poll conducted during the forum indicated that most of those present believed that it was a good idea to have a 'National Day celebration initiated by the Christian community', but that they did not think the year 1996 was 'good timing'.[5]

After the forum, *Christian Times Weekly* became a forum for debate between supporters and opponents of the proposed service, with the latter outnumbering the former. Supporters claimed that the proposed service would serve as an 'alternative National Day celebration', in which Christians could acknowledge their Chinese national identity and at the same time express their expectations of the nation courageously (Ying 1996). Opponents, however, doubted whether the expression of any alternative Christian viewpoint was possible given the predominantly official, and essentially Communist, nature of the National Day celebration. Articles in opposition to the proposed service published during this period focused mainly on five points: whether it was necessary for the churches to hold such a service in 1996 (Ho 1996; C.-w. Wu 1996); whether the rationale of the proposed service was realistic (C.-w. Wu 1996); that the sponsors were not truly patriotic and that patriotism cannot replace reason (C.-w. Wu 1996); and, that the negative effects of the proposed service would be far greater than the positive effects (Yuen 1996).

A report in *Ming Pao* aroused even wider media attention, and the proposed service became a subject for columnists in other newspapers and magazines. For example, Yu Kam-yin of the *Hong Kong Economic Journal* questioned the motive of the sponsors and held that it was inappropriate to use the name of 'Protestantism' to provide justification for the activities of small number of church leaders (K. Yu 1996). Mau Chi-wang of *Singtao Daily* held that the event showed how the Chinese government was influencing the Church (Mau 1996). When a reporter asked one of the sponsors, Carver Yu, whether the service was being contemplated in response to a request by the *Xinhua,* Yu responded, 'As Chinese, it is only sensible for us to show solidarity with our compatriots and express approval of the reunification. If Hong Kong were reuniting with Taiwan, I would also celebrate the Double Ten [10 October].'[6] Yu's remark invited instant, ruthless criticism from a commentator in the *Hong Kong Economic Journal,* who labeled him an opportunist and criticized him for bowing to the Chinese government:

> Any Chinese in mainland China, Taiwan or Hong Kong, regardless of his or her political position, would agree that 1 October is the National Day for Communist China. It is simply hypocritical to ignore history and put aside our emotions and celebrate a China that exists in abstract, and to insist that celebrating 1 October does not suggest approval of the current regime. If we want to express solidarity with our compatriots, why should we have waited until today? Does it mean that the Church in the past was claiming solidarity with colonialism? These are just lies! To put it simply, the saints of the Church bear the same cross as the rest of mortal mankind; they both must compromise with certain political systems in order to survive (Fan 1996).

In June 1996, seven Christian social groups launched campaigns in opposition to the proposed service.[7] On 14 June they hosted a forum entitled: 'Road to Reunification: the Decision of the Church', and invited lay Christians to participate in the discussion. More than 100 people attended the forum, including reporters from the local and international media. Most of the participants disapproved of the proposed service. Sponsors Raymond Fung and Gideon Yung also attended the forum to defend their cause. Fung explained that the sponsors' intention was precisely to avoid holding official, government-style celebrations. Yung pointed out that over the previous 40 years there had been events in China also worth 'celebrating' such as the emergence of personalities like Wei Jingsheng, Wang Xizhe and Wang Dan, and the 5 April movement and 1989 Tiananmen Square protests; events which he referred to as embodying the 'national quintessence' of China. According to Yung, national celebrations could encapsulate mourning and lament as well as praise. He suggested that the criticism directed against the sponsors was based on 'superficial and one-sided sentimental impressions'.[8]

Raymond Fung, 1988. Courtesy of the Hong Kong Christian Council.

Reverend Chu Yiu-ming, a well-known pro-democracy Protestant clergyman, publicly spoke out against the proposed service. He said that the proposed service had divided the Christian community. The silent majority, as distinguished from the supporters, he argued, would be accused of not celebrating the National Day, while the opponents, including himself, would be obliged to become 'die-hard' antagonists.[9] The opposition campaign upset the mobilization plans of the sponsors, and extensive reporting in the media of Chu's sharp opposition also made Protestants in general, further question the idea of an alternative Christian service.[10]

In July 1996 a number of lay church members took the unusual step of voicing criticism of the sponsors for their lack of rational discussion. Carver Yu's patriotic sentiments were criticized in an article written by a group calling themselves 'Grassroots Christians':

Chinese people born and raised in Hong Kong, like Carver Yu, might feel exhilarated about the reunification, which enables them to reaffirm their national identity as Chinese. From a Hong Kong perspective, however, grave concerns are felt about this 'exhilaration'. Such concern is fully justified ... How can anyone share the generalized, abstract patriotic sentiments of Carver Yu when they are confronted with facts and realities that trouble them? (Grassroots Christians 1996)

One comment was specifically directed at Gideon Yung's criticism of lay members:

Some leaders said that national celebrations held by the Church might be in the form of mourning, lamentation and confession, and that Christians should choose their own way of celebrating. But how would we be able to raise a toasting cup if we were lamenting? We simply cannot understand what kind of 'celebration' it would be. (Grassroots Christians 1996)

On 30 June 1996, the sponsors held a second 'Road to Reunification' forum for lay Protestants. More than 400 people attended the forum. Leaders of various Protestant churches shared their views with the participants and a poll was conducted. During the meeting the sponsors announced that the name of the proposed service would be changed from National Day Celebration Service to the National Day Service, a decision made after considering the views of lay members. It was also decided that *Xinhua* officials would not be invited and that a responsive prayer of penitence would replace the Rogation.[11] However, the sponsors reneged on their promise that they would consider the findings of the two polls when deciding whether the service would be held. Instead, they said they would consider only written opinions made during the meeting when deciding whether the renamed service would be held in 1996.[12] There was no consensus of opinion at the meeting. Some participants pointed out that the sponsors had been insisting on holding celebrations despite reservations expressed by a substantial number of lay Christians, undermining the lay communities' right to a veto.[13] Others expressed disappointment over the sponsors' use of the forum simply as an opportunity to clarify their position.[14] The poll conducted during the meeting showed that most lay Christians shared the view of the clergy. Most of them supported 'National Day celebrations initiated by Christians', but doubted whether 1996 was the right time.[15]

Debate continued in *Christian Times Weekly* after the 'Road to Reunification' forum for lay Christians. Some lay Christians accepted the views of the sponsors and threw their support behind the renamed service (Shen 1996; W.-f. Leung 1996). One of the Christian social groups, Christians for Hong Kong Society, changed its position and became more open to the hosting of the renamed service.[16] Nonetheless, some Christians continued to oppose holding a National Day Service (Chu 1996; Lo 1996). A Christian challenged the theology of the sponsors and cast doubt on the idea of national identity:

> Clergy and pastors have been citing the priests and prophets of the Old Testament for their patriotism and recalling how the priests offered atonement for sins on behalf of the nation. But the context of Israel in the Old Testament was different from ours in two ways. Israel in the Old Testament practiced theocracy, whereby political authority and religious authority were but two sides of the same coin. The love for God and the love for one's nation were inseparable. Secondly, the priestly office is valid only in a country that worships God. It would be irrelevant in an atheistic nation. ... Tibet was conquered and annexed by China several hundred years ago. If Hong Kong Christian should learn from the patriotism of the people of Israel, then Tibetan Christians should also demand the independence of Tibet. They should call for the building of their own country, as did the prophets of Israel (Y.-l. Chan 1996).

Other critics provided further comments on the possible undesirable outcome of the National Day celebration:

> Electing to express alternative views on 1 October, a highly symbolic date, is time-sensitive. But precisely because of the date's symbolic nature, largely in association with the Chinese communist regime, the deliberate choice of this date for celebration would require a clear political position, otherwise any celebration would be perceived as singing the praise of the current regime. Celebration held without a stated objective might be interpreted as an act glorifying the ruling regime (K.-w. Chan 1996).

The renamed service was finally held on 1 October 1996 but only 120 people attended.[17] On 1 October 1997, the sponsors held a second National Day Service, but fewer than 30 people attended.[18]

The following observations can be made about the National Day service.

While liberal church leaders and lay Christians continued to play the role of prophet, a group of church leaders made another attempt to develop a third form of Church-State relations. Firstly, the church leaders concerned sought a means to secure survival after 1997 by affirming the sovereignty of the Communist regime. The National Day Service had a double function, to accept the power of the State and at the same time clearly mark the boundaries of the Protestant churches. From this point of view, the proposed or renamed service per se, was an attempt to find a balance between religious principle and political reality. Secondly, the church leaders concerned tried to organize the clergy and lay Protestant Christians as a whole to take part in the service. In doing so it is possible to say that they intended to mobilize the Protestant churches to support the third form of Church-State relations. Finally, the church leaders concerned expressed strong national sentiment and identity — at least they did so in public and in front of the media. However, debate surrounding the service seemed to reveal that most of the clergy and lay Christians, particularly the members of Christian social groups who were largely younger people, did not share the same sense of national sentiment or identity. In sum, judging from the number of participants at the services, the idea was not well supported by the Protestant community and the efforts of certain church leaders to mobilize the churches were not successful. Despite this, these church leaders became more decisive in advocating the third form of Church-State relations after the incident. In 1998, the church leaders attempted to mobilize the Protestant churches to become involved in the Election Committee, and controversy was once again sparked in the Protestant community.

Representation on the Election Committee

In May 1998, the first HKSAR Legislative Council (Legco) elections were held. Up for election were 60 Legco seats, of which 20 were to be directly elected by the people of Hong Kong, 30 were to be elected by the members of various functional constituencies, and 10 were to be chosen by the Election Committee (EC). In the 800-member EC, 40 seats were reserved for representatives of the religious sector. The religious sector included six religions in Hong Kong: Catholicism, Protestantism, Buddhism, Taoism, Confucianism and Islam. The government allowed the HKCC to nominate its own representatives. A lottery system was used to divide up the 40 places among the six religions and the Protestant community was allocated 7 representatives. Sixty seats on the EC were reserved for representatives of the Hong Kong members of the National

Committee of the Chinese People's Political and Consultative Conference, 77 seats were reserved for the Hong Kong deputies to the National People's Congress and members of the Provisional Legislature.

The HKCC organized two meetings, on 10 December 1997 and then 12 January 1998, and invited Protestant leaders, representatives from church organizations and social groups to discuss how to nominate the Protestant representatives for the EC. Attendance was poor, with only 20 to 30 people attending the two meetings. At the first meeting, Simon Sit, chairman of HKCC, expressed support for the EC, but various social group leaders opposed the idea. The opponents of church participation in the EC argued that the undemocratic body was a 'rubber stamp' controlled by the government and at the same time deprived Hong Kong people of the right to elect their own leaders. They added that Christians should publicly voice their opposition and debunk the hypocritical nature of the HKSAR government.[19] Reverend Kwok Nai-wang wrote an article criticizing the EC in *Ming Pao*. He called for a boycott of the undemocratic election (N.-w. Kwok 1997). On the same day as the second meeting in January, various Christian social groups published an article in *Ming Pao* expressing their opposition to the Church becoming involved in the EC. In the article, three objections were raised: firstly, that the EC was undemocratic and that as a result Christian organizations should not take part in it; secondly, that by nominating Christian individuals to sit on the committee the churches would sacrifice their integrity and offer support to the lies of the HKSAR government; thirdly, that the HKCC did not have the right to make decisions for Christians in Hong Kong in regards to the EC and 'demanded that the Council organize an open forum to discuss whether the Protestant churches should participate and not to make the assumption that Christians in Hong Kong have agreed. What they need to do is consider the technical problems involved in nominating representatives'.[20]

In the face of widespread opposition, the executive committee of the HKCC decided to elect seven Protestant representatives by means of a general election in the Protestant community. The election was set for 13 January 1998. It was also decided that another election would be held so as to allow Protestants to choose the 10 best members of the EC to enter Legco. The Protestant representatives in the EC were expected to consider the results of this second election when casting their votes for the Legco seats. With the support of the HKCC, the 'Working Committee for the General Election of Hong Kong Protestants' was set up with Reverend Lo Lung-kwong as chairman. On 21 January, Lo sent a letter to all the Protestant denominations, independent churches, church organizations and theological seminaries inviting them to take part in the Protestant general election. The letter said that the Christian general election would 'express the principle of equity in election and deepen the consciousness of democracy among Hong Kong Protestants …'[21] Attached to the letter was a statement explaining the position of the HKCC on the EC. There were five main points in the statement:

1. We have grave reservations over the institution and composition of the Election Committee as promulgated by the SAR government. That an 800-member body is given power to return 10 legislators is clear indication of the 'inner circle' nature of the 1998 election, far short of the spirit of popular democracy. Nevertheless, we are willing to give the benefit of the doubt to the SAR government that it does desire to pursue a step-by-step democratization process in accordance with the Basic Law. We are willing, as it is, to cooperate with the authorities in ways that will quicken the pace of democratization. Therefore we are prepared to play the role of a bridge in generating, for the 7 seats allocated to us, the most widely representative electors for the Christian (Protestant) sub-sector, to ensure the presence of a Protestant voice in the Election Committee.

2. While the HKCC membership covers 21 main-line denominations and organizations, representing some 100,000 believers, and embraces over 50 different nationalities, we make no claim to exclusive representation of Hong Kong's entire Protestant community. But we are willing to be a channel to develop sound and feasible ways to help with the emergence of Christians with a sense of civic commitment to Hong Kong and the electoral process.

3. As a church organization, the HKCC will in no case engage in direct participation in political power structures. Our responsibility lies in encouraging and assisting Christian individuals to participate in the process of the Election Committee.

4. We disagree strongly with the view that with 40 of the 800 seats allocated to the Religious Sector, or 5 per cent of the Election Committee, non-religious people are being 'unfairly treated' or 'discriminated against'. We wish to affirm the value of the voice of the religious community in the Election Committee.

5. The HKCC deeply believes that the active participation of

> Christians in the exercising of their civic responsibility can
> only help to enhance a high degree of autonomy for Hong
> Kong, leading to a Special Administrative Region that is more
> free, more democratic, more prosperous and stable and more
> of a blessing to nation and people.

The statement on the EC released by the HKCC immediately triggered intense debate in the Protestant community. The church leaders who supported the position held that the Christian general election would only nominate Protestant representatives to take part in the EC, not the Legislative Council, so the Christian general election did not jeopardize the principle of Church-State separation.[22]

Cheng Yuk-tin, Executive Secretary of the Hong Kong Christian Institute, wrote an article in *Christian Times Weekly* pointing out two major flaws in the statement presented by the HKCC. One was that it was willing to cooperate with the authorities because it would quicken the pace of democratization. Cheng responded by saying that the Christian general election would not help to realize the goal of democratization. The other was that the Christian general election 'treated unfairly' or 'discriminated against' non-religious people, and that such an election model had neglected the principle of political equity. Cheng stated that the statement did not provide convincing explanation although it denied the criticism (Cheng 1998). The Christians for Hong Kong Society also expressed opposition to the Council's arguments in a statement published in *Christian Times Weekly*. The society said that the Christian general election would only legitimize the unfair and unjust Election Committee (Christian for Hong Kong Society 1998). Christian theologians soon joined the debate. Chan Sze-chi, Assistant Professor of Religion and Philosophy at Hong Kong Baptist University, pointed out that the principle of Church-State separation held by Christian tradition was that the Church did not take part in the establishment of or participate in the formation and operation of political or state organizations in any form. At the same time, the Church had to monitor and criticize the State in accordance with Christian faith and conscience. He strongly criticized the church leaders who supported the Christian general election:

> To say that this election does not violate Church-State separation
> not only breaks the line between black and white and [would be
> like] pointing to a horse and saying that it is a deer, but it is also a
> betrayal of the spirit of Church-State separation in the Christian
> tradition (S.-c. Chan 1998).

The church leaders who supported the Christian general election defended their position, and the debate spilled over into the wider media, especially in *Ming Pao*.[23] In the course of the debate, an opponent called for the introduction of the form of Church-State relations put forth by the Hong Kong Christian Sentinels in 1987 (see chapter 5), and accused the HKCC of being 'ambiguous' (C.-w. Wu 1998a, 1998b).

The church leaders further elaborated their argument for a Protestant general election in the media-based debate. For example, Raymond Fung suggested that the election was 'only to expand the democratic element in the election in the existing limited situation' (R. Fung 1998). In the article, Fung argued in favour of exploring the third form of Church-State relations proposed by some church leaders:

> My goal is to find and explore a middle line between the paths represented by Peter Kwong and Kwok Nai-wang. They have similarly chosen to walk independently and neglected the churches in Hong Kong. I do not believe that theirs are the paths that Hong Kong Christians should choose after 1997 (R. Fung 1998).

In the face of claims by the opposition that a Protestant general election would 'grant political legitimization to the unfair Election Committee' (S.-h. Chan 1998b, 1998c), Lo Lung-kwong elaborated upon the idea of a third form of Church-State relations:

> In the democratization process of Hong Kong's political system, my view is that it is important to take part in the unfair election and to protest against it. By doing so we can expand upon the democratic element in the election ... As an institutional arrangement, all elections in the past violated the principle of fairness, but we believe that through criticism and participation we have helped make Hong Kong more democratic. This is the way to 'enlarge' the democratic element and ... finally help make the electoral system fairer (L.-k. Lo 1998).

The Protestant general election took place despite continuing heated debate in the community. On 15 March 1998, nearly 9,000 Christians cast their votes to elect 7 Protestant representatives from among 20 candidates.[24] On 17 May, approximately 3,000 Christians took part in the 'shadow election' and cast their votes to elect the 10 best candidates for Legco from 25 members from the EC.[25] The Protestant representatives were expected to cast their votes according to the results of the 'shadow election'. Interestingly, *Ming Pao* took a critical tone when reporting on the Christian general election, and described the activity as an 'a small election of a very select circle'.[26] The debate surrounding the EC ceased following the end of the first Legislative Council election on May 24.

Emergent Phenomena of Church Involvement in Social Issues After 1997

Leading up to 1997 handover discussions about the new role of the Church in the Hong Kong SAR were common in the Protestant churches. Shun-hing Chan, an Assistant Professor of Religion and Philosophy at Hong Kong Baptist University, and one of the authors of this volume, suggested that the churches might use the theory of civil society to develop a new role and possible way of contributing in new HKSAR social context. In a series of articles entitled 'SAR Classroom' in the *Christian Times Weekly*, he analysed in detail the issues behind and social significance of the 'National Day Celebration Service' and suggested that the Church could assume the role of 'arbiter'. He held that the best outcome of the 'National Day Celebration Service' controversy would have been if the sponsors and their opponents had been able to carry out discussions on collective political-religious action on a basis of equality. He argued that they should have been able to provide good arguments and eventually reach a consensus after rational-critical discourse, and that if during this process a common identity had gradually emerged, some kind of agreed collective action could have been implemented. The rational-critical discourse and collective action of the Protestant community would then have become an example for other social groups to follow, encouraging them to join hands in promoting a civil society in Hong Kong (S.-h. Chan 1997a). He lamented that the Protestant churches had lost a valuable opportunity to help build such a society in Hong Kong.

Regarding the new HKSAR social context, Chan stated that Hong Kong people feared that the excellent elements of Hong Kong society would gradually disappear after 1997. For example, people feared that the problem of corruption would re-emerge, the values of a pluralistic society and the spirit of tolerance would fade, public influence in society and politics would shrink and that the term 'social justice' would become meaningless. In the HKSAR, he deemed that the Protestant churches could play the role of 'arbiter'. In other words, Chan argued, the churches could take a stance on issues outside the political establishment and that this would help safeguard the excellent elements of Hong Kong society and culture.

Chan went further to point out that there would have been practical significance to the Protestant churches' role as arbiter. Firstly, the duty of an arbiter is to make just and moral judgments and such judgments could mobilize public opinion, values and social forces to support the side that promotes social justice. In this way the churches would have contributed to the safeguarding of the excellent elements of Hong Kong society and culture. He argued that in Hong Kong the churches had the legitimacy to provide such judgments. Secondly, in the role of arbiter the churches would be able to transcend the two political poles of pro-China and anti-China and maintain their independence, according to Chan. If controversies emerged, the churches could support one side and criticize the other by making a moral judgment in the public arena. Therefore, depending on the issue, the churches could support or criticize the government or any political party, interest group or social organization and through its arguments on the issue make some impact on Hong Kong society (S.-h. Chan 1997b). Chan's argument shows that the Protestant churches could make some effort to explore what possible roles they could play in the new HKSAR political environment.

A number of new phenomena emerged in the Protestant churches around and after 1997. Such phenomena might affect Church-State relations in the future and deserve further investigation and discussion. They are, firstly, the implications of Anglican Archbishop Peter Kwong's change of attitude towards the HKSAR government. And secondly, the rise of the social activist movement in the evangelical churches, in particular the Society for Truth and Light and the Christian and Missionary Alliance, which began to take part in debates on a variety of social issues.

In the 1980s and 1990s, Bishop Kwong was more conservative politically and always sided with the government on matters of Church and State. After 1997, Bishop Kwong surprisingly changed his political stance and began to criticize the social policies of the HKSAR government. His Christmas and New Year Messages contained points criticizing the government. For example, in his 1999 Christmas message, Bishop Kwong lamented that Hong Kong's social system was becoming inhuman and that it was threatening humanity because it was turning people into slaves of economic progress. He said, 'The new trend in society is that more and more workers have to work overtime, some even need to work until midnight. What kind of phenomenon is this? ... In this era there are many forces that are destroying humanity, ... [they] live as robots or animals and we cannot pretend to not know about this, ... we have to reflect on the question whether our lives are truly human or whether we just live as slaves.'[27] In Bishop Kwong's 2001 Christmas message, he criticized the

HKSAR government for being more concerned about the economy than people in economic distress and called on the government to take into account both the economy and the livelihood of Hong Kong people. He stressed that 'the government should not only care about economic development and neglect the needs and livelihood of Hong Kong people ... We should not help only the economy and forget the people. We have to help the people first ... Priority should be given to the people and to solve their problems.'[28] The messages were praised by local social activists. For instance, Ho Hei-wah, Director of the Society for Community Organization, commented that Bishop Kwong's messages were important and could help stop the government from going astray. He said that he hoped the government would make an effort to improve the livelihood of the people. Lee Cheuk-yan, General Secretary of the Hong Kong Confederation of Trade Unions, praised Bishop Kwong's message and said that they reflected social realities. He suggested that the government should review Hong Kong's social security system.

In the right of abode controversy in 1999, Bishop Kwong took the same stance as Cardinal John Baptist Wu Cheng-chung of the Catholic Church. He criticized the HKSAR government's decision to invite the National People's Congress (NPC) in Beijing to re-interpret the Basic Law. On 29 January 1999, the Hong Kong Court of Final Appeal ruled that the children of Hong Kong citizens born in mainland China were legally allowed to reside in Hong Kong. In February, the secretary for justice, Elsie Leung Oi-sie, asked the NPC Standing Committee to re-interpret Article 22 and 24 of the Basic Law in an attempt to restrict the Mainland-born children of Hong Kong citizens from immigrating to the territory. On 28 April, the secretary for security, Regina Ip Lau Suk-yee, claimed that under the Basic Law almost 1.67 million Mainlanders would be allowed to come and live in Hong Kong and so a re-interpretation of the law was necessary. The large number of people claimed by the secretary alarmed the people of Hong Kong and caused many to change their attitude on the right of abode issue. A survey conducted by the Chinese University of Hong Kong revealed that 65.9 per cent supported the government in restricting the children from moving to Hong Kong and only 34.1 per cent supported the decision of the Court of Final Appeal.[29]

Cardinal Wu and Coadjutor Bishop Joseph Zen of the Catholic Church questioned the move of the HKSAR government. Cardinal Wu pointed out that the issue of right of abode fell into the realm of self-governance and that therefore the Hong Kong people should be the ones to interpret the Basic Law. The HKSAR government's decision to seek a reinterpretation from the NPC amounted to 'destroying the legal base of the SAR, shaking the foundation of family of Hong Kong people and will make people doubt the promises of "one country, two systems" and a high degree of autonomy made by the central government.'[30] On 9 June 1999, Bishop Kwong told the media that he completely agreed with Cardinal Wu. He held that since the Court of Final Appeal had already ruled on the issue it was a matter for the Hong Kong people deal with and that the HKSAR government should solve the problem step-by-step using administrative measures. To shift the responsibity to the NPC was unjustified and at the same time stirred up suspicion that the central government was intervening in the affairs of Hong Kong.[31]

In 2001, Bishop Kwong openly criticized the government for failing to consult the public and for causing confusion over educational reform. In January, the Director of Education Fanny Law Fan Chiu-fun sent a letter to the Grant Schools Council, which represented some 22 elite schools, most of which were Anglican primary and secondary schools. In the letter Law stated that Hong Kong society was unhappy with the elite schools and thought they were 'old fashioned' and 'too restricted'. She demanded that the council 'review current practices' so that the schools could improve themselves and satisfy the expectations of society.[32] On 10 February, Bishop Kwong called for an urgent meeting with more than 100 principals and supervisors of Anglican schools to discuss Law's criticisms. After the meeting, he criticized Law for underestimating the contribution of the elite schools and said that it was unfair of her to compare local schools with international schools in Hong Kong because the two school systems were significantly different. He went further to criticize the HKSAR government for being too hasty in its education reform programs, which, he said, failed to address the practical problems schools faced and thus made implementation of the reforms difficult. He called for the representatives of Anglican schools not to be a 'silent lambs' and urged them to voice their opinions to the government if they found the reform programs unfeasible.[33] On 6 May 2001, Bishop Kwong again criticized the HKSAR government's program of reform and said that its educational policy was causing confusion. He said that the educational policy did not take into consideration individual differences in schools. Furthermore, he criticized the Education Department for not considering suggestions put forward by the schools during the consultation period.[34]

The above Christmas messages, his stance on the right of abode issue and his outspokenness on educational reform suggest that Bishop Kwong had switched from his previously conservative unwillingness to criticize the government to becoming one of its most active critics. The reasons behind

Bishop Kwong's change of attitude toward the government after 1997 need further investigation.

Another phenomenon also deserving further attention was the emergence of well-organized social activist movements among the evangelical churches, in particular, the Society for Truth and Light and some denominations, which began to take an active part in debates on social issues.

In the 1970s, some Christian organizations became more socially active while engaging in evangelism. The evangelical churches at that time, however, placed much emphasis on evangelism but were suspicious of any social involvement that might get in the way of their evangelism work. Consequently, this limited the social activism of Protestants in the evangelical churches (W.-l. Kwok 2002). During the 1980s and 1990s, many evangelical churches and organizations took action to oppose pornography and what they considered 'obscene elements' in the media. This consequently brought some evangelical Christians together and led to the formation of the Society for Truth and Light (STL). The STL was established in May 1997 with the objective of bringing about change in the social culture in Hong Kong by means of research, action, education and coordination. They focused their work on the area of cultural norms and attitudes towards sex, the media and social ethics and so a result began to take part in many debates on social issues in Hong Kong.

From 1997 to 2002, the issues that the STL focused on included: Opposing the government's introduction of an anti-discrimination law regarding bias on sexual preference, opposing the culture of gang violence affecting families and youth, opposing the promotion of prostitution, pornography and obscene literature in the media, supporting the establishment of an press council independent of the government, opposing the Jockey Club's promotion of horse betting among young people, opposing the legalization of soccer betting.[35] What is notable is that the Christian and Missionary Alliance and the Baptist Convention of Hong Kong were very outspoken on some issues, in particular on the legalization of soccer betting.[36]

As the evangelical churches became more involved in social issues so too did they become more critical of the government and its social policies. This could be interpreted as a sign an attempt by the Protestant churches to influence the government and its policies and thereby help promote the building of a civil society in Hong Kong. However, the evangelical social movement tended to become engaged specifically in issues related to social ethics. The churches distanced themselves from issues related to democratization and political reform.[37] Whether the evangelical social movement will ever extend their focus from social ethics to political-based issues and begin to support democratic reform will need to be closely watched and studied. If it does happen the evangelical churches could further influence a change in Church-State relations in Hong Kong.

Concluding Remarks: New Church-State Relations in the Hong Kong SAR

In summary, it is possible to make some observations about the controversies surrounding the involvement of the churches in the Selection Committee (SC) (see chapter 4), the National Day Celebration Service and the Election Committee (EC), and how that affected Church-State relations. Some conservative church leaders made public statements and became involved in the SC on the grounds that they were acting as individuals and not on behalf of their church communities. In doing so they directly and indirectly supported the government. For example, Anglican Bishop Peter Kwong was a member of the Hong Kong SAR government Preparatory Committee, which was commissioned by the Chinese Government, and at the same time he competed for a seat on the SC. Moreover, the bishop joined hands with Shi Jiao-guang in a deliberate attempt to influence who would be chosen to sit on the SC. Liberal Protestant church leaders, such as Reverend Kwok Nai-wang, and lay Christians continued to play the role of 'prophet' by monitoring and criticizing the government and at the same time challenged conservative church leaders when they were seen to violate the principle of Church-State separation.

What is worth noticing is how the three controversies led to the emergence of a third form of Church-State relations. This new form of relations had several characteristics. Firstly, these church leaders expressed strong national sentiment and a sense of Chinese identity — at least they did so in public and in front of the media. This was evident during the deliberation over whether to hold a National Day Celebration Service. Secondly, the church leaders affirmed the sovereignty of the Communist regime in Hong Kong after 1997 and were willing to play a limited role, under certain conditions, in the political system. Their action was an attempt to find a balance between political reality and religious ideal. For example, they supported the government by sending Protestant representatives to take part in the SC and EC while emphasizing that their participation was given only under 'certain conditions'. Thirdly, the church leaders tried to organize the clergy and lay Protestant Christians as a whole to support their participation in the SC, the National Day Celebration Service and the EC. By doing so, it is possible to say that they intended to mobilize the Protestant churches to support this new third form of Church-State relations. These church leaders believed that they could take part in politics and at the same time criticize the government. It was argued that participation and criticism could go hand-in-hand and would prove to be a successful means by which the churches could help 'expand' the democratic element under restrictive circumstances.

It is possible to better understand the political attitude of these church leaders and this new form of Church-State relations if their behaviour is seen in the context of what was happening in Hong Kong at the time. Compared to more conservative church leaders such as Bishop Peter Kwong, both of them were willing to cooperate with the government. The difference is, the conservative church leaders took part in the political establishment as individuals, whereas these church leaders sought to mobilize the whole Protestant community to back their involvement in politics. In the process of participation, the conservative church leaders openly supported and defended the government, while these church leaders held that their participation was under certain 'conditions' and that they were still willing to mildly criticize government policy.

Compared to more liberal church leaders such as Reverend Kwok Nai-wang, both of them held that political participation was important. The liberal church leaders, however, insisted that the church should strictly comply with the principle of Church-State separation. These church leaders held that the church could take part in some aspects of politics but only 'indirectly' and under certain 'conditions'. This, they argued, would not violate the principle of Church-State separation. Participation, these church leaders maintained, would allow the church to monitor the government and the political establishment. They held that participation in the political system and criticism of the government could go hand-in-hand.

The above analysis suggests that this third form of Church-State relations as advocated by the church leaders falls between being a state 'contractor' and a critical 'prophet'. Only close observation of future Church-State interaction will reveal whether such a form of Church-State relations will become dominant in the Hong Kong SAR.

The church leaders who advocated the third form of Church-State relations believed that participation and criticism was possible and that it would prove a means by which they could communicate and cooperate with the government and further the process towards full democracy. The problem, however, lies in the inherent tension caused by cooperating with the government and being critical of it at the same time; the results will not always be fruitful. In the controversy surrounding the SC, the National Day Celebration Service and EC, some critics pointed out that the high profile church leaders who supported the above events were not so willing to publicly voice their criticism of government. This imbalance between participation and criticism gave Hong Kong society the impression that the Protestant community had sided with the SAR government. Furthermore, it gave the government and the undemocratic political system a form of legitimacy. The absence of loud criticism from the church leaders meant that their participation in the political system did not inspire political reform.

Secondly, those church leaders who advocated the third form of Church-State relations believed that although the SAR government's election system was 'far short of the spirit of popular democracy', they could 'enlarge' the democratic element and help make the system fairer. To take the EC as an example, 10 Legco seats were to be elected from the EC. In the 800-member EC, 60 seats were reserved for Hong Kong members of the National Committee of the Chinese People's Political and Consultative Conference, 77 seats were reserved for the Hong Kong deputies to the National People's Congress and members of the Provisional Legislature. It was generally considered in Hong Kong society that the EC was an 'inner circle' election controlled by the government. There were only seven seats reserved for Protestant representatives in the EC. Yet, the church leaders believed that these seven representatives could 'expand the democratic element in the election in the existing limited situation' and 'enlarge the democratic element and ... help make the electoral system fairer'. This theory lacked solid foundation. If the EC was set up in such a way as to deliberately limit democracy in the general electoral system, participation in the EC would decrease rather than increase the democratic element. Furthermore, Protestant participation in the EC gave the impression that the churches were prepared to put their names behind and give credibility to the undemocratic body. In other words, the catchy slogan 'criticism in participation' as advocated by the church leaders, in reality came to be interpreted as a sign of the Protestant churches' support for a series of undemocratic political arrangements concocted by the SAR government. Paradoxically, it seems that the church leaders and their followers did not understand the consequences of their actions, or they simply chose not to believe the results of their actions.

CHAPTER EIGHT

Summary and Conclusions

Church-State relations in Hong Kong, compared to those in some Western and socialist countries, are unique in terms of complexity and variety. The territory's colonial history and political structure have significantly helped to shape the form and development of Church-State relations. This study has sought to show how the Catholic and Protestant churches were influenced by the wider socio-political or 'macro' environment and to what extent this environment helped define the relationship between the churches and government. The churches' adoption, although unintentionally, of the role of 'contractor' or 'deputy' to the government after the 1950s, and their outspokenness in the 1980s, strongly illustrate how the socio-political environment affected Church-State relations in Hong Kong. However, differences in the organizational structure between the Catholic and Protestant churches also helped determine how they independently approached Church-State relations and how they each responded to change. The varying approaches adopted by the various Christian churches became apparent during the 1990s as Hong Kong prepared for the 1997 handover to mainland China. Moreover, in the years following Hong Kong's establishment as a Special Administrative Region of China, differences in attitude among the churches towards the new administration and its policies also emerged. Hence, this study started with empirical research within the local context. To simply borrow the 'Church-State separation' model found in the

United States, or the 'state domination of the church' model found in many socialist/Communist countries, and apply it to Hong Kong would be inappropriate and ineffectual.

Over the past fifty years, three types of Church-State relations have predominated in Hong Kong. The first emerged during the 1950s, when the churches accepted the invitation of the Hong Kong government to take part in social development. This resulted in a mutually beneficial partnership, or what is termed here a 'contractual' or 'deputy' relationship. The second emerged during the 1980s in the lead-up to the transition of Hong Kong's sovereignty in 1997. During this period, some progressive church leaders urged the colonial government to introduce political reform and promote democratization before 1997. Increasingly, church leaders and lay members began to participate in Hong Kong's socio-political affairs. These church activists openly criticized the leadership of the churches who, they said, had become part of the political establishment. To use a term borrowed from Christian theology, the progressive church activists assumed the role of the outspoken prophet. The third form of Church-State relations emerged during the 1990s and spanned the handover. During this period the churches sought to find ways to relate to the new HKSAR government and exhibited an increasing tendency towards 'criticism in participation'.

The above types of Church-State relations were largely determined by Hong Kong's unique and ever-changing social environment. The first type of Church-State relations arose during the political turbulence of the 1950s. The Hong Kong government at that time was deeply concerned about protecting its authority and colonial rule in the face of political challenges from pro-nationalist and pro-Communist forces in Hong Kong. It was also confronted by overwhelming social problems caused by the arrival of hundreds of thousands of refugees from the Mainland. As a result of this precarious situation the churches, as social organizations, came to enjoy a privileged position. Moreover, in comparison to the Chinese religious organizations, they had a closer cultural affinity with the colonial regime. Another factor at play behind the privileged status was the churches access to abundant resources and funds from overseas Christian communities. For the government, the churches were social organizations that did not threaten the colonial regime and also had the potential to become important partners in social development. The education and social services provided by the churches helped the government solve many social problems. At the same time, by being allowed to become active in education and social services, the churches were given the chance to both serve the people and preach the gospel, two fundamental missions of the Christian faith.

The Catholic Church

In Britain the strong Christian cultural heritage ensures a close relationship between Church and State — the Anglican Church is considered Britain's 'national church'. Although relations between the British Government and Catholic Church were strained for centuries, today the relationship is far less antagonistic. By contrast, in China, all religions are irreconcilable with the ideology of Marxism-Leninism. It would be anathema, therefore, for the Chinese Communist Party (CCP) to endorse any religious belief. As patriots and nationalists, the CCP leaders from the early days of the establishment of Communist China could not be seen to support Christianity, which was labelled a 'foreign religion'. The Chinese government's relationship with the Catholic Church was further aggravated by the Vatican's claiming the sole right to exercise authority over all Catholic clergy, both in terms of organization and theology. The Vatican's sovereign status in international law was another factor affecting smooth relations between the Catholic Church and Chinese government (B. Leung 1998).

Shortly after the arrival of the British in Hong Kong in 1841, Catholic missionaries were invited to serve the spiritual needs of the British army. As soon as they arrived they began to establish, with financial assistance from the colonial government, Catholic schools and a variety of social services including reformatory work (Ticozzi 1997, 77). The government was quick to realize that the churches could run a number of high quality social services and educational institutes at a lower cost than the government. The efforts and contributions of many devout Catholics in Hong Kong, and funds from overseas Catholic communities, allowed the churches to expand their services, enhance their ability to evangelize and generally strengthen their position to influence colonial Hong Kong society.

This working relationship between the churches and Hong Kong government is defined here as an 'unintended contractual relationship' which evolved without a governmental agenda. However, it cannot be referred to as a 'partnership' because over the whole colonial era, the Catholic Church and the Protestant churches had no say over the formulation of government policy on education and social services. Instead, the churches became effective and efficient contractors used to implement and execute government policies.

After World War II, the contractual relationship between the churches and government expanded greatly. Determined to block Communist infiltration into the colony, the government encouraged the Christian churches to provide services to the thousands of Chinese refugees fleeing the Mainland. They were seen as reliable allies in the government's efforts to block the spread of Communism, and were encouraged to help oust atheistic Communist influence in education. This became very evident following the colonial government's crackdown on the Communist underground network following the 1967 riots. In the 1970s, traditional Chinese associations such as the Po Leung Kuk and Tung Wah Hospital Group were embraced and began to act likewise as government 'contractors'. As time passed, the special privileges granted mainly to the Christian churches gradually began to diminish.

The Catholic Church, however, had to pay a high price to secure its position as a 'government contractor'. Firstly, its long desire to establish its own tertiary education institute was sacrificed. Secondly, on institutional level, it was not able to adopt the more socially active role with respect to justice and peace issues that Vatican II advocated, although individual clerics were involved in pressure groups. It was not until the 1980s that the Church was able to become more outspoken on socio-political issues and this was in part made possible by the growing leniency of the colonial government and increasing social unease as the handover neared. The Catholic Church's willingness to sacrifice its tertiary education ambitions and socio-political involvement indicates the extent to which it valued its contractual relationship with the government, with the purpose to serve the people. In the 1980s, it became more involved in socio-political issues and adopted the role of outspoken prophet largely due to the 'China factor' — the CCP's atheist views and its harsh treatment of the Catholic Church on the Mainland. The Church's increasing socio-political involvement eventually led to the development of a new form of Church-State relations.

During the colonial era there was little contact between the Hong Kong Catholic Church and Beijing officials. This belied a mutual lack of trust and would later complicate the building of Church-State relations between the Catholic Church and the HKSAR government after the handover. Many Hong Kong Catholics' sense of distrust and fear towards the Mainland stemmed from Beijing's long and well recorded harsh treatment of religious believers. General Catholic support for the pro-democracy movement in Hong Kong also reflected anti-Communism leanings. This naturally attracted the attention of CCP leaders in Beijing. Thus the position of the Hong Kong Catholic Church was to further complicate the already tense Sino-Vatican relations (B. Leung 1992b). Moreover, Beijing generally interpreted Hong Kong Catholic assistance to Mainland Catholics as interference in China's internal affairs and at odds with CCP interests.

In the lead-up to the handover, Beijing expressed concern about Christian activities in Hong Kong by allowing the contractual relationship between the government and churches in the field of education and social services to continue in the HKSAR, but asking for the elimination, or at least reduction of certain kinds of Hong Kong Christian 'assistance' to Mainland Christians, and calling for the end of church participation in Hong Kong's socio-political affairs.

Shortly before the handover, on various occasions the Hong Kong Catholic Church's leadership was caught in a dilemma vis-à-vis China's expectations of Christian churches. The leaders of the Catholic Diocese were prepared to make some concessions in an effort to ensure good Church-State relations with the HKSAR government. This included the elimination of Catholic involvement in the pro-democratic movement, and downscaling the promotion of the 1995 Legislative Council Elections as had been done in 1992. However, these same leaders were not prepared to reduce the Church's assistance to Mainland Catholics despite Beijing's warnings.

Soon after the handover, efforts by the new HKSAR government to introduce reforms in the education and social service sectors unsettled the Catholic Church, which interpreted them as a threat to the previously accepted 'contractual' terms. Coadjutor Bishop Joseph Zen Ze-kiun, consecrated in December 1996, was to take the lead in the gradual redrawing of Church-State relations in the days leading up to the handover and the years immediately following it.

The Catholic Church was involved in a series of controversies following the handover: it supported Mainland applicants in the 'Right of Abode' row; the diocese decided to participate passively in the Legislative Council Elections in 2000; the semi-dormant parish social concern movement was reactivated and it strongly supported the canonization of the 120 China Martyrs; and it voiced its concern about religious freedom in the HKSAR apropos the Falun Gong movement. The Church joined political dissent to oppose the implementation of Article 23 of the Basic Law. All of these reflected the church's increasing political activism. As the church began more and more to play the role of prophet by becoming a vocal conscience of society and intensifying its promotion of social justice, Church-State relations began to worsen.

The downgrading of the Christian churches in the government's Precedence List (from fifth to ninth position), the decreasing representation of Catholics in government educational and social reform committees, and the indirect government refusal to allow a papal visit to the HKSAR, reminded the Catholic Church not to be naïve about preserving close Church-State relations. The less than smooth relations actually forced the Church to stop sitting on the fence.

Bishop Joseph Zen, the successor of Cardinal Wu, was forced to make more clear-cut decisions regarding the Catholic position on various socio-political issues and to become more outspoken as a social 'prophet'.

The sharp change in relations between the Catholic Church and government was for the most part the result of major shifts in Hong Kong's socio-political environment due to the change of sovereignty. Within the Catholic Church there are different opinions concerning Church-State relations. The Catholic tradition allows internal discussions and arguments through its own mass media.[1] However, no open disputes were heard due to the teaching authority and culture of obedience within the Church. In 1999, the Catholic leadership decided to organize a synod in an effort to chart a new future path for the Church. Due to the rough socio-political environment and fundamental incompatibility of atheism with religious beliefs, the Church needed to consider policy adjustments.

The Protestant Church

Over a period of 50 years, the Hong Kong Government and Protestant churches were able to build a firm and close relationship. Even today, the contractual relationship between the government and churches continues to benefit both parties. This particular type of Church-State relationship is referred to here as a 'channelled partnership'. The support of the colonial government, however, disappeared when Hong Kong became a Chinese SAR in 1997 and a new form of Church-State relations began to emerge. One challenge came from the increasingly close relationship between the new HKSAR government and Chinese religious organizations.

The second type of Church-State relations emerged during the era of rapid social change in the 1980s. The 'problem of 1997' made many people in Hong Kong long for democratic political reform. It was in this social environment that a group of reformed Protestant church leaders and lay Christian activists became more active in socio-political issues and began urging the colonial government to implement democratic reforms. From the early 1980s to mid-1990s, these church activists openly expressed their concerns to the Chinese government regarding the future of religious freedom in Hong Kong. They also sought to secure the continuation of the churches' involvement in education and social services after the handover and demanded that the colonial Government speed up the pace of democratic reform before 1 July 1997.

The above demands were made in three statements issued by the Protestant churches in 1983: the 'Proposed Statement of Faith for Hong Kong Christians in the Face of Social and Political Change'; the 'Statement on Religious Freedom by the Protestant Churches of Hong Kong'; and 'Opinions of the Hong Kong Protestant Delegation to Beijing on the Future of Hong Kong'. Reverend Kwok Nai-wang of the Hong Kong Christian Council supported the position that in 1988 the Legislative Council choose the members on the basis of fully democratic and direct elections. Another well-known Protestant figure, Reverend Fung Chi-wood, led a movement protesting against the building of the Daya Bay nuclear plant in 1986.

In December 1986, a pro-Beijing 'social critic', Xin Weisi, warned the reformed church leaders that their involvement in political issues was tantamount to recreating a western middle ages-type of Church-State relations. His comments triggered an intense debate that continued for many months and greatly hampered the development of the Protestant socio-political movement. In 1986 and 1987, the conservative church leaders who held the reins of power in the Hong Kong Christian Council attempted to silence the voice of the reformed church leaders. Furthermore, they sought to remove any clergy who supported democratic reform in the Hong Kong Christian Council. In 1987, the Anglican Church demanded that Reverend Fung Chi-wood stop expressing his 'secular' views in public and asked him to travel overseas to study for two years. In 1988, Reverend Kwok Nai-wang left the Hong Kong Christian Council and founded the Hong Kong Christian Institute where he continued his battle for democratic reform with limited resources. This form of Church-State relations is here referred to as one of 'critical opposition'.

In the 1990s, as Hong Kong entered the final stages of the power transition, the opportunities for the churches to become involved in socio-political issues declined, and the struggle for democratic reform became more difficult. It is likely that the churches' new position of 'critical opposition' will prove effective only after substantial political reform in the Mainland. This will in turn affect the political attitude of the Hong Kong SAR government.

The third type of Church-State relations emerged in the mid-1990s. A group of church leaders sought ways to deal with the future Mainland-dominated, pro-Communist HKSAR government. Their efforts to mobilize the collective action of the Protestant community triggered intense debate among the Christian churches. An attempt was made to encourage churchgoers to participate in the debate surrounding the choosing of Selection Committee members, the National Day Celebration Service and Christian participation in the Election Committee. The group of church leaders held similar ideas and a common political position. They shared a strong sense of national consciousness and identity, sought to influence the political structure of Hong Kong in the face of the future rule of a Beijing appointed government, attempted to mobilize the Protestant community to respond to the 'problem of 1997' and an array of social and political problems. They also advocated an attitude towards politics that emphasized both criticism and participation.

These church leaders sought to find a balance between the struggle for reform and a willingness to compromise for the greater good — this position has been described here as one of 'criticism in participation'. This new approach falls somewhere between the churches previous relationship of 'channelled partnership' with the government and their increasing move towards one of 'critical opposition'. Research conducted by the authors suggests that the leaders of the Protestant churches granted legitimacy to the new HKSAR government by encouraging Protestant participation in the Selection Committee and Election Committee. Although these same church leaders argued that by taking part in the two undemocratic bodies they would be able to ensure some fairness and be a voice of criticism, their influence proved to be severely limited and largely ineffectual. The authors also point out that the arguments put forth by the church leaders in favour of participating in the political arrangements behind the setting up of the post-colonial government was untenable. The resulting form of Church-State relations is referred to here as one of 'organized dependence', which describes a kind of political relationship in which the Church is willing to stand behind and mobilize the Protestant community to support the government in order to win a friendly attitude in return. Moreover, it is expected that this relationship of organized dependence is likely to continue in the near future. The HKSAR government, it appears, welcomes the support of the churches and knows well the considerable influence the church leaders exert over the general Protestant community. However, we anticipate that compromise would outweigh the struggle to reform in the future interaction between these church leaders and the Hong Kong SAR government.

Implications to Democratization and the Building of Civil Society in Hong Kong

The three types of Church-State relations that have emerged over the past half-century have seriously impacted the political development of Hong Kong and will continue to do so in the future. In the West, the Christian churches are often seen to be very active in social affairs and at times pressuring governments to implement political reform. In Hong Kong, the churches' position as a government 'contractor' fundamentally determined Church-State relations and the churches' exercise of power. While both Church and State benefited from this contractual relationship, the churches' hands were tied and they were forced to sacrifice their role as critical prophet when dealing with the government. The government secured a faithful, and dependent partner and reduced the risk of the churches challenging its social policies. Indirectly, the government was able to use the churches to exert control over potentially critical segments of society. Further study is needed to determine the extent to which the government was able to channel its policies through the churches and, apart from the churches, to discover what other social organizations were drawn into the government's net. Particular attention should be given to the growing influence of certain Chinese religious organizations and their relationship with the new HKSAR government.

In addition to the 'institutional channelling strategy' employed by the government, Church-State relations can shed light on the development of civil society and the process of democratization in Hong Kong. Contemporary sociologists argue that democratization is a key factor behind the building of civil society. Craig Calhoun has suggested that civil society is a political community organized by citizens that stands outside the State (Calhoun 1993). Civilian members of society hold rational-critical discourse on political issues in the public sphere, and the criteria for such discourse is 'good' argument through which they reach consensus, build identity and become an organized social movement. This process of rational-critical discourse can expand its 'democratic inclusiveness', and recognize and accept members with different identities in a civil society. One question that arises when applying the theory of civil society to the study of Hong Kong Church-State relations is whether the Christian community has a part, or can play one, in the development of a civil society in Hong Kong. This study reveals that the second type of Church-State relations in Hong Kong — referred to here as 'critical opposition', where certain reformed church leaders and lay Christians struggled for social justice and political democratization — reflects an attempt by the churches to help build civil society. The controversy surrounding the churches' involvement in the Selection Committee, National Day Celebration Service and Election Committee exposed serious divisions within the Christian community and saw the emergence of a group of clergy and lay Christians who were prepared to stand up for their political ideals and principles and openly criticize the government. By taking part in debates on socio-political issues the churches have the potential to develop a Christian social movement and as such help build a civil society in Hong Kong.

Theoretical Reflections

From the study of Church-State relations in Hong Kong, it is possible to examine further the contributions and limits of the theory of institutional channelling. As shown in the previous analysis, studying the relationship between State and society is an effective starting point on which to build a theoretical framework of Church-State relations. Moreover, institutional channelling is also a heuristic concept that can help expose the pattern of interaction between the government and churches on an organizational level. John McCarthy and his colleagues point out that the State or government is a rational social actor that uses the mechanisms of taxation, the law and various policies to control and influence social movement organizations (McCarthy, Britt and Wolfson 1991). This study shows that the Hong Kong government was able to manipulate effectively the churches into becoming part of the government establishment. John McCarthy and his colleagues also point out that grassroot social movement organizations can escape the net of institutional channelling because tax laws and government policies affect them less. This study shows that those Christian social groups operating outside the formal church establishment were able to preserve their prophetic character and critical voice because they did not rely on government resources.

The theory of institutional channelling is analysed here and suggestions are made for possible revision. John McCarthy and his colleagues discovered from their research in the United States that state tax laws and policies can function as a net through which the government can exert control over social movement organizations. The research behind this book found that the Hong Kong government used its allocation of funds and resources in the fields of education and social services to exert control over the churches and other civil organizations. The implication is that a government can use a variety of means to exert control over potentially threatening civil organizations.

Secondly, the theory of institutional channelling suggests that the government is an active social actor whereas most social movement organizations are passive agents controlled, or at least influenced, by the former. Those social movement organizations that operate within the net of government influence are largely forced to comply with its policies while those movements outside the net are able to escape the State's controlling mechanisms. It is possible to argue that McCarthy and his colleagues' analysis neglected the fact that social movement organizations can be rational social actors rather than merely passive agents. This study shows that churches can respond to the government's attempts to control them in two ways.

The first can be called 'tacit compliance'. In chapter 5 it is argued that some Protestant church leaders developed a kind of patron-client relationship with the Hong Kong colonial government. When confronted, however, with the reality of a major change in Church-State relations following Hong Kong's handover to the Mainland, the church leaders had to consider new ways to relate to the new pro-Communist, Beijing-appointed HKSAR government. This reveals the churches' ability to become rational social actors — the church leaders assessed change in the external environment and responded by altering the way they interacted with the new government.

The second can be called 'strategic action' — opposing the State's channelling mechanism. McCarthy and his colleagues noted that local grassroot organizations can escape the net of the government. This study found that such organizations were able to do so not simply because of their location but as a matter of choice and conscious decision. For example, the establishment of the Hong Kong Christian Institute, as described in chapter 5, was due to Reverend Kwok Nai-wang's controversial departure from the Hong Kong Christian Council. Under pressure from the Mainland government, the Council attempted to restrict his involvement in socio-political affairs. In 1988 he founded the grassroots Hong Kong Christian Institute and continued his social and political participation outside the established church. This shows that some social movement organizations are not simply passive agents. On the contrary, they are active and rational social actors, like Bishop Joseph Zen of the Catholic Church, who battle against the government in order to secure social and political reform on humanitarian grounds.

Cardinal John Wu's 'Statement on Religious Freedom After 1997' in 1984

Sunday Examiner   **24 August 1984**

The Most Reverend John Baptist Cheng-Chung Wu, Bishop of Hong Kong, on behalf of the Catholics in the local diocese, has sent to the Government of China, through the Hong Kong Branch of the Xinhua News Agency, a statement of the Catholic's position on the future of Hong Kong.

This statement was prepared after half a year of careful reflection and careful discussion of information and ideas. The draft was revised again and again.

In the past two years, the Catholic Diocese of Hong Kong has expressed its position on the future of Hong Kong on various occasions and in various media. This, however, is the first complete statement officially discussed and issued.

In offering this statement, Bishop Wu, the leader of over 270,000 Catholics in Hong Kong, has at heart not only the Catholic community but the whole of Hong Kong. It is hoped that the statement will help all the people of Hong Kong, Catholics and non-Catholics alike, to reflect upon and to strengthen their confidence in and their hopes for the future of Hong Kong.

The full text of the statement follows.

Statement

on

The Catholic Church and the Future of Hong Kong
The Most Reverend John Baptist Cheng-Chung Wu
Catholic Bishop of Hong Kong

1. In 1997 China will resume sovereignty over Hong Kong and make it a special administrative zone. Facing this historical change, I, as Catholic Bishop of Hong Kong, have consulted separately with my Diocesan Board of Consultors, the Council of Priests, Pastoral Council, Executive Committee of the Central Council of Catholic Laity, Chinese Priests' Association, and the Association of Men and Women Religious Superiors. We reflected on and discussed this matter together in the light of faith and in the spirit of the Gospel, and now I make the following statement and express our sincere desire to continue to work with and for the people in freedom and in harmony.

2. As Chinese, we are proud of our heritage — of our long history and our rich culture, which we treasure. Its high moral values and noble ideas have been repeatedly admired and praised by the Catholic Church which respects and embraces all the positive elements present in every culture.

3. As people of Hong Kong we want to work, in solidarity with all fellow members of the community, for the good of Hong Kong and for the well being of society. Our special concern and love go out to the weak, the poor, the sick, the elderly and the lonely, and those in any way deprived or disabled. We are particularly committed to improving the quality of life — a quality of life which promotes the total development of the human person — body, mind, and spirit. In short, we will continue to strive to make Hong Kong a better and more humane place in which to live.

4. As Catholics we worship God and love our fellow men. We believe in Christ who is the Mediator between God and man, the Redeemer of mankind. He preached and suffered, died and rose again. He founded the Church on Peter to teach all nations and bring good tidings to the world. We are called to continue this mission of preaching Christ and proclaiming the Gospel by loving service to all people.

5. As the Catholic Bishop of Hong Kong, I assert unshakeably the right to religious freedom. This is a basic human right, given by God, and is now enjoyed by all people in Hong Kong. This right is demanded by man's dignity and is inherent in the very nature of man. It is essential that this basic right, and the free exercise of that right, which has been solemnly declared by the United Nations, be clearly enshrined, explicitly expressed and effectively guaranteed in the Sino-British Joint Declaration and in the Basic Laws of Hong Kong. This will help to strengthen the confidence of the people.

6. Religious freedom as we enjoy it in Hong Kong includes the following rights:

   a. The right to have or to adopt a religion or belief of one's choice, and to manifest it in worship, observance, practice and teaching.

   b. The right of the individual to worship in private and public, alone and with fellow believers.

   c. The right to make one's religion known to others, and to instruct those who are interested in this religion by the spoken and written word.

   d. The right of parents to provide religious instruction in bringing up their children.

   e. The right of religious communities and associations and to hold meetings and to promote educational, cultural, charitable and social activities.

   f. The right to appoint personnel, to train them and to send them abroad for specialized studies and at the same time the right to utilize, if and when necessary, the services of personnel from abroad.

   g. The right to erect and/or use building for religious purposes and to acquire such property if necessary.

   h. For the Catholics, in particular, the right to maintain their existing links and their existing unity with the universal Church, through union with the Pope and also with the Bishops and Catholic communities in other parts of the world. This unity is basic to the Catholic Church's belief.

7. The Catholic Church has been established in Hong Kong for over 140 years. Inspired by God's love for the world and for mankind, we have tried to fulfil Christ's Mission of Evangelization and to follow His example — to serve and not to be served. Throughout those years we have been working with and for the people of Hong Kong, doing our utmost to contribute in the fields of education, medical care and social welfare, without discrimination of sex, race, or creed. This is evidenced by the fact that over 95% of those who have availed themselves of the services provided by the Catholic Church are non-Catholics. Now and in the future we will continue to contribute actively to the all-round well being of the community in the same spirit of love and service within the limits of our competence and our resources. We will keep on striving to help in building up Hong Kong into an even more dynamic and even more highly developed and just society of which we shall always be proud to be members. We believe that a genuine and faithful Catholic is also a genuine and good citizen.

+ John Baptist Cheng-Chung Wu
  Catholic Bishop of Hong Kong

The Assumption of the Blessed Virgin Mary,
15th August, 1984

Cardinal Wu's Pastoral Letter
on the 1991 Election

Dear Brothers and Sisters in Christ,

1991 marks a significant milestone for the people of Hong Kong when, for the first time, we will be able to exercise our right to vote in direct elections to the Legislative Council. This is not only our right but also our duty. The Second Vatican Council tells us: 'Let all Christians appreciate their special and personal vocation in the political community. This vocation requires that they give conspicuous example of devotion to the sense of duty and of service to the advancement of the common good' (Church in the Modern World n.75). Pope Paul VI puts it even more explicitly, 'lay people should take up as their own proper task the renewal of the temporal order … so as to infuse a Christian spirit not only into the mentality and customs of the people, but also into the laws and structures of the community in which they live' (Pop. Prog. n.81).

In 1991 we also celebrate the 150th Anniversary of our Diocese. The theme of the celebration — 'hand-in-hand towards the future' — emphasizes that we want to walk in solidarity with all the people of Hong Kong in the years ahead. Let us now put our words into action by taking an active part in the elections, eagerly casting our vote, so that, by just and fair means, Hong Kong's transition may be accomplished in stable and orderly manner, leading to healthy development. This is the duty of all citizens; but as Christians it is an obligation of our faith, a necessary step in our co-operation with God to care for, renew and sanctify the world.

But to take an active part in the elections requires, first of all, that we register as electors. Thus I exhort all Catholics, eligible to vote, to register immediately — the deadline is 20th November, 1990. Parishes should appeal to their parishioners to do their utmost to fulfil this duty, even organizing ways of facilitating the faithful to register in time.

May Mary, Mother of God and our Mother, pray for the success of the elections, for peace and prosperity, democracy and freedom for Hong Kong.

Our Lady of the Rosary 1990

+ John B. Card. Wu

Proposed Statements of Faith for Hong Kong Christians in the Face of Social and Political Change

Introduction

The expected political consequences of Hong Kong's return to Chinese sovereignty in 1997 have brought major trauma to the territory, causing panic among Hong Kong citizens. As the People of God, we feel compelled at this particular time to re-affirm the faith of the church as handed down from of old, to identify our unique role and mission at this historical turning point and to consider the future direction of the church's witness. Following several meetings, where earnest discussions took place, and guided by God's grace we have reached some consensus on a Christian response to the current issues facing our faith. These are summarized in the following 10 statements, to be published for the reference for of all members of the local Christian churches:

I. Our Views on Social and Political Change

We affirm that God, the Lord of creation, redemption and judgment, is the master of history, therefore any future change in Hong Kong shall take place under His countenance. With this belief we shall remain steadfast and shall endeavour to fulfill what God intends us to fulfil with peaceful minds.

Meanwhile, as citizens of Hong Kong, we are obliged to develop an objective view on historical change and face reality with the wisdom that God gives us, proactively undertaking our responsibilities as Christians.

II. Unchanging Principles of the Church amid Social Change

We shall accept the Bible as the supreme authority of our faith, life and service, regardless of the social or political environment.

In times of social turmoil we are bound to face challenges and temptations and we might even fall in our weakness. Therefore we should ensure that we remain loyal to Christ in every circumstance without compromising, whatever external changes occur, or sacrificing Biblical principles for the sake of expediency. By virtue of God's mighty power we should bear witness to God in times of crisis and glorify His name by steadfastly observing the covenant that He had made with us and absolutely obeying His commandments.

III. The Nature and Mission of the Church

We believe that the church is a visible, spiritual group appointed by God through the Gospel of Jesus Christ. She is the body of Christ and Christ is alive in her. The church was founded by God in this world to honour His name, to serve the people, to testify and expand His Kingdom and fulfil the purpose of His creation and redemption through Christ. This is realized particularly through the following three functions:

1) Preaching the Gospel of God's salvation at home and in other parts of the world;
2) Fostering spirituality among the Christian community through worship, fellowship, pastoral care and spiritual discipline; and
3) Assuming the role of being 'the light and the salt' in this world to promote social and cultural progress.

This is a mission entrusted to the church by Christ. Therefore the church should endeavour to ensure the wholeness of this mission irrespective of circumstantial changes, without allowing for any deviation or partial omission driven by human intention or political influence.

IV. Christian Responsibility Towards and Expectations for Hong Kong

As citizens of Hong Kong we are assured that Christians have a role, together with the wider community, to play in shaping the future of Hong Kong so that it will become a democratic society underpinned by the rule of law, where human rights are respected, freedom and equality are protected and stability and prosperity are maintained. At this historical moment we should undertake the responsibility of preaching the Good News to the people of Hong Kong so that they might enjoy the grace of God and live fuller lives.

We expect that after 1997 Hong Kong will continue to experience a high degree of autonomy and that its people will still enjoy the human rights and freedoms bestowed by God, including freedom of speech, press, association, assembly, travel and religion, etc., to the extent that Hong Kong might contribute positively to the modernization and democratization of China as a whole.

V. Hong Kong Christians' Commitment to China

As Chinese, our historic identity is inextricably related to that of the Chinese people as a whole. Therefore we should not be concerned only with the interests of Hong Kong but should also care for and participate in the development of mainland China. We look forward to the Chinese people at large being able to share the human rights and freedoms bestowed by God, to the extent that China will become a nation where people live in prosperity and where justice is upheld. We hope that more Chinese will come to know God the Creator and claim the benefits of His redeeming grace. We are prepared to do our utmost to achieve this goal.

VI. The Hong Kong Church and the Ecumenical Church

We believe that the church in Hong Kong is an integral part of the ecumenical church, spiritually united with the church in China and churches in other parts of the world. Therefore we should maintain communication with and work together to assist each other and undertake the mission of preaching the Gospel.

While we acknowledge the common spiritual life of the church of Hong Kong and the church in China and other parts of the world, we also recognize that there is diversity among different local churches. Therefore the Hong Kong church should endeavour to enhance its uniqueness as a local church while remembering its Chinese cultural background. It should maintain administrative independence while actively participating in missionary programs around the world.

VII. Our Views on Church-State Relations

We believe that the authority of the government comes from God and that we should obey the government on matters that fall within the scope of its due authority. However, if the government requires what God forbids we should submit to God's will. The authority of the government has a definite scope. God endows the government with the duty of maintaining law and order and the stability of the society so that people are protected. On this basis, the government should be accountable to the people under the constitution. Christians should assume a prophetic role in society and actively encourage the government to do justice and work towards the well being of the people.

VIII. Social Change and Church Renewal

We believe that the church in Hong Kong has made positive achievements over the past few decades in terms of evangelism, parish development, education and social service. However, we acknowledge that we have not been sensitive enough to the rapid changes experienced in Hong Kong, to the point where the pattern of church life has lacked innovation. At this historical moment, the church should reflect on itself and seek renewal in order to turn crisis into opportunity. The following represents some possible key areas of focus:

1) Learning more about history in order to understand the present;
2) Preaching messages that are relevant to the times and faithful to the truth;
3) Emphasizing the fostering of faith and love in action for the spiritual betterment of Christians;
4) Strengthening discipleship training;
5) Emphasizing the role of preachers and lay leaders; and
6) Developing relevant church models and patterns of Christian service.

IX. Ecumenical Witness

In these changing times the church may be prone to schism and strife because of external pressures and lack of agreement internally. At this particular moment in time we should reaffirm our Christian unity in Jesus Christ and extend to each other mutual acceptance and trust on the basis of our common faith. We should deal with differences through dialogue and endeavour to foster concrete plans for co-operation, because by offering each other mutual support we shall be able to stand united in the face of challenge.

X. Integrity and Faithfulness of the Church

We should maintain the chastity of the church and pledge our loyalty to Christ in anticipation of His return. We should guard the church against the infiltration of secular elements and the influence of any powerful parties and should love one another to build the Body of Christ and glorify His name.

Concluding Remarks

At this moment of significant social change, we should make additional efforts to grasp the opportunity offered for preaching the Gospel and testifying to the name of the Lord. Having said that, we are well aware of our own weaknesses and that there is no way we can stand firm alone in the face of trials and challenges. We have to rely on the mighty power and faithfulness of the Father, the love of Christ and the presence of the Holy Spirit to protect our faith and guide us through the way ahead.

16 April 1984

Statement on Religious Freedom by the Protestant Churches of Hong Kong

The Protestant Churches of Hong Kong are earnestly concerned with future religious freedom in the territory and would like to make the following statement:

Introduction

The measure of religious freedom is closely related to the openness of a society, and religious freedom is evidence of progress in a society. We affirm that genuine religious freedom is based on human rights. Human rights are the birthrights of all men and women granted by God. Therefore, all governments have the responsibility to safeguard human rights.

The protection of religious freedom hinges upon respect for human rights by society as a whole. Human rights are specifically expressed in the freedoms of thought, speech, press, organization, assembly and action. We believe that genuine freedom for religious faith and activities is only possible in a society that respects human rights.

Current Religious Freedom of the Protestant Churches of Hong Kong

The citizens of Hong Kong have always been entitled to freedom of religious faith and activity, and the religious faith and activities of the Protestant churches of Hong Kong include:

I. For the individual

1) The freedom to believe without being discriminated against by society or prejudice to one's civic rights.
2) The freedom to choose different denominations, churches, theological persuasions and rituals.
3) The freedom to buy and own religious publications.
4) The freedom to preach a religious faith.

II. For the family

1) The freedom to procure one's children to accept religious faith and rituals according to one's religious traditions.
2) The freedom to hold worship services and provide religious education at home.
3) The freedom to hold religious rituals for birth, marriage and death, etc. of family members at chapels, funeral homes or on other premises at different stages of life.

III. For the Church as a whole

1. Church gatherings
   (a) The freedom to organize religious activities at different hours and venues and in different forms, such as worship services, prayer meetings, Sunday school, fellowship, seasonal conferences, Bible study classes, catechism classes, crusades, morning prayers and baptisms, etc.
   (b) The freedom to hold meetings for the purposes of evangelism or spiritual cultivation, such as crusades, spiritual admonitions, dramas and concerts, at lawfully leased public venues.
   (c) The freedom to organize or support the organization of Christian fellowships in various professional sectors for the purposes of evangelism and spiritual cultivation.
2. Spiritual cultivation and evangelism
   (a) The freedom to produce and broadcast programs for the purposes of evangelism and spiritual cultivation through electronic media such as movies, radio, television, CD-ROM recordings, tapes and slide shows, etc.
   (b) The freedom to print and disseminate literature for the purposes of evangelism and spiritual cultivation such as the Bible, hymns, ritual orders, journals, monographs, teaching kits and leaflets, etc.
   (c) The freedom to preach and provide teachings on the substance of the Christian faith to people of different age groups for the purpose of their conversion.
   (d) The freedom to send missionaries abroad to engage in missionary activity.

3. Witness through service
    (a) The freedom to set up social welfare organizations, social services and medical institutions as a manifestation of the holistic concern of the Christian churches for society and individuals.
    (b) The freedom to run education institutions such as kindergartens, primary schools, secondary schools, post-secondary colleges and vocational schools as a manifestation of the holistic concern of the Christian churches for society and individuals.
    (c) The freedom to establish organizations for the purpose of taking part in the drawing up of public policies, caring for people's livelihood and promoting social justice as a manifestation of the holistic concern of the Christian churches for society and individuals.
4. Human and other resources
    (a) The freedom to inherit, manage, apply and retain monetary donations and properties in Hong Kong or abroad for the purpose of religious activities or social service.
    (b) The freedom to liaise on religious matters, share resources, allocate staff and exchange thoughts with other churches and individual Christians in Hong Kong or abroad on the basis of mutual respect.
    (c) The freedom to run theological seminaries and research centres for the academic study of religion and the training of human resources.
    (d) The freedom to appoint and ordain clergy in accordance with the traditions of various Christian denominations.
5. Organization and management
    (a) The freedom for each denominational church to formulate its organizational structure, qualifications for membership and operational rules in accordance with its own traditions and constitutions.
    (b) The freedom for local churches and international missionary bodies to lawfully purchase, manage and utilize property, such as chapels, offices, rectories, schools, hospitals, social service centres and retreat houses, etc.
    (c) The freedom to own and manage cemeteries.

IV. The freedom to engage in other lawful and related ministries not mentioned above

The aforesaid represents a rough description of what the Christian churches in Hong Kong are currently doing and is seen as the physical manifestation of religious freedom in Hong Kong. We earnestly hope that Hong Kong will continue to enjoy the aforesaid freedom of religious faith and activities after 1997.

Concluding Remarks

We acknowledge that Christians should be committed to maintaining and developing a society that respects human rights. This would ensure that Hong Kong will enjoy even more freedom, stability and prosperity under Chinese sovereignty as a society that shows full respect for human rights and promotes democracy thus making an active contribution to the future well being of the entire Chinese nation.

As a symbol of God's presence in the world, the church is prepared to walk hand-in-hand with the citizens of Hong Kong, encouraging Christians to make a concerted effort to develop the territory. We are committed to becoming 'the light and the salt' through which God's love, peace and justice shall be manifested. We pledge to bring service to the needy, assistance to the weak and comfort to people in sorrow. We shall honour our responsibilities to our society, country and nation, fulfil the mission entrusted by our Lord and strive towards the goal that all people might hear the Gospel and lead godly lives.

1984

Opinions of the Hong Kong Protestant Delegation to Beijing on the Future of Hong Kong

Introduction

Hong Kong is set to revert to Chinese sovereignty in 1997, which is an undisputable and rightful development. We believe that the implementation of a high degree of autonomy, namely the self-governance of Hong Kong people based on the principle of 'one-country, two-systems' is a practicable solution to this historical issue. At this historical moment, we Christians are prepared to work hand-in-hand with all the citizens of Hong Kong to ensure the territory's continued prosperity and stability, the modernization of China and the well being of the whole Chinese race, while continuing to fulfil the mission of preaching the Gospel.

To this end, we are prepared to visit Beijing at the invitation of the PRC State Council Bureau of Religious Affairs to exchange views with the Chinese authorities in order to enhance mutual understanding.

Our Views on Hong Kong Society

By preaching the Gospel and providing various kinds of social service Hong Kong Christians have always stood in solidarity with the wider Hong Kong community in facing the future. Given the principle of the self-governance of Hong Kong people we have the following views on the future of Hong Kong after 1997:

1. Leveraging on its unique strengths in geographic and political terms, Hong Kong has made enormous economic achievements over the past few decades despite limited human resources, winning recognition and respect from the international community. We believe that Hong Kong owes these achievements to the collaborative efforts of its general public as well as investors and the professional sector.

2. Freedom, openness and the rule of law, as well as the policy of active non-interference adopted by the government in general matters have been important factors contributing to Hong Kong's economic success.

3. While Hong Kong's economy continues to prosper, the foundations of its social morality have been facing severe challenges. Social problems caused by the sex industry, gambling and drug abuse, etc., as well as other criminal activities, are seen as aggravating. The younger generation is characterized by blurred moral values. Society fails to provide comprehensive protection for the less competitive nor does it uphold the dignity of the underprivileged. The contribution of the general public to Hong Kong's prosperity and stability is not fully acknowledged. We see these problems as the shortcomings of the Hong Kong society that should be rectified over time by the people of Hong Kong working together in a more proactive manner.

4. We recognize that in order to ensure the continued prosperity and stability of Hong Kong in future, it is imperative to establish a government with strong credibility. This government should be directly accountable to the citizens of Hong Kong. It should be concerned not only with economic development, but also with the interests of the silent majority. Meanwhile it should maintain its legislative, judicial and administrative independence.

5. The structure of Hong Kong's government has been in effect for a long time and has proved to be very efficient. While continuous fine-tuning should be made and new developments sought on the existing basis, any dramatic reshuffling is deemed undesirable.

6. Hong Kong's international connections should be maintained and furthered after its return to Chinese sovereignty. Hong Kong people's right to travel freely to and from the territory is essential if Hong Kong wants to keep its status as an international city. The Chinese government should negotiate with other countries after 1997 to ensure that Hong Kong citizens who do business or travel abroad will be treated fairly and will continue to enjoy freedom of entry and departure.

7. We believe that the citizens of Hong Kong should have the right to participate in the formulation and future revision of the Basic Law. The government should seek the approval of Hong Kong citizens for any subsequent revision of the Basic Law after its formulation. The provisions of the Basic Law should be based on guiding principles such as freedom, open-mindedness, the rule of law and the respect of human rights.

8. The industrial and commercial sectors of Hong Kong are expected to develop in

increased pace in future. While continuing its effort to promote Hong Kong's economic development, the government should not be biased towards the interests of investors and professionals at the expense of the rights and needs of the working class. The basic rights of workers, such as the freedom to choose one's job and career, vocational protection, protection from unreasonable dismissal and non-payment of wages, the right to engage in industrial actions, the right to organize and participate in workers' unions and the right to carry out class negotiations, should be safeguarded in order to ensure respect for human dignity and values.

9. Investment in education is indispensable for maintaining the future economic and social progress of Hong Kong in tandem with the modernization of China. We believe that our education system should be developed on a diversified basis with a view to training human resources for different sectors. Post-secondary education should be expanded with institutions maintaining their international orientation and standards. Primary education should be enhanced with the introduction of a bilingual education policy underpinned by the priority of the Chinese language and the use of the English language on a complementary basis. Meanwhile, moral education should be strengthened so that Hong Kong citizens can secure greater support to develop for themselves sound moral values and noble virtues.

10. Hong Kong should develop a comprehensive social security system in future for the benefit of and to offer protection for the basic living of all citizens.

11. A democratic political institution should start to be implemented now to prepare the people of Hong Kong for self-governance.

Our Views on the Hong Kong Church

Over the years, the church has taken root in different communities and classes in Hong Kong through its ministries in evangelism, medical care, education and social service, as well as its role in the formulation of public policies. We are prepared to continue our servanthood for the people of Hong Kong. Please refer to the 'Proposed Statements of Faith for Hong Kong Christians in the Face of the Social and Political Change' tabled by a group of Christians as an account of Christian loyalty to God and responsibility to Hong Kong.

We have the following views on the church in Hong Kong after 1997:

1. The future Hong Kong should not only maintain its freedom and openness in economic activities: it should also maintain the same freedom in ideology and religion, so that the Hong Kong Church will be able to continue to make a contribution to society.

2. Religious freedom has a broad scope that includes freedom of personal belief, public worship, preaching, religious education, assembly, speech and the press. In this connection, a 'Statement on Religious Freedom by the Protestant Churches of Hong Kong' has been submitted to the Chinese authorities by a group of

Christians. We propose the detailed incorporation of the current scope of religious freedom enjoyed by Hong Kong citizens in the Basic Law.

3. Although Christians in Hong Kong (excluding Catholics) account for only 5% of the total population, they are undertaking a significant share of the responsibility in medical care, education and social welfare. The churches currently run 200 kindergartens, 175 primary schools, 120 secondary schools, 15 theological seminaries, 3 schools for the deaf, 5 hospitals and numerous social service centres, such as homes for the elderly, youth centres and elderly centres. The churches' undertaking is inspired by their faith and driven by a genuine desire to help meet the needs of society. The churches have been shouldering this responsibility since the early years of Hong Kong's development, when the government was unable to provide sufficient educational opportunities and social services. Because of their rigorous attitude and their emphasis on moral education and the cultivation of virtues, they have won the trust and support of the people of Hong Kong. In fact, the churches have been pioneers in Hong Kong's education and social service sectors. We believe that the churches should continue to make contributions in this regard so as to improve and advance society in terms of morality and spirituality.

4. Currently, the responsibility of funding developments in education and the social services is largely taken up by the Hong Kong government, which grants subsidies to schools and social services managed by religious groups on a full or partial basis. The government shows respect for and trusts the religious groups and allows them to run their schools and social services according to their own principles and objectives. We believe that the future government of Hong Kong should continue to adhere to this policy.

5. Although the churches in Hong Kong are deeply rooted in Hong Kong society, the catholic and ecumenical character of the churches means that they have an intimate fellowship with Christians and churches all over the world, sharing in Christ's hardships as well as happiness with each other. As a member of the global Church, we shall share the work and hope of Hong Kong people with people in other nations through the international church, so that they may come to respect Hong Kong and deal with us on an equal basis.

6. While most churches in Hong Kong are independent and autonomous, they are closely related to their denominational affiliates in other parts of the world in terms of tradition and history. This is a relationship that we ardently treasure. We hope that the churches will be able to interact with churches and Christians of other countries in mutual respect after 1997.

Concluding Remarks

As Hong Kong Christians, we would like to reiterate our loyalty to God and our obligation to Hong Kong society and the Church. We confess our Chinese identity; we love our state and nation and we are prepared to stand in solidarity with our Chinese compatriots, for better or for worse. The livelihood of our one billion compatriots and the overall development of China shall remain a pressing concern on our part. Apart from prayers and care, we are also prepared to undertake responsibility by engaging in concrete actions for the betterment of Hong Kong. We believe that the progress of the territory shall in its own way contribute to China's development. We are convinced that the current delegation to Beijing shall be conducive to this cause.

1984

Cardinal Wu's Pastoral Letter 'God is Love' in 1999

Dear Brothers and Sisters in Christ,

'You were called to freedom, only do not use your freedom as an opportunity for the flesh, but through love be servants of one another. For the whole law is fulfilled in one word, You shall love your neighbour as yourself' (Gal 5: 13–14). 1999, the third and final year of preparation for the Great Jubilee will be aimed at broadening the horizons of believers, so that they will see things in the perspective of Christ: in the perspective of the 'Father who is in heaven', from whom the Lord was sent and to whom he has returned. The whole of the Christian life is like a great pilgrimage to the house of the Father, whose unconditional love for every human creature we discover anew each day. This pilgrimage takes place in the heart of each person, extends to the believing community and then reaches to the whole of humanity. It will therefore be necessary, especially during this year, to emphasize the theological virtue of charity, recalling the significant and lapidary words of the First Letter of John: 'God is love'. Charity, in its twofold reality as love of God and love of neighbour, is the summing up of the moral life of the believer (cf. Tertio Millennio Adveniente, nos. 49–50).

These perspectives ought to provide us with a new way of looking at the question of the right of abode of children born in the Mainland to Hong Kong parents, a new way of discussing the question and its consequences. In the long term, these children cannot without permission be reunited with their families in Hong Kong and we should pay special attention to this.

In fact, a large number of adult Hong Kong residents came from the Mainland to settle here in the 1950s and 1960s. Hong Kong at that time was not blessed with a strong economy or firm social structure. Nevertheless, when faced with a continuous flood of refugees, there was no hesitation and doors were opened to welcome them. At the present time, the economic outlook is not so bright. Yet, compared with the rest of the world Hong Kong is seen to be particularly blessed and is still the envy of many. Based on the belief that 'blood is thicker than water', that 'all within the four seas are one family', the Chinese people have always shown kindness to others and taken delight in sharing. Faced then today with the question of children born to Hong Kong parents in the Motherland, how can we harden our hearts, look on with indifference and a lack of humanity, and use 'interpretation' to deny them hope?

The Government of the S.A.R., in its concern for Hong Kong and its sense of responsibility, is to be respected. But when it seeks the long term prosperity of Hong Kong by requesting the Standing Committee of the N. P. C. for re-interpretation of the Basic Law in order to limit the right of abode of children born in the Mainland to Hong Kong parents, then it engenders a certain resistance on the part of Hong Kong residents to Mainland people, with lamentable consequences. Diligent and resourceful, benevolent and caring, the people of Hong Kong are well known both within and beyond China for their generosity and open-handedness in helping wherever disaster strikes and causes human suffering, whether within Hong Kong itself, in China, or in other countries. Given sufficient time, and provided with adequate information and proper arrangements, Hong Kong's zealous people, philanthropists, voluntary bodies and church communities could deal with the present question of right of abode, and, united in hand and in heart, could respond to the limits of their ability to face the challenge and to meet the difficulties, could grasp the opportunity to develop a spirit of love and create a new miracle. Let it be seen that the people of Hong Kong are loving and its society is a caring one.

In accordance with the principles of 'one country, two systems' and 'a high degree of autonomy', the Central Government's solemn commitment to the Hong Kong S.A.R., and with reference to the provisions of the scope of self governance of the Hong Kong S.A.R., the N. P. C. gave Hong Kong courts the right to interpret its own laws. This right is the established basis of Hong Kong's system of law and of government. Hong Kong is home to more than six million people, an international city belonging to the community of nations, an important window for our Motherland. It is extremely important that the basis of law and government be maintained in all its integrity. The present question of the right of abode belongs within the competence of Hong Kong's autonomy. The S.A.R. should itself give its own interpretation, but it has not done this. Asking for a reinterpretation from the Standing Committee of the N. P. C. cannot help but damage the foundation of the autonomy of the S.A.R., shake the foundations of the Hong Kong family, raise doubts in people's minds about the Central Government's promise of 'one country, two systems with a high degree of autonomy', undermine the confidence of the international community towards Hong Kong. Who can be sure how far-reaching the effects will be?

Dear brothers and sisters, facing this present situation do we feel helpless? That is understandable! Can nothing be done? Remember our faith. Pray more, open ourselves, believe firmly. God helps those who help themselves, because His 'power working in us can do more than we can ask for or imagine. Glory be to Him from generation to generation in the church and in Christ Jesus for ever and ever, Amen.' (Eph 3:20–21)

Visitation of Our Lady 1999

+ John B. Card. Wu

Notes

Foreword   Faith, Citizenship and Colonialism in Hong Kong

1. See, for example, the scriptural citations in A Plé, 'Les textes de l'écriture sur la charité fraternelle', in A Plé (ed.), *L'Amour du Prochain*, Paris: Les Éditions du Cerf, 1954.
2. Wong Man-fong *China's Resumption of Sovereignty over Hong Kong*, Hong Kong: Hong Kong Baptist University, n.d., 40–3.
3. See Commentator, *Renmin Ribao*, 15 and 25 May, 2, 10 and 13 June 1967.
4. Benjamin K. P. Leung, 'The Student Movement in Hong Kong: Transition to a Democratizing Society', in Stephen Wing-kai Chiu and Tai-lok Lui (eds), *The Dynamics of Social Movement in Hong Kong*, Hong Kong: Hong Kong University Press, 2000, 214–6.
5. On Sir Alexander Grantham's views, see Steve Tsang (ed.), *A Documentary History of Hong Kong: Government and Politics*, Hong Kong: Hong Kong University Press, 1995, 291–2.
6 Until 1977, Hong Kong judges were not selected from among barristers in private practice, as they would have been in the United Kingdom, but from the Colonial Legal Service.
7 Patrick Yu Shuk-siu, *Tales from No. 9 Ice House Street*, Hong Kong: Hong Kong University Press, 2002, 12–3, 57. His account has been supplemented with information from Jesuit archives.

8. See James 2. 15–6.

9. Peter Hodge, 'The Politics of Welfare', in John F. Jones (ed.), *The Common Welfare: Hong Kong's Social Services*, Hong Kong: Chinese University Press, 1981, 17–9.

10. See, for example, the role of Protestant and Catholic clerics in the educational field during the 1950s in Anthony Sweeting, *A Phoenix Transformed: The Reconstruction of Education in Post-War Hong Kong* (Hong Kong: Oxford University Press, 1993), chapter 5. Christian professionals were active, amongst other fields, in the development of medical care for children and those suffering from tuberculosis, as well as in the creation of youth and community services.

11. *Codex Iuris Canonici Pii X Pontificis Maximi*, Rome: Typis Polyglottis Vaticinis, 1965, canons 1372–4; and *Codex Iuris Canonici Auctoritate Ioannis Pauli Pp. II Promulgatus*, Rome: Libreria Editrice Vaticana, 1983, canon 226.

12. Catherine Jones, *Promoting Prosperity: The Hong Kong Way of Social Policy,* Hong Kong: Chinese University Press, 1990, 222–5.

13. David Baird, 'Hongkong: Christians in Revolt', *Far Eastern Economic Review*, 21 May 1970.

14. David Baird, 'Thy Will Be Done', *Far Eastern Economic Review*, 29 January 1970.

15. Denny Ho Kwok-leung, *Polite Politics: A Sociological Analysis of an Urban Protest in Hong Kong*, Aldershot: Ashgate, 2000, 67–8.

16. Bernard H. K. Luk, 'Custom and Religion', in Richard Y. C. Wong & Joseph Y. S. Cheng (eds), *The Other Hong Kong Report 1990*, Hong Kong: Chinese University Press, 1990, 575–6.

17. Alvin Y. So, *Hong Kong's Embattled Democracy: A Societal Analysis*, Baltimore: John Hopkins University Press, 1999, 107–9.

18. Tai-lok Lui and Stephen Wing-kai Chiu, 'Introduction — Changing Political Opportunities and the Shaping of Collective Action: Social Movements in Hong Kong', in Chiu and Lui, *The Dynamics of Social Movements in Hong Kong*, 12.

19. E.g., Romans 13. 1–8; 1 Peter 1. 13.

20. 'De ecclesia in mundo hujus temporis', *Concilium Oecuminicum Vaticanum Secundum,* Taipei: Catholic Central Bureau, 1966, 196–200.

21. John Paul II, *Sollicitudo Rei Socialis*, London: Catholic Truth Society, 1988, 83; and *Centesimus Annus,* Vatican City: Libreria Editrice Vaticana, 1991, 44. For an example of the very different approach to social relations in the 1950s, see Edwardus E. Bezzina, *De Valore Sociali Caritatis secundum principia S Thomae Aquinitatis*, Naples: M. D'Auria, 1952.

22 *New China News Agency*, 17 June 2002.

23 Though not an overwhelming or unambiguous majority. See the thoughtful analysis in Joseph Man et al., *Education and Principle-based Opinion: A Study of the Right of Abode Controversy in Hong Kong*, Hong Kong: Hong Kong Institute of Asia-Pacific Studies, 2000, 15–9.

24 *South China Morning Post*, 6 February 2001 and 16 January 2002.

25   *Renmin Ribao*, 23 July 1999.
26   Legco Panel on Home Affairs, *Minutes of special meeting: 20 February 2001*, LC Paper No. CB(2)1673/00–01.
27   *Renmin Ribao*, 20 February 2001.
28   *New China News Agency*, 2 October 2000.
29   Lam Wun-kwong, Secretary for Home Affairs, avoided expressing any view on either the canonization or the Liaison Office's intervention when questioned in the legislature. *Government Information Services*, 18 October 2000.
30   The Chief Executive's official tribute was only two sentences long, however. *Government Information Services*, 23 September 2002.

Chapter 1   Introduction

1.   See Robertson (1987) for a general discussion on study of Church-State relations. On Marxist tradition, see Marx and Engels (1957), Hamilton (1998, 166–220). On Durkheimian tradition, see Pickering (1984), Alexander (1988), Chan (1999a) and Nielsen (1999). On Weberian tradition, see Schlucher (1989), Lemmen (1990), and S.-h. Chan (1999b).
2.   On Latin America, see Levine (1981), Fleet (1985), Fleet and Smith (1997), and S.-h. Chan (2000b). On Africa, see Villa-Vicencio (1990, 1996), Walshe (1995).
3.   We borrow these concepts from Anthony Gill (1998, 9–10).

Chapter 2   Church-State Relations Models

1.   Based on experiences of the European Communism, Pedro Ramet developed a theory of Church-State interaction. In his theory, Ramet outlines seven areas, which he calls 'clusters', which should be investigated in the study of Church-State relations. They are 'religion and modernization', 'religion and nationalism', 'geneticism-monism', 'religious culture and political culture', 'factionalism in Church-State interaction', 'organization theory' and 'institutional needs of religious organizations'. See Pedro Ramet (1987, 184–95).

Chapter 3   Rendering Education and Social Services While Assisting the Government in Defending Hong Kong from Communism

1.   *Dates and Events Connected with the History of Education in Hong Kong, 1877*, Hong Kong Catholic Diocesan Archive, 22–3.
2.   Hong Kong was officially classified as a Prefecture in the Catholic hierarchical

structure by Propaganda Fide, Rome. See Ryan (1959, 2) and Ticozzi (1983, 1–4).

3. Hong Kong Record Series, 147 2/1, Hong Kong Public Records Office.
4. Information Service Department, ed. 1997. *Hong Kong 1997*, Hong Kong: Hong Kong Government, 409.
5. For discussion of the expulsion of missionaries for political reasons, see B. Leung (1992a, 73–103).
6. *South China Morning Post*, 15 December 1949, 5; 19 December 1949, 3; 10 April 1950, editorial.
7. On 10 October 1956, in what later became known as the 'Kowloon Riot', the Nationalists attacked Communist affiliated schools, trade unions, factories and shops, resulting in casualties of over 300 people. In April 1966, a 5-cent fare increase by the Hong Kong Star Ferry triggered large-scale protests. In 6 May 1967 a workers' protest at a plastic flowers factory in San Po Kong led to a confrontation between the Hong Kong Government and the Communist Workers' Union. The Hong Kong Government took actions to suppress dissident activities and announced a curfew order. See Hong Kong Government, *Report on the Kowloon and Tsuen Wan Riots: 10–12 October, 1956* (Hong Kong: Cheng Ya, 1956) and Hong Kong Government, Commission of Inquiry, *Kowloon Disturbance, 1966* (Hong Kong: Government Printers, 1967).
8. An elderly resident in Sai Kung who joined the guerrilla warfare described the Chinese Communists to this writer and how the British worked secretly during WWII to combat the Japanese occupation of Hong Kong and southern China. The guerrilla leader Zeng Sheng recorded this conflict in his memoirs. Zeng (1992, 378–513).
9. Sir Alexander Grantham to Secretary of State for the Colonies, British Government, 1103 top secret, 30 November 1948, quoted by Sweeting (1993, 199).
10. *South China Morning Post*, 16 December 1948, 7.
11. 'Grantham to SofS, 311 secret, 1 April 1949'. In CO537/4824, Hong Kong Public Record Office.
12. 'Grantham to SofS, 384 secret, 30 April 1949'. In FO371/5839, Hong Kong Public Record Office.
13. See 'The Letter of Bishop R.O. Hall, Bishop of Hong Kong and South China to the Secretary of the Board of Education. 16 September 1950'. Hong Kong Record Series, 147 2/2 (1), 119, Hong Kong Public Records Office.
14. See 'Letter of Secretary of Board of Education to the Rt. Rev. R.O. Hall, the Bishop of Hong Kong, Ref. E.D. 3/2106/45'. Hong Kong Record Series, 147 2/2 (1), 120, Hong Kong Public Records Office.
15. This was due to the influence of successive British Education Acts in 1870, 1902 and 1944. See McClelland (1988).
16. Hong Kong Record Series, 147 2/2 (2), Hong Kong Public Records Office.
17. See 'The Report on Registration of Children Without Schooling'. Hong Kong

Record Series, 147 2/2 (1), 119, Hong Kong Public Records Office.

18. The crackdown was not known about by many. It was discussed by the former head of the Xinhua News Agency, Xu Jiatun in 1995. See Xu (1995, 75).

19. Major J. L. Hillard, Commissioner, Essential Services Corps, 'Survey of Strikes — June 1967', ESC 90/67, 15 September 1967, mimeo, 64, 74.

20. *Shenzhen Tequ Bao (Shenzhen Daily)*, 12 December 1996; and Wang (1997, 31).

21. For the social and educational services provided to girls by the French Sisters, see 'Sisters of St. Paul de Chartres File' of Hong Kong Catholic Diocesan Archives. For the education services provided to boys see: 'Father Teruzzi File' and 'Father Mangieri File' of Hong Kong Catholic Diocesan Archives, *Dates and Events Connected with the History of Education in Hong Kong 1877*, by the St. Louis Institute of Rehabilitation, a Catholic missionary institute, which provides details of the education services offered on behalf of the Government by the Christian churches during the period 1857–1877. See Ticozzi (1983, 108–12).

22. See also Maryknoll Archive, no. MPBA, Hong Kong 9/8.

23. Hong Kong Catholic Diocesan Archives, HK-DA S.6–01, F/03.

24. Stephen Law, 'Social Commitments of the Catholic Church in Hong Kong Education', manuscript, 23. This was confirmed by Father Mencarini who was Vicar General during the 1950s and '60s with responsibility for the building of churches and schools to cope with the expansion of the Catholic population. He was interviewed by Beatrice Leung on 6 May 1997.

25. Information given by Father Mencarini during an interview by Beatrice Leung on 6 May 1997.

26. 'Statistics of the Diocese of Hong Kong'. In *Hong Kong Catholic Directory: 1997*, Hong Kong: Catholic Truth Society, 1997, 553.

27. In a survey taken in September 1999, 48 of the 57 government's directors and vice directors indicated they had gone to church schools before taking university degrees.

28. Recalled by Father Mencarini, the Bishop's assistant in educational affairs (1950s–1980s) when he was interviewed by Beatrice Leung in April 1997. Bishop Francis Hsu, in private correspondence also mentioned the abortive plan to set up a Catholic tertiary educational institute in Hong Kong. See Fang (1977, 37–8) and Hong Kong Catholic Diocesan Archives, HK-DA, S.6–02, F/01.

29. For the social and education services provided to girls by the French Sisters, see 'Sisters of St. Paul de Chartres File', Hong Kong Catholic Diocesan Archives. For the education services provided to boys, see 'Father Teruzzi File', and 'Father Mangieri File', Hong Kong Catholic Diocesan Archives.

30. *Almost as Old as Hong Kong*, 3, quoted in Stephen Law, 'Social Commitments of the Catholic Church in Hong Kong: Social Service', manuscript, 5.

31. Stephen Law, 'Social Commitments of the Catholic Church in Hong Kong: Social Service', manuscript, 5.

32. 'Brief History'. In *Caritas-Hong Kong: Annual Report 1984–85*, 6–7.

33. *Caritas-Annual Report 1968–1969*, quoted in Stephen Law, 'Social Commitments of the Catholic Church in Hong Kong: Social Service', manuscript, 7.

34. Stephen Law, 'Social Commitments of the Catholic Church in Hong Kong: Social Service', manuscript, 1–2.

35. Recalled by a key participant of that controversial group.

36. Appeared in the first draft of the document entitled 'Jiaohui zhi shehui guang' [教會之社會觀, The Social Outlook of the Church], 9–10.

37. Reviewed by an informant who was close to the British Hong Kong Government.

38. *Ibid.*

39. Hong Kong Diocesan Convention, *Social Dimension of the Church* (Hong Kong: Diocesan Convention, n.d.). See also Ticozzi (1997, 186–90).

40. In an interview in the 1990s, an anonymous Catholic refugee recalled how in the 1950s the immigration official at the US Consulate questioned him about the situation in his home Chinese village. He said that this official even took out a detailed map to double-check the authenticity of the information given.

41. Businessmen and government officials had different views on the provision of education to children. Businessmen believed that education should be aimed at making better workers, while the government wanted education to cultivate law-abiding citizens, so it could reduce the funding allocation to the police force. See Sweeting (1993, 197–8).

42. Ng Shui-lai, Director of Hong Kong Christian Service, remarked: 'Under such circumstances, the Church can no longer provide both the financial and human resources in social welfare as it did in the past. So what will become of the duty of the Church? Or if the Church will not be able to do anything significant except remaining purely as the deputy of the government, what role will she have?' See Ng (1990, 23).

Chapter 4   Hong Kong Christian Churches Defend Religious Freedom and Choose Representation on the Selection Committee During the Transition Period (1984–1997)

1. The official interpretation of religious freedom is recorded in Document 19 (1982) issued by the Party Central of the CCP. See MacInnis (1989, 1–26).

2. Jane Chui gives a detailed description of how liberal church leaders and lay Christians responded to the Basic Law. See Chui (1992, 37–9, 42–7).

3. Each version of the Chinese constitution has pledged 'religious freedom', yet for non-religious reasons, religious believers have been arrested. The Chinese leaders have their own interpretation of 'religious freedom' and religious activities are circumscribed by regulations issued by the CCP. See Document 19 (1982) in Documentation Centre of Party Central and Policy Section of Religious Affairs Bureau (1995, 53–73).

4. *Green Paper: The Further Development of Representative Government in Hong Kong* (1984).

5. For more about the NCNA, see the memoirs of its former director Xu Jiatun. See Xu (1995).

6. See annex 3, appendix 7 in *Report of the Survey Office, Public Responses to Green Paper: The 1987 Review of Developments in Representative Government*, Part II (1987).

7. Following the United Front principle, since 1980 the Communists in Hong Kong have been assigning one or two contact persons to meet various Catholic Church leaders to convey Beijing's view to them in an informal manner. The open criticism of Xin Weisi had more weight than these private meetings.

8. See Beatrice Leung (2000) and China Catholic Communication, *Guide to the Catholic Church in China 2000*, Singapore, 2000, 14.

9. Established by the Chinese government, the function of HKSAR Preparatory Committee was to help set up the first HKSAR government. Out of the 150 members in the Preparatory Committee, 94 were Hong Kong delegates appointed by the Chinese government. On 26 January 1996, a total of 148 members of the Preparatory Committee went to Beijing to receive a certificate of appointment presented by the Chinese government.

10. *Ming Pao*, 18 May 1996.

11. The nine Christian social groups are: the Hong Kong Christian Institute, Hong Kong Women's Christian Council, Hong Kong Student Christian Movement, Hong Kong Christian Industrial Committee, Christians for Hong Kong Society, Social Concern Group of the Breakthrough Youth Centre, Justice and Peace Commission of the Hong Kong Catholic Diocese, Hong Kong Catholic Labour Committee and the Catholic Youth Council.

12. See *Extra* (8 May 1996, 2), jointly published by the Hong Kong Christian Institute, Hong Kong Women's Christian Council, Hong Kong Student Christian Movement, Hong Kong Christian Industrial Committee, Christians for Hong Kong Society, and the Justice and Peace Commission of the Hong Kong Catholic Diocese.

13. *Ibid.*, 4.

14. The eight Christian social groups were: the Hong Kong Christian Institute, Hong Kong Women's Christian Council, Hong Kong Student Christian Movement, Hong Kong Christian Industrial Committee, Christians for Hong Kong Society, Justice and Peace Commission of the Hong Kong Catholic Diocese, Social Concern Fellowship of Shum Oi Church of the Church of Christ in China, and the Catholic Youth Council.

15. The seven Christian social groups were: the Hong Kong Christian Institute, Hong Kong Women's Christian Council, Hong Kong Student Christian Movement, Hong Kong Christian Industrial Committee, Christians for Hong Kong Society, Justice and Peace Commission of the Hong Kong Catholic Diocese, and the Catholic Youth Council.

16. *Ming Pao*, 17 May 1996.

17. *Hong Kong Economic Journal*, 17 May 1996.
18. *Hong Kong Economic Journal*, 18 May 1996.
19. *Hong Kong Economic Journal*, 17 May 1996.
20. *Christian Times Weekly* 472, 15 September 1996.
21. The 14 candidates who intended to compete for the seats on the Selection Committee were: Peter Kwong (Archbishop, Diocese of Hong Kong and Macau, Anglican Church), Simon Sit Poon-ki (Chairperson, Hong Kong Christian Council), Louis Tsui (Bishop of East Kowloon and East New Territories, Anglican Church), Thomas Soo (Bishop of West Kowloon and West New Territories, Anglican Church), Tsang Kwok-wai (Diocesan Archdeacon, Anglican Church), Andrew Chan (Diocesan General Secretary, Anglican Church), Lam Chun-wai (Diocesan Deputy General Secretary, Anglican Church), Moses Cheng Mo-chi (Chairperson, Committee on the Promotion of Civic Education), Pang Cheung-wai (Supervisor, *Sheng Kung Hui* Kei Lok Primary School), Mok Yiu-kwong (Chairperson, Diocesan Welfare Council, Anglican Church), Yau Chung-wan (Supervisor, Emmanuel Lutheran College), Alice Yuk Tak-fun (General Secretary, the Hong Kong Young Women's Christian Association), Choi Chi-kan (Director of Education, Assemblies of God) and Tony Lau Yat-chiu (Business Manager, the Lutheran Church, Hong Kong Synod).
22. The candidates who were recommended by Bishop Peter Kwong and Shi Jiao-guang included: Peter Kwong, Simon Sit Poon-ki, Louis Tsui, Thomas Soo, Tsang Kwok-wai, Andrew Chan, Pang Cheung-wai and Yau Chung-wan. See Peter Kwong and Shi Jiao-guang, 'Reference to elect members of religious sector in the Selection Committee of the Hong Kong SAR, China' [中華人民共和國香港特別行政區第一屆推選委員會宗教界推委參考文件] 4 October 1996. Bishop Peter Kwong emphasized that clergy should only take part in political activities on an individual basis, and yet he included a group of Anglican clergy in a list of names recommended for seats on the Selection Committee. This raises the question: Did these clergy take part in the Selection Committee on an individual basis, or did they take part as representatives of the Anglican Church?
23. *Hong Kong Economic Journal*, 9 October 1996.
24. Pang Cheung-wai, one of the candidates and a Protestant affiliated to the Anglican Church, was also a member of the pro-China political party the Democratic Alliance for the Betterment of Hong Kong. See Chan Ka-wai (1996).
25. See A Group of Christian University Students and Graduates, 'An open letter to Bishop Peter Kwong, Elder Simon Sit Poon-ki, Ms Alice Yuk Tak-fun and other Christian members of the Selection Committee' [致鄺廣傑主教、薛磐基長老、郁德芬女士及推委會內基督徒委員的公開信]. *Ming Pao*, 11 December 1996.
26. *Christian Times Weekly* 487, 29 December 1996.
27. Reverend Lo Lung-Kwong, a member of the Hong Kong Christian Council suggested that if the Protestant representatives on the Selection Committee violated the principles stipulated by the Hong Kong Christian Council, the nomination

committee could issue an open statement to condemn him/her. However, the nomination committee was dissolved at a later period and moreover, the Protestant representatives were not chosen by the committee. If anyone violated the agreed principles there was no procedure or legitimate grounds to condemn them.

28. In every version of the Chinese constitution 'religious freedom' has been included, yet for non-religious reasons, religious believers continue to be arrested. Chinese leaders have their own interpretation of 'religious freedom' and religious activities are circumscribed by regulations issued by the CCP. See Document 19 (1982) in Documentation Centre of Party Central and Policy Section of Religious Affairs Bureau (1995, 53–73).

29. The official of Xinhua News Agency in Hong Kong Branch echoed Beijing's view to the author, soon after the news of the creation of Cardinal Wu was announced.

30. See *The Tablet* (London), 19 May 1984, 471.

31. *Kung Kao Po*, 23 December 1983.

32. Revealed in an interview by Beatrice Leung with a priest in the Hong Kong Catholic diocese in 1990.

33. *Hong Kong Catholic Directory 2000*, Hong Kong: Catholic Truth Society, 2000, p. 62.

34. On the row between China and the Vatican over the controversy of Archbishop Deng Yiming, see Leung (1992a: 189–256).

35. Bishop Jin presented this argument to Beatrice Leung when he visited Hong Kong in 1989.

36. *Sunday Examiner*, 25 October 1996; *Kung Kao Po*, 25 October 1996.

37. Bishop Joseph Zen gave details of the ordination when Beatrice Leung interviewed him in January 2002.

38. Explained to one of the authors by NCNA cadres after the consecration.

39. Bishop Jin, Catholic bishop of Shanghai, dissuaded Beatrice Leung and some other Hong Kong Catholics when he visited Hong Kong in 1994.

40. The Catholic Diocese of Hong Kong was requested to nominate candidates to represent the Catholic Church to the Selection Committee in the religious subgroup within the grassroots sector.

41. *Kung Kao Po*, 19 April 1996; 26 April 1996; *Ming Pao*, 17 May 1996; 31 August 1996.

42. *Ming Pao*, 17 May 1996.

43. Pope John Paul II, in his speech to the Chinese in Manila, expressed that a good Christian should be a good citizen. See *Sunday Examiner*, 1 February 1981.

44. Report was issued from the Chancellery Office, and appeared in the Catholic official paper. See *Kung Kao Po*, 23 August 1996.

45. *Ibid.*

46. *Ming Pao*, 17 May 1996.

47. Interview with Mary Yuen Mei-yin, Executive Secretary of the Justice and Peace Commission of the Hong Kong Catholic Diocese, by Beatrice Leung in May 1998.

Chapter 5 Non-traditional Relations Between the Hong Kong Government and Christian Churches

1. Council Fathers are those key theologians upon whose theological views Vatican II's orientation was built.
2. *Kung Kao Po*, 12 June 1981, 3.
3. 'Justice and Peace Commission of the Hong Kong Catholic Diocese', promotional pamphlet published by the Justice and Peace Commission of the Hong Kong Catholic Diocese.
4. The Catholic diocese encouraged the social participation of the Church only in the 1980s, at the time when Hong Kong society was anxious about the Sino-British negotiations on the future of Hong Kong.
5. *Kung Kao Po*, 7 December 1990.
6. Minutes of the Annual General Meetings of the Justice and Peace Commission of the Hong Kong Catholic Diocese between 1981 and 1989.
7. Noted in the *Committee Report of the Justice and Peace Commission of the Hong Kong Catholic Diocese, 1981–82*. Hong Kong: Justice and Peace Commission of the Hong Kong Catholic Diocese.
8. Some of these women literally lived on boats that were afloat in the waters between Hong Kong and China.
9. UCAN News, *Asia Focus*, 22 December 1995.
10. Bishop Deng Yiming has a chapter on this event in his memoirs. See Tang (1991: 126–30). Cardinal Casaroli went to Hong Kong to greet Bishop Deng Yiming who was released in 1981 after 22 years of imprisonment in China. as the first overture from the Vatican.
11. 'Draft Agreement between the Government of the United Kingdom and North Ireland and the Government of the People's Republic of China on the Future of Hong Kong', 26 September 1984.
12. *Sunday Examiner*, 5 July 1996; *Yi: China Message* (issue 166) XV–XVII, 6 (August 1996): 12–3.
13. Explained by Bishop Joseph Zen who was responsible for Catholic education at the Diocese, on May 2000.
14. Letter from the Chancellor, Catholic Diocese to Catholic leaders on participation in elections, 25 July 1988.
15. *Kung Kao Po*, 9 March 1991. The Prelate's pastoral letter was reprinted in the parishes.
16. A Chinese religious congregation of the Hong Kong diocese re-scheduled the congregation's feast day in order that the Chinese nuns of that congregation could join the rally.
17. Acknowledged by the former head of *Xinhua*, Hong Kong Branch. Xu Jiatun explained that all the events in the rallies in supporting the pro-democratic movement in China were taped and all of these tapes were sent to Beijing. See Xu (1995, 363–98).

18. *Kung Kao Po*, 8 September 1995.
19. Justice and Peace Commission of the Hong Kong Catholic Diocese, *Dao Jai Zenggang Zhong* (The Word in the Political Platform: A Social Analysis and Suggestions for Improvement), Hong Kong: Justice and Peace Commission of the Hong Kong Catholic Diocese, July 1995. An abridged version of this book together with the original text was distributed to Catholics in all the parishes of the diocese to help Catholics choose candidates according to their merits and performance. Another booklet provided was *Xuanju yu Ni* (The election and you). Hong Kong: Justice and Peace Commission of the Hong Kong Catholic Diocese, July 1995.
20. This was revealed by Msgr. Claudio Celli, Director of China Desk, State Council, Vatican, when he was interviewed in March 1986.
21. Beatrice Leung, 'The Catholic Bridging Effort with China', *Religion, State and Society* (UK) 28 (June 2000): 185–95.
22. Circular on 'Stepping Up Control Over the Catholic Church to Meet the New Situation', Central Office Document, 1989, no. 3 (produced by the Central Office of the CCP with the State Council and transmitted to the Central Government's United Front and Religious Affairs Bureau of the State Council). See Beatrice Leung (1992, 376–83).
23. *Sunday Examiner*, 5 July 1996; *Yi: China Message* (issue 166) XV–XVII, 6 (August 1996): 12–3.
24. *Asian Focus* 13, 18 (9 May 1997).
25. *Ta Kung Pao*, 1 September 1984.
26. *Ta Kung Pao*, 17 April 1984.
27. *Ta Kung Pao*, 1 September 1984.
28. There were initially four delegates of Protestant leaders on the trip to Beijing. One of the delegates, Reverend Philip Teng (滕近輝) who represented the evangelical churches, was absent on the trip.
29. *Ta Kung Pao*, 8 September 1984.
30. On 25 October 1998, the Hong Kong *Sheng Kung Hui* was established as the 38th Province of the Anglican Communion, and Peter Kwong was installed as the Archbishop of the Hong Kong *Sheng Kung Hui* at the Grand Hall of the Hong Kong Convention and Exhibition Centre.
31. *South China Morning Post*, 7 January 1986.
32. *South China Morning Post*, 24 July 1997.
33. *Ecumenical News International Bulletin* 14, 23 July 1997, 34.
34. *Ibid.*
35. *South China Morning Post*, 24 July 1997.
36. *South China Morning Post*, 5 January 1981.
37. *Wen Wei Po*, 9 December 1981.
38. See open letter of the Joint Committee for Monitoring Public Facilities.
39. *Christian Weekly* 861, 22 February 1981, 2.

40. The speeches made at the forum were later compiled into a book. See Commission on Public Policy, Hong Kong Christian Council (1982).
41. *Wahkiu Yatbo*, 26 February 1984.
42. In the Hong Kong Christian Council 1987 newsletter, there were articles discussing the problems of immigration in the Church. See 'Face the Problems of Immigration' [正視移民], *Message*, October 1987.
43. See Christian Sentinels for Hong Kong (1988). Christian Sentinels was also a member of the Joint Committee for the Promotion of Democratic Government (JCPDG).
44. *Hong Kong Economic Journal*, 22 January 1986; *South China Morning Post*, 28 January 1986.
45. *Wahkiu Yatbo*, 11–13 February 1986.
46. Those who issued the statement included: the Hong Kong Student Christian Movement, the Social Concern Group in the Society of Religion of the Chinese University of Hong Kong, West Kowloon Community Church, Fellowship of Theological Graduates, Christian Social Concern Fellowship of Tsuen Wan and Kwai Chung, Social Concern Fellowship of Shum Oi Church, Church Workers Association, Society of Chung Chi Theology Division Students, and the Community Church of Kwun Tong. See Chui (1992, 34).
47. In *The Draft of the Basic Law*, it was stated that religious organizations in China and Hong Kong should comply with the three principles of mutual non-subordination, mutual non-interference and mutual respect.
48. See also *Ming Pao*, 5 August 1988; *Kuai Bao*, 5 August 1988; *South China Morning Post*, 5 August 1988.
49. See *Hong Kong Economic Journal*, 5 October 1987; *Hong Kong Standard*, 28 December 1987; *South China Morning Post*, 31 August 1988; *Hong Kong Economic Times*, 2 September 1988; *Oriental Daily*, 12 September 1988; *Christian Times Weekly* 58, 9 October 1988.
50. *Hong Kong Economic Journal*, 5 October 1987.
51. *Hong Kong Economic Journal*, 1 May 1988.
52. *Hong Kong Standard*, 3 December 1987; *South China Morning Post*, 12 December 1987; *South China Morning Post*, 15 December 1987.

Chapter 6   The Hong Kong SAR Government and the Catholic Church

1. Of 114 schools, 100 were requested by the Government to teach in English while 14 were granted this privilege after an appeal.
2. The policy however proved unsuccessful when in November 2000, the government allowed ten Chinese-medium schools to have one out of ten courses taught in English. The Hong Kong educated Nobel Prize winner, Professor Cui Qi, suggested bilingual education was best for Hong Kong. See *Ming Pao*, 7 December 2000.

3. A number of mission school principals and supervisors of religious congregations who run prestigious mission schools did not agree with the change to mother tongue teaching as the means to resolve the language problem among Hong Kong students.

4. Archbishop Adam Exner of Vancouver, Canada also attended this synod because ethnic Asians constitute two thirds of his region.

5. 'Excerpts from Pope John Paul II's Homily at the Asian Synod's Opening Mass', *Tripod* 105, May-June 1998, 26–8.

6. *Sunday Examiner*, 3 May 1998; *Kung Kao Po*, 3 May 1998; 'Intervention of Coadjutor Bishop of Hong Kong, Joseph Zen', *Tripod* 105, May-June 1998, 38–40.

7. *Ibid.*

8. 'Intervention of John Tong, Auxiliary Bishop of Hong Kong', *Tripod* 105, May-June 1998, 41–4.

9. Bishop Zen said that he was politely but firmly told not to visit seminaries in China. The interview was held in February 1998.

10. For details of the bridging effort see Beatrice Leung, 'Inter-Church Relations Within the Universal Church: A Study of Bridging Efforts with China'. Paper presented at the Third European Catholic China Conference 'The Catholic Church in China — Message, Response and Commitment', 15–19 September 1999, Krynica Morska, Poland.

11. *Hong Kong Economic Journal*, 7 June 1999.

12. Callers on radio phone-in programs were very vocal.

13. *Kung Kao Po*, 13 June 1999.

14. *Kung Kao Po*, 16 May 1999; 30 May 1999; 13 June 1999; and 20 June 1999.

15. *Ming Pao*, 17 June 1999.

16. *Ming Pao*, 26 June 1999.

17. *Sunday Examiner*, 4 July 1999.

18. *Sunday Examiner*, 8 August 1999.

19. *Ibid.*

20. See chapter 4 of this book for a detailed discussion of this question.

21. *Kung Kao Po*, 25 July 1999.

22. *Kung Kao Po*, 18 July 1999.

23. 'An Interview Report on Bishop Joseph Zen', *Kung Kao Po*, 8 July 1999.

24. The years between 1984, the year of the signing of the Sino-British Agreement on the Future of Hong Kong to 1 July 1997 were called the transitional period.

25. See chapter 4 of this book for a detailed discussion of this question.

26. *Hong Kong Economic Journal*, 10 August 1999; *Ming Pao*, 10 August 1999.

27. *South China Morning Post*, 10 August 1999.

28. In their August issues, *Economist, Asiaweek* and *Times* all commented on this event.

29. Lin is regarded as a leading Chinese critic in Hong Kong on socio-political as well as economic affairs (translation by the author).

30. *Kung Kao Po* and *Sunday Examiner*, 18 July 1999.

31. *South China Morning Post*, 10 August 1999.
32. Falun Gong is a combination of breathing exercises, Buddhism and Taoism. The CCP from April to September 1999 tried hard to eliminate it due to its defiant nature. See Beatrice Leung, 'China and Falun Gong : Party and Society Relations in the Modern Era'. *Journal of Contemporary China* 11, 33 (2002:761–84). See Shaw (1999, 17). The struggle between the CCP and Falun Gong received wide coverage in international media publications, for example, *Time, The Economist, Far Eastern Economic Review, New York Times, Asian Week*, and others.
33. *Renmin Ribao,* 1 October 2000.
34. *Xinhua*, 2 October 2000.
35. The story was featured on *TVB News Hong Kong*, 1 October 2000. Unless the Chinese clerics and religious sisters were commanded by the government to attend the early morning (6:00 am) National Day (1 October 2000) Flag Raising Ceremony, they would not go there voluntarily by themselves because it is their general practice to be engaged in morning prayers and/or morning mass between 6:00–8:00 am before breakfast and before they start their daily work.
36. *Xinhua*, 26 September, 2 October 2000. Reported in 'News in Brief'. *Religions in China* 24, 5 (October 2000): 33–6.
37. Several international mass media organizations asked Beatrice Leung to comment on whether they are saints or criminals, and on who was correct — the Vatican or Beijing authorities?
38. Some Hong Kong Catholics gave these opinions when interviewed in October 2000.
39. *Sunday Examiner*, 15 October 2000. The original article, written in Chinese, was published by *Ming Pao*, 4 October. *Sunday Examiner* published the English translation.
40. Two days later, both *Kung Kao Po* and *Sunday Examiner*, 6 October 2000 issues both published Bishop Zen's article.
41. *Sunday Examiner*, 15 October 2000.
42. *Hong Kong Economic Journal*, 6 October 2000.
43. Robert Chung publicly revealed that he had been asked by the Hong Kong University President to stop releasing the results of opinion polls on the public image of the Chief Executive. A public hearing was held at the University of Hong Kong in March 2000 and the process was made public. The President of the University resigned when the public accused him of not only failing to protect academic freedom, but of bending to pressure from a private assistant of the Chief Executive. The academic community at the University of Hong Kong demanded his resignation. The case was widely covered by international and local news media.
44. *Hong Kong Economic Journal* and *Ming Pao*, 9 November 2000.
45. On the struggle between the Party-Catholic in organizational control see: Beatrice Leung, 'Sino-Vatican Interplay of Institution Control: in Preparing Church Leaders', manuscript.

46. Revealed by a Chinese bishop when interviewed in July 2000.

47. Beatrice Leung, 'China and Falun Gong: Party and Society Relations in the Modern Era'. *Journal of Contemporary China* 11, 33 (2002:761–84).

48. *Hong Kong Economic Journal*, 10 February 2001.

49. *Kung Kao Po*, 17 June 2001, editorial.

50. S. Lee (2001). Major Chinese newspapers in Hong Kong covered the clash between Bishop Zen and the SAR Government. See also *Apple Daily*, *Oriental Daily*, and *Ming Pao*, 8 December 2001.

51. Much is written about Bishop Zen's desire to employ 'civil disobedience' as means to fight for the schooling of these children. See *Apple Daily*, *Oriental Daily*, *Ming Pao*, 19 December 2001.

52 Nearly all newspapers in Hong Kong covered the news and gave analysis. *Apple Daily* (24 September 2002, editorial) was pro-bishop and the church; *Wen Wei Po* (24 September 2002) was pro-China. *Sing Tao Daily* (25 September 2002) struck the middle ground. *Sunday Examiner* collected views of church-related persons on Zen's stance (27 October 2002, 3).

53 *South China Morning Post*, 21 September 2002.

54 Liang Yin-cheng, 'C. H. Tung's Prejudice on Religion', *Hong Kong Economic Journal,* 12 October 2002, 22.

55 *Kung Kao Pao*, 3 October 2002, 1.

56 *Kung Kao Pao*, 27 October 2002, 1, 23–4.

57 Security Bureau, *Proposal to Implement Article 23 of the Basic Law: Summary of Consultation Document*. Hong Kong: Security Bureau, Hong Kong SAR Government. September 2002.

58 Ambrose Leung, 'Date is Set for Draft Bill on Article 23', *South China Morning Post*, 12 December 2002.

59. Explained by a Hong Kong priest who is close to Catholic top leaders.

60. Bishop Joseph Zen expressed this opinion to one of the authors when he was interviewed in October 2000.

61. On 5 March 2001, Bishop Zen was invited to give a lecture to the General Education Program at Hong Kong University. That month he was also guest speaker at a luncheon organized by the Hong Kong Democratic Foundation.

62. Pro-China priests such as Fr. Luke Tsui, openly disagreed with the political stance of Zen. See Ambrose Leung, 'Discordant Voice in the Church Choir', *South China Morning Post*, 8 January 2002.

63. *Kung Kao Po*, 23 May 1999.

64. *Kung Kao Po* and *Sunday Examiner*, 25 July 1999.

Chapter 7　The Hong Kong SAR Government and Protestant Churches

1. Raymond Fung, who called on Gideon Yung, Lo Lung-kwong and Kwok Nai-wang

to discuss the matter, proposed the idea of the National Day Celebration. See Yu (1997).

2. According to Raymond Fung, the Christian National Day celebration was based on a 'priesthood theology'. He explained, 'The Church should fulfill its priestly duties and petition God on behalf of the nation. A priest raises the cup of thanksgiving to God, not to the political regime. He offers repentance, intercession and joyous thanksgiving on behalf of the nation rather than singing the praises of the regime in power.' See R. Fung (1996a).

3. *Ming Pao*, 8 May 1996, A1.

4. *Christian Times Weekly* 457, 2 June 1996, 1–2.

5. *Ibid.*

6. *Ming Pao*, 1 June 1996.

7. The seven Christian groups were: the Hong Kong Christian Institute, Hong Kong Student Christian Movement, Christians for Hong Kong Society, Hong Kong Women's Christian Council, Hong Kong Christian Industrial Committee, Catholic Youth Council and the Justice and Peace Commission of the Hong Kong Catholic Diocese.

8. *Ming Pao*, 15 June 1996; *Hong Kong Economic Journal*, 15 June 1996.

9. *Ibid.*

10. *Hong Kong Economic Journal*, 1 July 1996.

11. *Ibid.*

12. *Christian Times Weekly* 462, 7 July 1996.

13. *Hong Kong Economic Journal*, 1 July 1996.

14. *Ming Pao*, 1 July 1996.

15. *Christian Times Weekly* 462, 7 July 1996.

16. *Hong Kong Economic Journal*, 1 July 1996.

17. *Christian Times Weekly* 475, 6 October 1996, 1.

18. *Christian Times Weekly* 528, 12 October 1997, 2.

19. *Christian Times Weekly* 528, 12 October 1997, 2. The Christian groups who issued the statement were: the Hong Kong Christian Institute, Hong Kong Women's Christian Council, Christians for Hong Kong Society, and the Hong Kong Student Christian Movement. *Christian Times Weekly* 538, 21 December 1997, 2.

20. See 'Representing Christianity, What Do They Represent?' *Ming Pao*, 12 January 1998. The undersigned of the article include: Hong Kong Christian Institute, Hong Kong Women's Christian Council, Christians for Hong Kong Society, Hong Kong Student Christian Movement, Hong Kong Christian Industrial Committee, and the Church Workers' Association.

21. See the open letter on Christian General Election, 1.

22. The speaker is Reverend Luk Fai of the Church of Christ in China. See *Christian Times Weekly* 545, 8 February 1998, 2.

23. Raymond Fung wrote an article to clarify the position of the church leaders who supported the Christian General Election with the name 'Fung Yuen' in *Ming Pao*.

See Fung Yuen (1998).

24. *Christian Times Weekly* 551, 22 March 1998, 1.

25. *Christian Times Weekly* 560, 24 May 1998, 1.

26. See the special issue: 'A Small Election of A Very Select Circle' [非常圈子小選舉]. *Ming Pao Weekly* 1534, 4 April 1998.

27. *Ming Pao*, 25 December 1999, A03.

28. *Ming Pao*, 25 December 2001, A02.

29. *Ming Pao*, 8 May 1999.

30. *Apple Daily*, 7 June 1999, A14.

31. *Christian Times Weekly* 616, 20 June 1999, 1.

32. *Ming Pao*, 9 February 2001, A07.

33 *Ming Pao*, 11 February 2001, A04.

34. *Ming Pao*, 7 May 2001, A13.

35. See various issues of *Zhu Guang Wan Luo* [燭光網絡], newsletter of the Society for Truth and Light.

36. See *Ming Pao*, 17 May 2002, A23 and 31 May 2002, A33. The Evangelical Free Church of China, which is considered among some Protestant circles to be 'fundamentalist', also spoke openly on the issues. *Ming Pao*, 21 May 2002, B14.

37. Sociological literature shows that the social movement organized by the evangelical churches have always been associated with right-wing Protestantism, otherwise known as the Christian Right. The Christian Right has tended to be in conflict with the social movements organized by the mainstream Protestant churches, or left wing Protestantism. See Wilcox (1992) and Herman (1997). The relation between the Christian Right and democracy in the United States context, see Jeffrey Isaac, Matthew Filner and Jason Bivins (1999).

Chapter 8 Summary and Conclusions

1. In the February and March issues of *Kung Kao Po*, Bishop Zen debated with a priest columnist on the issue of Sino-Vatican relations. Later a lay Catholic joined the debate.

Bibliography

Abbott, Walter. 1966, ed. *Document of Vatican II*. New York: Guild Press.

Baird, David. 1970a. 'Thy Will be Done'. *Far Eastern Economic Review*, 29 January.

_____. 1970b. 'Hong Kong: Christian in Revolt'. *Far Eastern Economic Review*, 21 May.

Barth, Karl. 1960. *Community, State, and Church: Three Essays*. Garden City, New York: Doubleday.

Bradley, Gerard V. 1987. *Church-State Relationships in America*. New York: Greenwood Press.

Brown, Deborah A. 1996. 'The Role of Religion in Promoting Democracy in the People's Republic of China and Hong Kong.' Pp. 79–114 in *Church and State Relations in 21st Century Asia*, edited by Beatrice Leung. Hong Kong: Centre of Asian Studies, the University of Hong Kong.

Calhoun, Craig. 1993. 'Civil Society and the Public Sphere.' *Public Culture* 5: 267–80.

Carino, Feliciano V. 1981. *Church, State and People, the Philippines in the 1980s: Report and Papers of a National Theological Dialogue, Manila, Philippines, November 10–13, 1980*. Singapore: The Commission on Theological Concerns, Christian Conference of Asia.

Chan, Alan Chor-choi. 1988. 'Bashi Niandai Xianggang Jiaohui Lianhe Sheguan Xingdong: Yidian Fansi' ['Reflections on the collaborative social concern actions of the churches in Hong Kong in the eighties']. *Si* [Reflection] 1: 11–3.
陳佐才。1988。〈八十年代香港教會聯合社關行動 —— 一點反思〉。《思》，第1期，頁11–3。

Chan, Che-po and Beatrice Leung. 1996. 'The Voting Behaviour of the Hong Kong Catholics in the 1995 Legislative Council Election'. Pp. 315–52 in *The 1995 Legislative Council Election in Hong Kong*, edited by Kuan Hsin-chi et al. Hong Kong: Hong Kong Institute of Asia-Pacific Studies, the Chinese University of Hong Kong.

———. 2000. 'The Voting Propensity of Hong Kong Christians: Individual Disposition, Church Influence, and the China Factor'. *Journal for Scientific Study of Religion* 39(3): 297–306.

Chan, Ka-wai. 1996. 'Jiaohui Haoxin zuo Huaishi' ['Evil result derives from the Church's good intention']. *Christian Times Weekly* 474, 29 September, 9.

陳家偉。1996。〈教會好心做壞事〉。《基督教時代論壇週報》，第 474 期。9月29日。頁 9。

———. 1996. 'Shuiren shi Jiaohui yu Qunzhong Gejue' ['Who is separating the Church from the people']. *Christian Times Weekly* 479, 3 November, 12.

陳家偉。1996。〈誰人使教會與群眾隔絕？〉。《基督教時代論壇週報》，第 479 期。11月3日。頁 12。

Chan, Shun-hing. 1995. 'Xianggang Zhengjiao Quanxi Fazhan de Qianjing' ['The future of Church-State relations in Hong Kong']. Pp. 139–148 in *Jidujiao Xinyang yu Xianggang Shehui Fazhan [Christian Faith and the Development of Hong Kong Society]*, edited by Agatha M.Y. Wong. Hong Kong: Hong Kong Christian Institute.

陳慎慶。1995。〈香港政教關係發展的前景〉。《基督教信仰與香港社會發展》，黃美玉編。香港：香港基督徒學會。頁 139–48。

———. 1997a. 'Gongmin Shehui Fazhan Cuoshi Liangji' ['Lost opportunity in building a civil society']. *Christian Times Weekly* 538, 21 December, 10.

陳慎慶。1997a。〈公民社會發展錯失良機〉。《基督教時代論壇週報》，第 538 期。12月21日。頁 10。

———. 1997b. 'Zai Tequ Chujing xia zuo "Zhongcairen"' ['To play the role as an arbiter in the Hong Kong SAR']. *Christian Times Weekly* 539, 28 December, 10.

陳慎慶。1997b。〈在特區處境下作「仲裁人」〉。《基督教時代論壇週報》，第 539 期。12月28日。頁 10。

———. 1998a. 'Xianggang Jidujiao Shehui Fuli Shiye de Fazhan' ['The development of Christian social service in Hong Kong']. *China Graduate School of Theology Journal* 25: 65–85.

陳慎慶。1998a。〈香港基督教社會福利事業的發展〉。《中國神學研究院期刊》，第 25 期。頁 65–85。

———. 1998b. 'Dui Jidujiao jie Puxuan Shijian de Pinglun (1)' ['Comment on the Christian General Election (1)']. *Christian Times Weekly* 570, 2 August, 9.

陳慎慶。1998b。〈對基督教界普選事件的評論 (1)〉。《基督教時代論壇週報》，第 570 期。8月2日。頁 9。

———. 1998c. 'Dui Jidujiao jie Puxuan Shijian de Pinglun (2)' ['Comment on the Christian General Election (2)']. *Christian Times Weekly* 571, 9 August, 9.

陳慎慶。1998c。〈對基督教界普選事件的評論（2）〉。《基督教時代論壇週報》，第 571 期。8月9日。頁 9。

_____. 1999a. 'Zongjiao, Daode yu Shehui Zhixu: Tu'ergan Shehui Lilun de Dangdai Lunshu' ['Religion, morality and social order: Emile Durkheim's Social Theory in contemporary perspectives']. *Logos and Pneuma* 10: 167–83.

陳慎慶。1999a。〈宗教、道德與社會秩序：涂爾幹社會理論的當代論述〉。《道風》，第 10 期。頁 167–183。

_____. 1999b. 'Zhongguo Zongjiao, Zibenzhuyi yu Xiandai Wenming: Weibo de Gongxian yu Juxian' ['Chinese religion, capitalism and modern civilization: the contributions and limitations of Max Weber']. *Journal of Social Theory* 2(2): 267–89.

陳慎慶。1999b。〈中國宗教、資本主義與現代文明：韋伯的貢獻與局限〉。《社會理論學報》，2(2)。頁 267–89。

_____. 2000a. 'Nationalism and Religious Protest the Case of the National Day Celebration Service Controversy in the Hong Kong Protestant Churches.' *Religion, State and Society* 28(4): 359–383.

_____. 2000b. 'Minzhu Guodu yu Gonggu: Jiduzongjiao zai Ladingmeizhou de Gongxian' ['Democratic transition and consolidation: the contributions of Christianity in Latin America']. Pp. 221–47 in *Jidujiao yu Jingdai Zhongxi Wenhua* [Christianity and modern Chinese-Western culture], edited by Lo Ping-cheung and Zhao Dun-hua. Beijing: Beijing University Press.

陳慎慶。2000b。〈民主過渡與鞏固：基督宗教在拉丁美洲的貢獻〉。《基督教與近代中西文化》，羅秉祥、趙敦華編。北京：北京大學出版社。頁 221–47。

Chan, Shun-hing and Anthony Lam Sui-ki. 2000. 'Dangdai Zhongguo Zhengjiao Guanxi de Zhuanbian yu Fazhan: Tianzhujiao Jiaohui de Gean Yanjiu' ['The transformation and development of Church-State relations in contemporary China: A case study of the Catholic Church']. *Hong Kong Journal of Sociology* 1: 103–29.

陳慎慶、林瑞琪。2000。〈當代中國政教關係的轉變與發展：天主教教會的個案研究〉。《香港社會學學報》，第 1 期。頁 103–29。

Chan, Sze-chi. 1998. 'Mushi Suowei Heshi? Jiaonei Puxuan zhi Shenxue Pinglun' ['What should the clergy do? Theological criticism of the General Election in the Protestant Church']. *Christian Times Weekly* 550, 15 March, 9.

陳士齊。1998。〈牧師所為何事？教內普選之神學評論〉。《基督教時代論壇週報》，第 550 期。3月15日。頁 9。

Chan, Yi-li. 1996. 'Cong Jidutu de Shuangchong Shenfen kan Guoqing Wenti' ['Look into the problems of National Day Celebration from Christian's double identities']. *Christian Times Weekly* 470, 1 September, 8.

陳以理。1996。〈從基督徒的雙重身份看慶祝國慶問題〉。《基督教時代論壇週報》，第 470 期。9月1日。頁 8。

Chang, Joyce S. H. 1996. 'Jiaohui cong Shehui Fuwu Huiying Shehui Bianqian de Tantao' ['A study of Catholic's response to social change: Catholic social service']. Pp. 209–24 in *Shehui Bianqian yu Jiaohui Huiying: Jiaoliuhui Lunweiji* [Church response to rapidly changing society], edited by Cheung Ka-hing. Hong Kong: Catholic Institute for Religion and Society.

陳秀嫻。1996。〈教會從社會服務回應社會變遷的探討〉。《社會變遷與教會回應：交流會論文集》，張家興編。香港：公教教研中心。頁 209–24。

Cheng, Yuk-tin. 1998. 'Qishi Weiyi de Lu? Ping Xianggang Jidujiao Xiejinhui dui Lifahui Xuanju Weiyuanhui de Lichang' ['Is it the only way? Comment on the position of the Hong Kong Christian Council on the Legco Election Committee']. *Christian Times Weekly* 548, 1 March, 8.

鄭鈺鈿。1998。〈豈是唯一的路 —— 評香港基督教協進會對立法會選舉委員會的立場〉。《基督教時代論壇週報》，第 548 期。3月1日。頁 8。

Ching, Frank. 1999. 'Scare Tactics.' *Far Eastern Economic Review*, May, 18.

Chow, Nelson. 1984. *Xianggang Shehui Fuli Zhengce Pingxi* [A study of Hong Kong's social welfare policy]. Hong Kong: Cosmos Books.

周永新。1984。《香港社會福利政策評析》。香港：天地圖書有限公司。

Christian Communications Ltd, ed. 1984. *Sanzi yu Xianggang Jiaohui Qianjing* [The Three-Self's and the prospects of the churches in Hong Kong]. Hong Kong: Christian Communications Ltd.

福音證主協會編。1984。《三自與香港教會前景》。香港：福音證主協會。

Christian for Hong Kong Society. 1998. 'Ma jiushi Ma, Lu jiushi Lu: Ping "Jidujaojie" Puxuan' ['A horse is a horse. A deer is a deer: Comment on Christian General Election']. *Christian Times Weekly* 550, 15 March, 8.

基督徒關懷香港學會。1998。〈馬就是馬、鹿就是鹿：評「基督教界普選」〉。《基督教時代論壇週報》，第 550 期。3月15日。頁 8。

Christian Sentinels for Hong Kong. 1988. *Guoduqi de Xianggang: Zhengzhi, Jingji, Shehui* [Hong Kong in transition: Politics, economy and society]. Hong Kong: Wide Angle Press Limited.

基督徒香港守望社。1988。《過渡期的香港：政治、經濟、社會》。香港：廣角鏡出版社有限公司。

Christian Social Groups. 1996. 'Yihan Xiejinhui Jiaru Tuiweihui' ['We condemn the Hong Kong Christian Council for taking part in the Selection Committee']. *Ming Pao*, 24 May.

基督徒前線團體。1996。〈遺憾協進會加入推委會〉。《明報》。5月24日。

Chu, Yiu-ming. 1996. 'Huigui Lushang' ['The road to reunification'] (in 4 parts). *Christian Times Weekly* 463–67 (14, 21 and 28 July, and 4 August): 2.

朱耀明。1996。〈回歸路上〉。《基督教時代論壇週報》(分四節)，第 463–67 期。7月14、21、28日及8月4日。頁 2。

Chui, Jane C. L. 1992. *Huiying Jiuqi: Jidutu Qunti de Jianzheng* [Some Christian responses on 1997 issues]. Hong Kong: Hong Kong Christian Institute.

徐珍妮。1992。《回應九七：基督徒群體的見證》。香港：香港基督徒學會。

Commission on Public Policy, Hong Kong Christian Council, ed. 1982. *Xianggang Jiaohui yu Xianggang Qiantu* [Hong Kong churches and Hong Kong future]. Hong Kong: Communications Department, Commission on Public Policy of Hong Kong Christian Council.

香港基督教協進會公共政策委員會編。1982。《香港教會與香港前途》。香港：香港基督教協進會公共政策委員會新聞部。

Copithorne, Maurice. 1998. 'The Last Governor: Chris Patten and the Handover of Hong Kong'. *Pacific Affairs*, 71(3): 416–19.

Curry, Thomas J. 1986. *The First Freedoms: Church and State in America to the Passage of the First Amendment.* New York: Oxford University Press.

Demerath III, N.J. and Rhys H. Williams. 1987. Pp. 77–90 in *Church-State Relations: Tensions and Transitions*, edited by Thomas Robbins and Roland Robertson. New Brunswick: Transaction Books.

Document Centre of Party Central and Policy Section of Religious Affairs Bureau, ed. 1995. Xinshiqi Zongjiao Gongzuo Wenxian Xuanbian [Selected documents on religious work of new age]. Beijing: Zongjiao Wenhua Press.
中共中央文獻研究室綜合研究組，國務院宗教事務局政策法規司編。1995。《新時期宗教工作文獻選編》。北京：宗教文化出版社。

'Draft Agreement between the Government of the United Kingdom and North Ireland and the Government of the People's Republic of China on the Future of Hong Kong'. 26 September 1984.

Dunbabin, J. P. D. 1994. *The Post Imperial Age: the Great Power and the Wider World.* New York: Longman.

England, Joe. 1971. 'Industrial Relations in Hong Kong'. Pp. 207–59 in *Hong Kong: the Industrial Colony*, edited by Keith Hopkins. Hong Kong: Oxford University Press.

England, Joe and John Rear. 1975. *Chinese Labour Under British Rule.* Hong Kong: Oxford University Press.

Fan, Chung-lau. 1996. 'Jiaohui Congsu ban Guoqing' ['Church to hold National Day Celebration in concurrence with popular trends']. *Hong Kong Economic Journal*, 7 June.
范中流。1996。〈教會從俗辦國慶〉。《信報》。6月7日。

Fang, Hao. 1977. *The Late Bishop Francis Hsu's Letters: An Incomplete Collection.* Tainan: Window Press.

Feige, Franz G. M. 1990. *The Varieties of Protestantism in Nazi Germany: Five Theological Positions.* Lewiston, NY: E. Mellon Press.

Feldman, Stephen M. 1997. *Please Don't Wish Me a Merry Christmas: A Critical History of the Separation of Church and State.* New York: New York University Press.

Fleet, Michael. 1985. *The Rise and Fall of Chilean Christian Democracy.* New Jersey: Princeton University Press.

Fleet, Michael and Brian H. Smith. 1997. *The Catholic Church and Democracy in Chile and Peru.* Notre Dame, Indiana: University of Notre Dame Press.

Fosh, Patricia, et al. 1999. 'Government Supervision of Trade Unions in Hong Kong: Colonial Powers, Patterns of Enforcement and Prospects for Change.' Pp. 239–54 in *Hong Kong Management and Labour: Change and Continuity*, edited by Patricia Fosh et al. London: Routledge.

Fung, Raymond. 1996a. 'Jishi xiang Shen Jubei' ['Raising the cup of thanksgiving: To God as his priest']. *Christian Times Weekly* 455, 19 May, 10.
馮煒文。1996a。〈祭師向神舉杯〉。《基督教時代論壇週報》，第 455 期。5月19日。頁 10。

———. 1996b. 'Jinle Shen de Yi Hou' ['After Fulfilling our Duties to God']. *Christian Times Weekly* 456, 26 May, 10.
馮煒文。1996b。〈盡了神的義後〉。《基督教時代論壇週報》，第 456 期。5月26日。頁 10。

———. 1996c. 'Weishenmo zai Jiuliu?' ['Why in 1996?'] *Christian Times Weekly* 460, 23 June, 10.
馮煒文。1996c。〈為甚麼在九六？〉。《基督教時代論壇週報》，第 460 期。6月23日。頁 10。

———. 1996d. 'Cizhi bao Caoshou' ['Sit should resign so that he could preserve his personal integrity']. *Christian Times Weekly* 485, 15 December, 10.
馮煒文。1996d。〈辭職保操守〉。《基督教時代論壇週報》，第 485 期。12月15日。頁 10。

———. 1998. 'Jiaonei Puxuan shitiao zenyang de Lu?' ['Where will the Christian General Election lead?'] *Christian Times Weekly* 550, 15 March, 8.
馮煒文。1998。〈教內普選是條怎樣的路？〉。《基督教時代論壇週報》，第 550 期。3月15日。頁 8。

Fung, Yuen. 1998. 'Minzhu Jincheng de Dongli' ['The dynamic of democratization process']. *Ming Pao*, 30 March.
馮元。1998。〈民主進程的動力〉。《明報》。3月30日。

Goodstadt, Leo F. 1967. 'Red Guards in Hong Kong.' *Far Eastern Economic Review*, 16–22 July.

Gill, Anthony. 1998. *Rendering unto Caesar: the Catholic Church and the State in Latin America*. Chicago: the University of Chicago Press.

Grassroots Christians. 1996. 'Aiguo de Beihou' ['Behind patriotism']. *Ming Pao*, 1 July.
一群基層基督教友。1996。〈「愛國」的背後〉。《明報》。7月1日。

Green Paper: The Further Development of Representative Government in Hong Kong. Hong Kong: Government Printer, 1984.

Ha, Louis. 1992. 'Catholicism in Hong Kong.' Pp. 527–41 in *The Other Hong Kong Report 1991*, edited by Sung Yun-wing and Lee Ming-kwan. Hong Kong: Hong Kong University Press.

Hamilton, Malcolm. 1998. *Sociology and the World's Religions*. London: Macmillan Press.

Hanson, Eric O. 1980. *Catholic Politics in China and Korea*. Maryknoll, NY: Orbis Books.

Herman, Didi. 1997. *The Antigay Agenda: Orthodox Vision and the Christian Right*. Chicago: University of Chicago Press.

Ho, Man-cheung. 1996. ' "Huigui Lushang" Jiaomu Tonggong Yantaohui Hougan'

['Reflections on the "Road to Reunification" Forum for clergy']. *Christian Times Weekly* 458, 9 June, 8.

何文祥。1996。〈「回歸路上」教牧同工研討會後感〉。《基督教時代論壇週報》，第 458 期。6月9日。頁 8。

Hong Kong Diocesan Convention. n.d. *Social Dimension of the Church*. Hong Kong: Diocesan Convention.

Hong Kong Diocesan Office. 1974. *The Diocese of Hong Kong and Macao 1949–1974: A Brief History and the 1974 List of Churches, Primary Schools and Secondary Schools, Social Welfare Centres*. Hong Kong: Hong Kong Diocesan Office.

Hong Kong Government. 1956. *Report on the Kowloon and Tsuen Wan Riots: 10–12th October, 1956*. Hong Kong: Cheng Ya.

Hong Kong Government, Commission of Inquiry. 1967. *Kowloon Disturbance 1966*. Hong Kong: Government Printer.

Hong Kong Welfare Department. 1972. *Plans for the Future Development of Hong Kong's Social Welfare*. Hong Kong: Hong Kong Government Printer.

Hong Kong Welfare Department. 1973. *The Five Year Plan for Social Welfare Development in Hong Kong, 1973–1978*. Hong Kong: Hong Kong Government Printer.

Howard, A. E. Dick. 1985. 'The Wall of Separation: the Supreme Court as Uncertain Stonemanson'. Pp. 85–118 in *Religion and the State: Essays in Honor of Leo Pfeffer*, edited by James E. Wood, Jr. Waco, TX: Baylor University Press.

Isaac, Jeffrey C., Matthew F. Filner, and Jason C. Bivins. 1999. 'American Democracy and the New Christian Right: A Critique of Apolitical Liberalism.' Pp. 222–64 in *Democracy's Edges*, edited by Ian Shapiro and Casiano Hacker-Cordón. Cambridge: Cambridge University Press.

Jiang, Zemin. 1992. 'Seminar on Party Theory'. Pp. 1–2 in *Dangwei Gongzuo Daquan*, edited by Li Zonglin et al. Beijing: Chinese Broadcast Press.

Jungel, Eberhard. 1992. *Christ, Justice and Peace: Toward a Theology of the State in Dialogue with the Barmen Declaration*. Edinburgh: T & T Clark.

Kang, Xiaogang. 1999. *Quanli de Zhuanyi* [The transfer of power]. Hanzhou: Zhejiang Renmin Chubanshe.

康曉光。1999。《權力的轉移》。杭州：浙江人民出版社。

Kei, Wan-sze. 1986. 'Huiying Xin Weisi zhi "Jibenfa yu Zongjiao Ziyou"' ['Response to Xin Weisi's "Basic Law and Religious Freedom"']. *Ming Pao*, 16 December.

姬雲思。1986。〈回應辛維思之「基本法與宗教自由」〉。《明報》。12月16日。

Ko, Tinming. 2000. *The Sacred Citizens and the Secular City: Political Participation of Protestant Ministers in Hong Kong during a Time of Change*. Aldershot: Ashgate.

Kwok, Nai-wang. 1993. *Wei Zhecheng qiu Shengming* [Seeking spirituality in a precarious city]. Hong Kong: Hong Kong Christian Institute.

郭乃弘。1993。《為這城求生命》。香港：香港基督徒學會。

_____. 1994. 'Jidujiao zai Xianggang Fazhan de Juese he Renwu' ['The role and mission of Christianity in Hong Kong's social development']. Pp. 75–93 in *Xianggang Jiaohui yu Shehui Yundong: Bashi Niandai de Fensi* [Social Movement and the Christian Church in Hong Kong: Reflections on the 1980s], edited by Shun-hing Chan. Hong Kong: Hong Kong Christian Institute.
郭乃弘。1994。〈基督教在香港發展的角色和任務〉。《香港教會與社會運動：八十年代的反思》，陳慎慶編。香港：香港基督徒學會。頁75–93。

_____. 1997. 'Jiaohui buying jiaru Xuanwei' ['The Church should not take part in the Election Committee']. *Ming Pao*, 27 December.
郭乃弘。1997。〈教會不應加入選委〉。《明報》。12月27日。

Kwok, Wai-luen. 2002. 'Qishi Niandai Xianggang Fuyinpai Qingnian Jidutu zhi Shehui Canyu' ['The social participation of Hong Kong young evangelicals in the seventies']. *China Graduate School of Theology Journal* 32: 145–90.
郭偉聯。2002。〈七十年代香港福音派青年基督徒之社會參與〉。《中國神學研究院期刊》，第32期。頁145–90。

Lam, Anthony Sui-ki. 1997. *The Catholic Church in Present-Day China*. Hong Kong and Leuven: Holy Spirit Study Centre and Ferdinand Verbiest Foundation.

Lam, Chi-shing. 1988. 'Miandui Jiuqi: Zongjiao Tuanti Juese de Mosuo' ['Facing up to 1997: Exploring the role of religious organization']. *Breakthrough Magazine* 159 (January-February): 4–5.
林志成。1988。〈面對九七：宗教團體角色的摸索〉。《突破雜誌》，第159期（1–2月）。頁4–5。

Lau, Emily. 1987. 'An unholy alliance: Protestant liberals accuse leaders of bowing to Beijing.' *Far Eastern Economic Review*, 24 December, 24.

Law Wang-sing. 1986. 'Lun Zongjiao yu Zhengzhi' ['On religion and politics']. *Ming Pao*, 30 December.
羅運承。1986。〈論宗教與政治〉。《明報》。12月30日。

Lee, Chee-kong. 1987. *Xianggang Jidujiaohuishi Yanjiu* [A study of Hong Kong Christian churches]. Hong Kong: Taosheng Publishing House.
李志剛。1987。《香港基督教會史研究》。香港：道聲出版社。

Lee, Chi-ping. 1987. 'Jiaohui zhong de Zhengzhi, Zhengzhi zhong de Jiaohui' ['Politics in the Church, the Church in politics']. *Pai-Shing Semi-Monthly* 144 (16 May): 21–3.
李致平。1987。〈教會中的政治、政治中的教會〉。《百姓》，第144期。5月16日。頁21–3。

Lee, Stella. 2001. 'Rebuff for Church offer of school places'. *South China Morning Post*, 8 December.

Lee, Wan and Cheung Chui-yung. 1986. 'Xianggang Jidujiao Gongye Weiyuanhui' ['Hong Kong Christian Industrial Committee']. Pp. 177–82 in *Zhongguo yu Xianggang Gongyun Zongheng* [Dimensions of the Chinese and Hong Kong labour movement], edited by Ming K. Chan. Hong Kong: Hong Kong Christian Industrial Committee.

李雲、張翠容。1986。〈香港基督教工業委員會〉。《中國與香港工運縱橫》，陳明錄編。香港：基督教工業委員會。頁 177–82。

Lemmen, M. M. W. 1990. *Max Weber's Sociology of Religion: Its Method and Content in the Light of the Concept of Rationality*. Hilversum: Gooi en Sticht.

Leung, Beatrice. 1991. 'The Triangular Relation: Hong Kong, China and the Vatican'. *Missiology* 2: 217–29.

———. 1992a. *Sino-Vatican Relations: Problems of Conflicting Authority, 1976–86*. Cambridge: Cambridge University Press.

———. 1992b. 'The Catholic Voter'. Pp. 151–84 in *Votes without Power: the Hong Kong Legislative Council Elections 1991*, edited by Rowena Kwok et al. Hong Kong: Hong Kong University Press.

———. 1996a. 'Sino-Vatican Negotiation: Old Problems for New Consideration'. Pp. 56–78 in *Church and State Relations in 21st Century Asia*, edited by Beatrice Leung. Hong Kong: Centre of Asian Studies, the University of Hong Kong.

———, ed. 1996b. *Church and State Relations in 21st Century Asia*. Hong Kong: Centre of Asian Studies, the University of Hong Kong.

———. 1997. 'The Uneasy Balance: Sino-Vatican-Hong Kong Relations after 1997'. Pp. 97–118 in *Hong Kong SAR: In Pursuit of Domestic and International Order*, edited by Beatrice Leung and Joseph Cheng. Hong Kong: The Chinese University Press.

———. 1998. 'The Sino-Vatican Negotiations: Old Problems in a New Context.' *China Quarterly* 153: 128–40.

———. 2000. 'Catholic Bridging Efforts with China.' *Religion, State and Society* 28(2): 185–96.

———. 2001. 'The HKSAR Catholic Church at the Crossroads.' Pp. 221–36 in *Political Development in the HKSAR*, edited by Joseph Cheng. Hong Kong: City University of Hong Kong Press.

Leung, Wai-fung. 1996. 'Woshi Zhongguo Guomin: Shenfen Gelie Zhitong' ['Am I Chinese? The agony of alienation']. *Ming Pao*, 9 July.
梁慧風。1996。〈我是中國國民：身份割裂之痛〉。《明報》。7月9日。

Levine, Daniel H. 1981. *Religion and Politics in Latin America: the Catholic Church in Venezuela and Colombia*. New Jersey: Princeton University Press.

———. 1992. 'From Church and State to Religion and Politics and Back Again.' Pp. 170–191 in *Politics and Social Change in Latin America: Still a Distinct Tradition?* Edited by Howard J. Wiarda. Boulder: Westview Press.

Li, Ng Suk-kay. 1978. *Mission Strategy of the Roman Catholic Church in Hong Kong, 1949–1974*. M. Phil. thesis, University of Hong Kong.

Li, Songlin, et al. 1992, eds. *Dangwei Gongzuo Daquan* [Handbook on the Work of Party Members]. Beijing: Chinese Broadcast Press.
李松林等編。1992。《黨委工作大全》。北京：中國國際廣播出版社。

Lin, Xingzhi. 1999. 'Zhengzhi Shenbu Youji, Jingji Youshi Jianshi' ['Politically it is not free, economically it is losing its edge']. *Hong Kong Economic Journal*, 16 August, 14.

林行止。1999。〈政治身不由己，經濟優勢漸失〉。《信報》。8月16日。
頁 14。

Liu, Peng. 1996. 'Church and State Relations in China: Characteristic and Trend.'
Pp. 41–55 in *Church and State Relations in 21st Century Asia*, edited by Beatrice
Leung. Hong Kong: Centre of Asian Studies, the University of Hong Kong.

Lo, Lung-kwong. 1998. 'Jidujiaojie Puxuan de Fensi' ['Reflections on the Christian
General Election']. *Christian Times Weekly* 578, 27 September, 8–9.
盧龍光。1998。〈基督教界普選的反思〉。《基督教時代論壇週報》，第
578 期。9月27日。頁 8–9。

Lo, Ping-cheung. 1996. 'Shiyi de Shuangchong Hanyi' ['The double implications of
October 1']. *Christian Times Weekly* 464 , 21 July, 7.
羅秉祥。1996。〈十一的雙重涵意〉。《基督教時代論壇週報》，第 464
期。7月27日。頁 7。

Lo, Shiu-hing. 1998. 'The Politics of Sustaining, Reversing and Constraining Private
Democratization in Hong Kong'. *Australian Journal of International Relations*
52(3): 273–283.

Luo, Kuang, ed. 1967. *Tianzhujiao Zaihua Chuanjiao Shiji* [The history of catholic
missions in China]. Tainan: Guangchi Press.
羅光編。1967。《天主教在華傳教史集》。台南：光啟出版社。

MacInnis, Donald. 1989. *Religion in China Today*. New York: Orbis Books.

Marx, Karl and Friedrich Engels. 1957. *Karl Marx and Friedrich Engels in Religion*.
Moscow: Foreign Language Publication House.

Mau, Chi-wang. 1996. 'Wuxing Zhishou zheng Ganyu Xianggang Jiaohui' ['An
invisible hand is influencing the Church in Hong Kong']. *Singtao Daily*, 30 May.
繆熾宏。1996。〈無形之手正干預香港教會〉。《星島日報》。5月30日。

McBrien, Richard P. 1987. *Caesar's Coin: Religion and Politics in America*. New York:
Macmillan.

McCarthy, John, David W. Britt and Mark Wolfson. 1991. 'The Institutional Channeling
of Social Movements by the State in the United States.' *Research in Social
Movements, Conflict and Change* 13: 45–76.

McClelland, V.A. 1988. 'Sensus Fidelium: the Developing Concept of Roman Catholic
Voluntary Effort in Education in England and Wales'. Pp. 61–88 in *Christianity
and Educational Provision in International Perspective*, edited by Colin Brock
and Witold Tulasiewicz. London: Routledge.

Miners, Norman. 1988. 'The Representative and Participation of Trade Unions in the
Hong Kong Government'. Pp. 40–5 in *Labour Movement in a Changing Society:
the Experience of Hong Kong*, edited by Y. C. Jao et al. Hong Kong: Centre of
Asian Studies, the University of Hong Kong.

———. 1991. *The Government and Politics of Hong Kong*. 5th Edition. Hong Kong:
Oxford University Press.

Montemayor, Jeremias U., ed. 1989. *Catholic Social Teaching*. Manila: Rex Books.

Newman, John Henry. 1947. *The Idea of a University*. New York: Longman.

Ng, Margaret Ngoi-yee. 2001. 'Where's the harm in being charitable?' *South China Morning Post*, 18 March.

Ng, Sek Hong and Victor Fung-shuen Sit. 1989. *Labour Relations and Labour Conditions in Hong Kong*. London: Macmillan.

Ng, Shui-lai. 1990. *Maixiang Jiushi Niandai de Shehui Fuli* [Social welfare into the 90's]. Hong Kong: Hong Kong Christian Service.
吳水麗。1990。《邁向九十年代的社會福利》。香港：香港基督教服務處。

Nielsen, Donald A. 1999. *Three Faces of God: Society, Religion, and the Categories of Totality in the Philosophy of Emile Durkheim*. Albany: State University of New York Press.

Parker, Donald Dean. 1938. *Church and State in the Philippines, 1896–1906*. Manila: University of the Philippines.

Paton, David M. 1985. *R.O.: The Life and Times of Bishop Ronald Hall of Hong Kong*. Hong Kong: The Diocese of Hong Kong and Macao and the Hong Kong Diocesan Association.

Pattnayak, Satya R., ed. 1995. *Organized Religion in the Political Transformation of Latin America*. Lanham, MD: University Press of America.

Pickering, W.S.F. 1984. *Durkheim's Sociology of Religion: Themes and Theories*. London: Routledge and Kegan Paul.

Po, Lo-to. 1986. 'Xianggang Jiaohui Jiji Canzheng de Yinyou' ['The reasons why Hong Kong churches actively participate in politics']. *Ming Pao*, 19 December.
布魯圖。1986。〈香港教會積極參政的因由〉。《明報》。12月19日。

Poon, Yuk-kuen. 2002. *Wang Bide Mushi zai Xianggang Gongzuo zhi Tantao* [A preliminary study of Reverend Peter Wang's Ministry in Hong Kong]. Hong Kong: Christian Study Centre on Chinese Religion and Culture.
潘玉娟。2002。《汪彼得牧師在香港工作之探討》。香港：基督教中國宗教文化研究社。

Ramet, Pedro. 1987. *Cross and Commissar: the Politics of Religion in Eastern Europe and the USSR*. Bloomington and Indianapolis: Indiana University Press.

———. 1988, ed. *Eastern Christianity and Politics in the Twentieth Century: Christianity Under Stress*. Vol. I. Durham and London: Duke University Press.

———. 1990, ed. *Catholicism and Politics in Communist Societies*. Durham and London: Duke University Press.

Ramet, Sabrina Petra, ed. 1992. *Adaptation and Transformation in Communist and Post-Communist Systems*. Boulder: Westview Press.

———. 1993. *Religious Policy in the Soviet Union*. Cambridge: Cambridge University Press.

———. 1998. *Nihil Obstat: Religion, Politics, and Social Change in East-Central Europe and Russia*. Durham and London: Duke University Press.

Report of the Survey Office, Public Responses to Green Paper: the 1987 Review of Developments in Representative Government. Hong Kong: Government Printer, 1987.

Robbins, Thomas. 1987. 'Church-State Tensions and Marginal Movements in the United States'. Pp. 135–149 in *Church-State Relations: Tension and Transition*, edited by Thomas Robbins and Roland Robertson. New Brunswick: Transaction Books.

Robbins, Thomas and Roland Robertson. 1987, eds. *Church-State Relations: Tension and Transition*. New Brunswick: Transaction Books.

Robertson, Roland. 1987. 'General Considerations in the Study of Contemporary Church-State Relationship.' Pp. 5–11 in *Church-State Relations: Tension and Transition*, edited by Thomas Robbins and Roland Robertson. New Brunswick: Transaction Books.

Ryan, Thomas. 1959. *The Story of a Hundred Years: the Pontifical Foreign Missions Institute in Hong Kong, 1858–1958*. Hong Kong: Catholic Truth Society.

Saich, Tony. 1997. 'Negotiating the State: the Development of Social Organizations in China'. *China Quarterly* 161: 124–42.

Schluchter, Wolfgang. 1989. *Rationalism, Religion and Domination: A Weberian Perspective*. Berkeley: University of California Press.

Schurmann, Franz. 1968. *Ideology and Organization in Communist China*. Berkeley: University of California.

Scott, Ian, ed. 1998. *Institutional Change and the Political Transition in Hong Kong*. New York: St. Martin's Press.

Selznick, Philip. 1960. *The Organizational Weapon: A Study of Bolshevik Strategy and Tactics*. Illinois: Free Press.

Shapiro, Ian and Casino Hacker-Cordon, eds. 1999. *Democracy's Edge*. Cambridge: Cambridge University Press.

Shaw, Sin-ming. 1999. 'Breathing's Easier than Believing.' *Time*, 9 August, 17.

Shen, Mo-ren (The Silent One). 1996. 'Zheshi wodui Guojiari Chongbai de Lichang' ['My position regarding the National Day Service']. *Christian Times Weekly* 466, 4 August, 8.
沈默人。1996。〈這是我對國家日崇拜的立場〉。《基督教時代論壇週報》，第 466 期。8月4日。頁 8。

Smith, Elwyn A. 1972. *Religious Liberty in the United States: the Development of Church-State Thought Since the Revolutionary Era*. Philadelphia: Fortress.

So, Daniel W. C. 1987. 'Searching for a Bilingual Exit'. Pp. 249–68 in *Language Education in Hong Kong*, edited by Robert Lord and Helen N. L. Cheng. Hong Kong: The Chinese University Press.

Stone, Ronald H., ed. 1983. *Reformed Faith and Politics: Essays Prepared for the Advisory Council on Church and Society of the United Presbyterian Church in the U.S.* Washington: University Press of America.

Sung, Yan-wing. 1986. 'Jibenfa yu Zongjiao Ziyou: du Xin Weisi de Huiying' ['Basic Law and religious freedom: A response to Xin Weisi']. *Ming Pao*, 15 December.
宋恩榮。1986。〈基本法與宗教自由：對辛維思的回應〉。《明報》。12月15日。

Swatos, Jr., William H. 1995, ed. *Religion and Democracy in Latin America*. New Brunswick, NJ: Transaction Publication.

Sweeting, Anthony. 1993. *A Phoenix Transformed: the Reconstruction of Education in Post-War Hong Kong*. Hong Kong: Oxford University Press.

Sze, Stephen Man-hung. 1996. 'The Social Awareness and Intended Role of Catholic Intellectuals in Face of 1997'. Pp. 150–62 in *Church and State Relations in 21st Century Asia*, edited by Beatrice Leung. Hong Kong: Centre of Asian Studies, the University of Hong Kong.

Tang, Dominic Yiming. 1991. *How Inscrutable His Ways, Memoirs 1951–1981*. Second Edition. Hong Kong: n.p.

Ticozzi, Sergio, PIME. 1983. *Xianggang Tianzhujiao Zhanggu* [Anecdotes of the Catholic Church in Hong Kong]. Hong Kong: Holy Spirit Study Centre.
田英傑。1983。《香港天主教掌故》。香港：聖神研究中心。

———. 1997, ed. *Historical Documents of the Hong Kong Catholic Church*. Hong Kong: Hong Kong Catholic Diocesan Archives.

Tung, Chee-Hwa. 1997a. 'A Future of Excellence and Prosperity for All'. Speech at the Ceremony to Celebrate the Establishment of the Hong Kong Special Administrative Region, 1 July.

———. 1997b. 'Building Hong Kong for a New Era'. Address at Provisional Legislative Council Meeting. 8 October.

Turner, Byran. 1991. *Religion and Social Theory*. Second Edition. Newbury Park, California: Sage.

Vallier, Ivan. 1971. 'The Roman Catholic Church: A Transnational Actor'. *International Organization* 3, 479–95.

Villa-Vicencio, Charles. 1990. *Civic Disobedience and Beyond: Law, Resistance, and Religion in South Africa*. Grand Rapids: Wm. B. Eerdmans.

———. 1996. *The Spirit of Freedom: South Africa Leaders on Religion and Politics*. Berkeley: University of California Press.

Vines, Stephen. 1998. *Hong Kong: China's New Colony*. London: Aurum Press.

Walder, Andrew G. 1986. *Communist Neo-Traditionalism: Work and Authority in Chinese Industry*. Berkeley: University of California Press.

Walshe, Peter. 1995. *Prophetic Christianity and the Liberation Movement in South Africa*. Pietermaritzburg: Cluster Publications.

Wang, Min. 1997. *Yidai Chuanwang Dong Jianhua* [Tung Chee Hwa: the Shipping Tycoon of his generation]. Beijing: Zhonghua Gongshuang Lianhe Chubnshe.
王旻。1996。《一代船王董建華》。北京：中華工商聯合出版社。

Webb, Paul. 1977. 'Voluntary Social Welfare Service'. Pp. 133–44 in *Chung Chi College 25th Anniversary Symposium*. Hong Kong: Chung Chi College, the Chinese University of Hong Kong.

Wickeri, Philip L. 1996. 'Confucian Culture and Church-State Relations in 21st Century East Asia'. Pp. 25–40 in *Church and State Relations in 21st Century Asia*, edited by Beatrice Leung. Hong Kong: Centre of Asian Studies, the University of Hong Kong.

Wilcox, Clyde. 1992. *God's Warriors: the Christian Right in Twentieth Century America*. Baltimore: John Hopkins University Press.

Wong Chi-wai. 1995. *Bashi Niandai Xianggang de Zhengjiao Guanxi: Judu Xinjiao dui* 'Jiuqi' Wenti de Huiying [Church State relations in the 1980s: Protestants' response to the problem of 1997]. M. Phil. thesis, The Chinese University of Hong Kong.
黃志偉。1995。《八十年代香港的政教關係：基督新教對「九七」問題的回應》。香港中文大學碩士論文。

Wong, Chong-gyiau. 1992. *The Emergence of Political Statements and Political Theology in the History of the Taiwanese Presbyterian Church.* Ph. D thesis. Boston University.

Woodman, Sophia, ed. 1997. *Hong Kong's Social Movement: Forces From the Margins.* Hong Kong: July 1 Link and Hong Kong Women Christian Council.

Wu, Chi-wai. 1996. 'Huigui Lushang Jingji Mantu' ['A thorny road to reunification']. *Christian Times Weekly* 462, 7 July, 8.
胡志偉。1996。〈回歸路上荊棘滿途〉。《基督教時代論壇週報》，第462期。7月7日。頁8。

_____. 1998a. 'Hunyao Buqing de Zhengjiao Guanxi?' ['Ambiguity in Church-State Relations?'] *Ming Pao*, 9 April.
胡志偉。1998a。〈混淆不清的政教關係？〉。《明報》。4月9日。

_____. 1998b. 'Zhengjiao Guanxi de Zaisi' ['Rethinking Church-State Relations']. *Christian Times Weekly* 557, 3 May, 13.
胡志偉。1998b。〈政教關係的再思〉。《基督教時代論壇週報》，第557期。5月3日。頁13。

Wu, John. 1984. 'Statement on the Catholic Church and the Future of Hong Kong'. Press Letter. 23 August. Released by Catholic Information Service.

_____. 1989. 'March into the Bright Decade: Pastoral Exhortation of Cardinal John B. Wu on the Pastoral Commitment of the Catholic Diocese of Hong Kong'. Released by Catholic Information Service.

_____. 1995. *Proclaim the Gospel of the Lord, Spread the Kingdom of God: March into the Bright Decade.* Interim report and proposal (Booklet circulated among Hong Kong Catholics). 4 June.

_____. 1999. 'God is Love'. Pastoral letter issued on 30 May. Reprinted in *Kung Kao Po* and *Sunday Examiner* (Hong Kong), 6 June 1999.

Xin, Weisi. 1986. 'Jibenfa yu Zongjiao Ziyou' ['Basic Law and religious freedom']. *Ming Pao*, 5 December.
辛維思。1986。〈基本法與宗教自由〉。《明報》。12月5日。

_____. 1987a. 'Zaitan Jibenfa yu Zongjiao Ziyou' ['Basic Law and religious freedom revisited'] (in 2 parts). *Ming Pao*, 3–4 February.
辛維思。1987a。〈再談基本法與宗教自由〉(分兩節)。《明報》。2月3–4日。

_____. 1987b. *Xin Weisi Zhenglunji* [Collected essays on politics by Xin Weisi]. Hong Kong: Ming Pao Publication Limited.
辛維思。1987b。《辛維思政論集》。香港：明報出版社。

Xu, Jiatun. 1995. *Xu Jiatun Xianggang Huiyilu* [Xu Jiatun's Hong Kong memoirs]. Taipei: Lienjin.
許家屯。1995。《許家屯香港回憶錄》。台北：聯經。

Yang, Nak Heong. 1997. *Reformed Social Ethics and the Korean Church*. New York: Peter Lang.

Ye, Xiaowen. 1996. 'Dangqian Woguo de Zongjiao Wenti' ['The contemporary religious questions of the Motherland']. *Zhonggong Zhongyang Danxiao Baogao Xuan* [Selected reports of the Party Central School]. 101(5): 9–23. (Internally circulated document.)

葉小文。1996。〈當前我國的宗教問題〉。《中共中央黨校報告選》，101 (5): 9–27。（內部傳閱文件）

Yeung, Caroline. 1987. 'Metamorphosis of the Yang Memorial Social Service Centre: Implementation of Social Policies and Achievements over Twenty Years (1967–87)'. Pp. 62–68 in *Mission and Care: Special Issue of Yang Social Service Centre's Twenty Years Anniversary*. Hong Kong: Yang Social Service Centre.

Ying, Fuk-tsang. 1996. ' "Guoqing" geiwo de tiaozhan' ['My "National Day" challenge']. *Christian Times Weekly* 461, 30 June, 8.

邢福增。1996。〈「國慶」給我的挑戰〉。《基督教時代論壇週報》，第 461 期。6月30日。頁8。

Yu, Carver Tat-sum. 1984. *Xinnianshu Zhushi* [Notes on Statement of Faith]. Enlarged Edition. Hong Kong: Fellowship of Evangelical Student.

余達心。1984。《信念書註釋》（增訂本）。香港：香港基督徒學生福音團契。

————. 1996. 'Reflection on Church-State Relations in Hong Kong.' Pp. 142–149 in *Church and State Relations in 21st Century Asia*, edited by Beatrice Leung. Hong Kong: Centre of Asian Studies, the University of Hong Kong.

————. 1997. 'Jiaomu Chouban Guoqing de Benyi yu Wuhui' ['The original intention behind proposing the National Day Celebration and subsequent misunderstanding']. *Ming Pao*, 27 June.

余達心。1997。〈教牧籌辦國慶的本意與誤會〉。《明報》。6月27日。

Yu, Fong-ying. 1987. *Tradition and Change in Chinese Education in Hong Kong*. Hong Kong: Chinese University Press.

Yu, Kam-yin. 1986. 'Xin Huashe de Xiezuo Banzi' ['The group of writers at the New China News Agency']. *Hong Kong Economic Journal*, 31 December.

余錦賢。1986。〈新華社的寫作班子〉。《信報》。12月31日。

————. 1996. 'Jiaohui Qingzhu Guoqing Fengbo yunao yuda' ['The Increasing conflict of the Christian National Day Celebration Controversy']. *Hong Kong Economic Journal*, 29 May.

余錦賢。1996。〈教會慶祝國慶風波愈鬧愈大〉。《信報》。5月29日。

Yuen, Mi. 1996. ' "Guojiari" Fengbo' ['The National Day Controversy']. *Christian Times Weekly* 461, 30 Jun, 2.

阮覓。1996。〈「國家日」風波〉。《基督教時代論壇週報》，第 461 期。6月30日。頁2。

Zheng, Sheng. 1992. *Zeng Sheng Huiyilu* [Memoirs of Zeng Sheng]. Beijing: Jiefanjun Chubanshe.

曾生。1992。《曾生回憶錄》。北京：解放軍出版社。

Glossary

Aberdeen Technical Institute, the	香港仔工業學院
Anti-Rise in Bus Fares Movement	反兩巴加價運動
Association of Major Superiors of Religious Men in Hong Kong	香港男修會會長聯會
Association of Major Superiors of Religious Women in Hong Kong	香港女修會會長聯會
Baker, Bishop J. Gilbert H.	白約翰會督
Baptist Convention of Hong Kong, The	香港浸信會聯會
Basic Law	基本法
Birthright Society	出生權維護會
Board of Diocesan Consulters	教區諮議會
Bolshevik	布什維克黨
Boxer Rebellion	義和團起義
Canossian Sisters	嘉諾撒仁愛女修會
Caritas-Hong Kong	香港明愛
Caritas Internationalis	國際明愛
Catholic American Foreign Missionary Society, the (Maryknoll Fathers)	美國天主教傳教會 (瑪利諾神 神父)
Catholic Chinese Weekly (Kung Kao Po)	《公教報》
Catholic Church, the	天主教
Catholic Institute for Religion and Society	公教教研中心
Catholic Marriage Advisory Council	公教婚姻輔導會

Catholic Youth Council	香港天主教青年聯會
Chai Wan	柴灣
Chan, Rev. Canon Alan	陳佐才法政牧師
Chan, Andrew	陳謳明
Chan, Anson	陳方安生
Chan Cho-wai, Joseph	陳祖為
Chan Shun-hing	陳慎慶
Chao, Rev. Jonathan	趙天恩牧師
Chen Yun	陳雲
Chenglung	乾隆
Cheng Mo-chi, Moses	鄭慕智
Cheung Man-kwong	張文光
Cheung Sha Wan	長沙灣
Chin Pak-tau	錢北斗
Chinese Church Research Center	中國教會研究中心
Chinese Catholic Patriotic Association	中國天主教愛國會
Chinese Communist Party	中國共產黨
Chinese People's Political Consultative Conference	中國人民政治協商會議
Choi Chi-kan, Rev.	蔡滋勤牧師
Choi Yuen-wan, Philemon	蔡元雲
Chow, Nelson	周永新
Christian and Missionary Alliance, The	基督教宣道會
Christian Communications Limited	福音證主協會
Christians for Hong Kong Society	基督徒關懷香港學會
Christian Sentinels for Hong Kong	基督徒香港守望社
Christian Social Concern Fellowship of Tsuen Wan and Kwai Chung	荃葵社關組
Christian Study Centre on Chinese Religion and Culture	基督教中國宗教文化研究社
Christian Times Weekly	《基督教時代論壇週報》
Christian Weekly	《基督教週報》
Chu Yiu-ming, Rev.	朱耀明牧師
Chung, Father Peter	鍾志堅神父
Church Workers' Association, The	教會工作者協會
Committee of the Christians Concerned for the Basic Law	香港基督教關注基本法委員會
Committee of the Christian Three-self Patriotic Movement	基督教三自愛國運動委員會
Commission on Public Policy (CPP)	公共政策委員會（政委會）
Community Chest	公益金
Community Church of Kwun Tong, The	觀塘社區教會

Community Church in West Kowloon, The	西九龍社區教會
Controversy of Chinese Rites	中國禮儀之爭
Council of Priests	司鐸議會
Court of Final Appeal	終審庭
Daya Bay	大亞灣
Democratic Party	民主黨
Deng Xiaoping	鄧小平
Deng Yiming, Bishop Dominic	鄧以明主教
Diamond Hill	鑽石山
Diocesan Convention	教區會議
Diocesan Liturgical Commission	教區禮儀委員會
Diocesan Pastoral Council	教區牧民議會
Diocesan Personal Commission	教區人事委員會
Duan Yinmin, Bishop Mathias	段蔭明主教
Electoral College	選舉團
Evangelical Free Church of China, The	中國基督教播道會總會
Falun Gong	法輪功
Fan sheng (Sharing)	《分享》
Fellowship of Baptist Students	浸會大學學生團契
Fellowship of Theological Graduates	朋輩團契
Fu Tieshan, Bishop Michael	傅鐵山主教
Fung Chi-wood, Rev.	馮智活牧師
Fung, Raymond	馮煒文
Guangdong Province	廣東省
Ha, Father Louis	夏其龍神父
Hall, Ronald O., Bishop	何明華會督
Ho Hei-wah	何喜華
Ho Sau-lan	何秀蘭
Hong Kong Catholic Labour Committee	香港天主教勞工事務委員會
Hong Kong Catholic Social Communications Office	香港天主教社會傳播處
Hong Kong Chinese University	香港中文大學
Hong Kong Christian Council (HKCC)	香港基督教協進會
Hong Kong Christian Industrial Committee	香港基督教工業委員會
Hong Kong Christian Institute	香港基督徒學會
Hong Kong Council of Catholic Laity	香港天主教教友總會
Hong Kong Diocesan Pastoral Sisters Association	香港教區牧職修女聯會
Hong Kong Policy Research Institute	香港政策研究社
Hong Kong Public Records Office	香港政府檔案署
Hong Kong Special Administrative Region (HKSAR)	香港特別行政區

HKSAR Preparatory Committee	香港特別行政區籌備委員會
Hong Kong Student Christian Movement	香港基督徒學生運動
Hong Kong Women's Christian Council	香港婦女基督徒協會
Hong Kong Economic Journal	《信報》
Hong Kong Economic Times	《香港經濟日報》
Hong Kong YWCA	香港基督教女青年會
Hsu Cheng-pin, Bishop Francis	徐誠斌主教
Hsu Tao-leung, Rev.	許道良牧師
Hsueh, Theodore	薛孔奇
Ip Lau Suk-yee, Regina	葉劉淑儀
Jesuits Fathers, the	耶穌會神父
Ji Pengfei	姬鵬飛
Jiang Zemin	江澤民
Jin Luxian, Bishop Louis	金魯賢主教
Joint Committee for Monitoring of Public Utilities	各界監管公共事業聯合委員會
Joint Committee for Monitoring of the Two Electricity Companies	各界爭取監管兩電聯合委員會
Joint Committee for the Promotion of Democratic Government (JCPDG)	民主政制促進聯合委員會（民促聯）
Joint Committee of Christians Concerned for the Review of Representative Government	基督徒關注政制檢討聯委會
Joint Conference for Shelving the Daya Bay Nuclear Plant	爭取停建大亞灣核電廠聯席會議
'Joint Statement of Christians Concerned on the *Green Paper: The 1987 Review of Developments in Representative Government*'	〈基督徒關注《八七政檢綠皮書》聯合聲明〉
Justice and Peace Commission of the Hong Kong Catholic Diocese, The (DCJP)	香港天主教正義和平委員會（正委會）
Kaifong Associations	街坊福利會
Kangxi	康熙
King's Park	京士柏
Ko Shan Theatre	高山劇場
Ko Tin-ming	高天明
Kuai Bao	《快報》
Kuan Hsin-chi	關信基
Kung Kao Po	《公教報》
Kwai Chung	葵涌
Kwok Nai-wang, Rev.	郭乃弘牧師
Kwong, Archbishop Peter	鄺廣傑大主教
La Salle Brothers	基督學校修士會
La Salle College	喇沙書院

Ng Shui-lai	吳水麗
North Point	北角
'Opinions of the Hong Kong Protestant Delegation Beijing on the Future of Hong Kong' (Beijing Delegation Statement)	〈香港基督徒北京訪問團對香港前途意見書〉（訪京團意見書）
Oriental Daily	《東方日報》
Pang Cheung-wai	彭長緯
Patten, Chris	彭定康
Po Leung Kuk	保良局
Pong Kin-son, Rev.	龐建新牧師
Pontifical Commission of Justice and Peace	宗座正義和平委員會
Pope John Paul II	教宗若望保祿二世
'Position Paper of Church Workers on the *Draft of the Basic Law*'	〈教會同工對《基本法（草案）徵求意見稿》的立場書〉
Pozzoni, Bishop Dominico	師多敏主教
PRC (People's Republic of China)	中華人民共和國
'Preliminary Proposal on Future Development of Representative Government in Hong Kong'	〈香港未來政制模式芻議〉
'Proposed Statement of Faith for Hong Kong Christians in the Face of Social and Political Change' (Statement of Faith)	〈香港基督徒在現今社會及政治變遷中所持的信念獻議〉（信念書）
Provisional Legislative Council	臨時立法會
Qing Dynasty	清朝
Religious Affairs Bureau	宗教事務局
Renmin Ribao	《人民日報》
Rennie's Mill	調景嶺
Salesians Fathers	鮑斯高慈幼會
Sai Kung	西貢
Second Vatican Council (Vatican II)	梵諦岡第二次大公會議
Sham Shui Po	深水埗
Shek Kip Mei	石硤尾
Sheng Kung Hui	聖公會
Shi Jiao-guang	釋覺光
Shum Oi Church	深愛堂
Sino-British Joint Declaration	中英聯合聲明
Sisters of St. Paul de Chartres	沙爾德聖保祿女修會
Sisters of the Precious Blood	耶穌寶血女修會
Sit Poon-ki, Elder Simon	薛磐基長老
Social Concern Fellowship of Shum Oi Church	深愛堂社關組
Social Concern Group in the Society of Religion, the Chinese University of Hong Kong	香港中文大學宗教系社關組
Social Concern Group of the Breakthrough Youth Center	突破青年中心社關組

Society for Truth and Light, The	明光社
Society of Chung Chi Theology Division Students	崇基神學組學生會
Soo, Bishop Thomas	蘇以葆主教
South China Morning Post	《南華早報》
St. Joseph's College	聖若瑟書院
St. Mary's Canossian College	嘉諾撒聖瑪利書院
St. Paul's Convent School	聖保祿學校
'Statement on Religious Freedom by the Protestant Churches of Hong Kong' (Statement on Religious Freedom)	〈香港基督教會有關宗教自由的聲明〉（宗教自由聲明）
Ta Kung Pao	《大公報》
Tai Wan Shan	大環山
Tai Wo Hou	大窩口
Taiwan	台灣
Tam Yiu-chung	譚耀宗
Teng, Rev. Philip	滕近輝牧師
Tiananmen	天安門
Tong, Bishop John	湯漢主教
Tong, Ronny	湯家驊
Trench, Sir David	戴麟趾爵士
Tsang, Donald	曾蔭權
Tsang, Father J. B.	曾慶文神父
Tsang Kwok-wai, Rev.	曾國偉牧師
Tsang Yin-ling, Iris	曾燕玲
Tse, Rev. John	謝約翰牧師
Tso Shui-wan, Rev. Josephine	曹瑞雲牧師
Tsuen Wan	荃灣
Tsui, Bishop Louis	徐贊生主教
Tsui, Father Luke	徐錦堯神父
Tung Chee-hwa	董建華
Tung Wah Hospital Group	東華三院
Union of the Hong Kong Catholic Organizations in Support of the Patriotic and Democratic Movement in China, The	香港天主教團體支援中國愛國民主運動聯合會
Wah Yan College	華仁書院
Wahkiu Yatbo	《華僑日報》
Wang Fengqiao	王鳳超
Wen Wei Po	《文匯報》
West Kowloon Community Church	西九龍社區教會
Wong Tai Sin	黃大仙
Wu Cheng-chung, Cardinal John Baptist	胡振中樞機

Wu, Rose	胡露茜
Wuhua	五華縣
Xin Weisi	辛維思
Xinhua News Agency	新華社
Xinjiang	新疆省
Xu Jiatun	許家屯
Xu Zhixuan, Bishop	徐之玄主教
Yang Memorial Social Service Centre	楊震社會服務中心
Yau Chung-wan	丘頌雲
Yau Ma Tei Typhoon Boat Squatters	油麻地避風塘艇戶
Ye Xiaowen	葉小文
Yi	《驛》
Yu Kam-yin	余錦賢
Yu Tat-sum, Rev. Carver	余達心牧師
Yuen Mei-yin, Mary	阮美賢
Yuk Tak-fun, Alice	郁德芬
Yung, Gideon	翁偉業
Yung Kok-kwong, Rev.	翁珏光牧師
Zen Ze-kiun, Bishop Joseph	陳日君主教
Zhao Ziyang	趙紫陽

Index